AUGUSTINE

OUTSTANDING CHRISTIAN THINKERS

Series Editor: Brian Davies OP

The series offers a range of authoritative studies of people who have made an outstanding contribution to Christian thought and understanding. The series will range across the full spectrum of Christian thought to include Catholic and Protestant thinkers, to cover East and West, and historical and contemporary thinkers. By and large, each volume will focus on a single 'thinker', but occasionally the subject may be a movement or a school of thought.

Brian Davies OP, the Series Editor, is Professor of Philosophy at Fordham University, New York. He was formerly Regent of Blackfriars, Oxford University and tutor of theology at St Benet's Hall, Oxford. He has taught at the University of Bristol, Emory University and the Beda College in Rome. He is Reviews Editor of *International Philosophy Quarterly*. His previous publications include: *Thinking about God* (Geoffrey Chapman, 1985); *The Thought of Thomas Aquinas* (Oxford University Press, 1992); and *An Introduction to the Philosophy of Religion* (Oxford University Press, 1982).

Already published:

The Cappadocians
Anthony Meredith SJ

Hans Urs von Balthasar
John O'Donnell SJ

Catherine of Siena
Giuliana Cavallini OP

Teresa of Avila
Archbishop Rowan Williams

Kierkegaard
Julia Watkin

Bultmann
David Fergusson

Lonergan
Frederick E. Crowe SJ

Karl Barth
John Webster

Reinhold Niebuhr
Kenneth Durkin

Aquinas
Brian Davies OP

The Venerable Bede
Benedicta Ward SLG

Paul Tillich
John Heywood Thomas

Paul
C. K. Barrett

AUGUSTINE

Mary T. Clark RSCJ

CONTINUUM
London and New York

Continuum
The Tower Building, 11 York Road, London SE1 7NX
370 Lexington Avenue, New York, NY 10017–6503

First published 1994
Reissued 2000

British Library Cataloguing-in-Publication Data
A catalogue record for this book is available from the British Library.

ISBN 0-8264-5087-3

Typeset by Colset Private Ltd, Singapore
Printed and bound in Great Britain by Biddles Ltd, Guildford and King's Lynn

Contents

Editorial Foreword

St Anselm of Canterbury (1033–1109) once described himself as someone with faith seeking understanding. In words addressed to God he says 'I long to understand in some degree thy truth, which my heart believes and loves. For I do not seek to understand that I may believe, but believe in order to understand.'

This is what Christians have always inevitably said, either explicitly or implicitly. Christianity rests on faith, but it also has content. It teaches and proclaims a distinctive and challenging view of reality. It naturally encourages reflection. It is something to think about; something about which one might even have second thoughts.

But what have the greatest Christian thinkers said? And is it worth saying? Does it engage with modern problems? Does it provide us with a vision to live by? Does it make sense? Can it be preached? Is it believable?

The Outstanding Christian Thinkers series is offered to readers with questions like these in mind. It aims to provide clear, authoritative and critical accounts of outstanding Christian writers from New Testament times to the present. It ranges across the full spectrum of Christian thought to include Catholic and Protestant thinkers, thinkers from East and West, thinkers ancient, mediaeval and modern.

The series draws on the best scholarship currently available, so it will interest all with a professional concern for the history of Christian ideas. But contributors also write for general readers who have little or no previous knowledge of the subjects to be dealt with. Its volumes should therefore prove helpful at a popular as well as an academic level. For the most part they are devoted to a single thinker, but occasionally the subject is a movement or school of thought.

Brian Davies OP

vii

Preface

My reading of Augustine has lasted throughout four decades, and I have many aspects of his thought to explore. Numerous are the learned monographs and articles on special Augustinian doctrines already published and continuing to appear all over the world from scholars on every continent. In the present volume my aim has been the modest, but difficult, one of introducing general readers and students to the main teachings developed by Augustine in response to the intellectual and religious challenges of his day. The harmony he sought between his understanding and his faith is reflected in these doctrines where scriptural statements and discursive thought happily mingle. As a personal attitude, faith embraces both heart and head. The vibrancy of Augustine's homilies to the faithful of Hippo is comprehensible only in the light of his appreciation of faith as loving trust in Christ, whose teachings gave to faith a content to be understood so that it could be fully lived by the whole human person.

In order to concentrate on what Augustine himself concluded regarding central philosophical and theological topics, I have made no effort to identify what his various predecessors contributed to his treatment of each topic, nor how his own solutions affected subsequent thinkers. But because of the permeation of fourth-century Roman culture by Neoplatonism, I offer an entire chapter to that Hellenistic philosophy which undoubtedly influenced Augustine's philosophical formation.

My basic exposition of the philosophical and theological thought of Augustine finds its justification in the fact that his writings are true classics in having something essential to say concerning human existence in any century. As Christian classics they shed religious light upon contemporary problems and ultimate concerns. Indeed, Augustine's efforts to understand what he believed were expended on behalf of all of us, so that we might grow in Christian understanding of how life is to be lived, namely, with truth and goodness united in the right use of freedom. For Augustine this means that all human knowing, loving and willing take place in relationship to God. Since relationships are inevitably concrete, there is for Augustine no absent God.

I hope that the cultural marks of Augustine's own age will not prevent any reader from appreciating the lasting value of his insights into the reality of human nature and divine grace. Those who read his *Confessions* usually end them with a deepened awareness of the presence of God in their lives. A further perusal of his writings can bring the conviction that 'in his will is our peace', an Augustinian teaching vividly portrayed in Dante's *Divine Comedy*. Augustine prayed, taught, wrote and worked for peace, the harmony of truth and goodness in action. From this great Christian believer who respected rational thought there is much to learn.

In the face of the obvious evils of the human condition of which Augustine was well aware (and yet did not see the *worst* of it in the twentieth century!), today's literature of despair is surely in need of his legacy of hope, made possible by faith in God and true love of neighbour. No other Christian teacher has so emphasized the essential role of joy in moral life. Human misery, rampant as it is, was never the intention of the Creator. The 'heart' and the 'book', pictured in most portraits of Augustine, indicate his appreciation of the human emotion of love which, nevertheless, he never exalted at the expense of intellectual truth.

It is a joy for me to thank all those colleagues — friends — who kindly read various chapters in their formative stages or the book as a whole. From each one I received valuable criticism and encouragement. Among them are: Roland Teske SJ of Marquette University: Avery Dulles SJ and Joseph T. Lienhard SJ of Fordham University; George Lawless OSA of the Institutum Patristicum 'Augustinianum'; Michael Scanlon OSA of Villanova University; John O'Meara of University College, Dublin; and most especially Brian Davies OP of Blackfriars, Oxford, who was exceedingly generous with his editorial expertise throughout the entire process.

Mary T. Clark RSCJ
Manhattanville College
Purchase, NY, USA
8 June 1993

Chronological table

	HISTORICAL EVENTS	BIOGRAPHICAL OUTLINE
354	Emperor Constantius, d. 360; last son of Constantine; Pope Liberius, d. 366	Birth of Augustine at Thagaste, 13 November
360	Emp. Julian the Apostate, d. 363	
361		In school at Thagaste; serious illness
363	Emp. Jovian, d. 364	
364	Emp. Valentinian I (West), d. 375; Valens (East), d. 378	
366–67	Emp. Gratian, d. 383; Pope Damasus, d. 384	At secondary school, Madaura
369–70		Year of idleness at Thagaste
370		Higher studies at Carthage
371		Takes a concubine
372	Revolt of Berber chief Firmus in Africa	Birth of Adeodatus, his son; father died
372–73	Consecration of Ambrose as Bishop of Milan	Reads Cicero's *Hortensius*; converted to philosophy; becomes a Manichee
374		Teaching rhetoric at Carthage
375	Emp. Valentinian II, d. 392, with Gratian	Returns from Carthage to teach at Thagaste
379	Emp. Theodosius I (East), d. 395	Death of friend; returns to Carthage
380		First work: On the Beautiful and Fitting
383	Emp. Maximus (Spain, Gaul, Britain), d. 388, murdered Gratian	Meets Faustus of Milevis; doubts the Manichee teachings; sails for Rome
383–84	Symmachus, Prefect of Rome	Teaches in Rome
384	Pope Siricius, d. 399	Became official orator in Milan
386		Reading of Platonic books; studies St Paul's epistles; visited by Ponticianus; converted to Christianity (fully); retires to Cassiciacum

387		Baptism at Milan; vision of Ostia; death of Monica
387–88		Returns to Africa; settles at Thagaste
388–91		Monastic life at Thagaste; deaths of Adeodatus and Nebridius
391	General edict against paganism	To Hippo to see candidate for monastic life; ordained priest; monastery at Hippo
392	Eugenius made Emperor	
394	Theodosius conquers Eugenius; unites Empire under one Emperor	
395	Emp. Honorius (West), d. 423; Emp. Arcadius (East), d. 408	Becomes coadjutor bishop at Hippo, with right of succession
396		Becomes Bishop of Hippo
396–400	Vandals enter Gaul; Visigoths attack Italy	
397	Death of Ambrose; Simplicianus succeeds	
399	Pope Anastasius I, d. 401	
401	Pope Innocent I, d. 417	
408–10	Emp. Theodosius II, d. 450; Vandals, Suevi enter Spain; Rome taken by Alaric	Rests a few months for sake of health at a villa outside Hippo
411	Condemnation of Donatists at Carthage	
412	Condemnation of Celestius, Pelagian, Africa	
417	Pope Innocent condemns Pelagius, Celestius; Pope Zosimus, d. 418	
418	Pope Zosimus condemns Pelagius, Celestius; Pope Boniface I, d. 422	
422	Pope Celestine I, d. 432	
425	Emp. Valentinian III (West), d. 455	
426		Names Heraclius to succeed him as bishop
429	Vandals enter Africa	
430	Siege of Hippo by Vandals	Death of Augustine

Augustine's works

The dates provided here are for the most part approximate ones.

AD		PL	CSEL	CCL	BA	English
386	*Contra academicos* Against the Sceptics	32, 905–958	63	29	4	FC 5; ACW 12
	De beata vita The Happy Life	32, 959–976	63	29	4	FC 5
	De ordine On Order	32, 977–1020	63	29	4.1	FC 5
386–387	*Soliloquia* Soliloquies	32, 869–904	89		5	FC 5; PN 7
	De immortalitate animae Immortality of the Soul	32, 1021–1034	89		5	FC 4
387–391	*De musica* On Music	32, 1081–1194			7	FC 4
387–389	*De moribus ecclesiae catholicae et Manichaeorum* The Catholic and Manichean Way of Life	32, 1309–1378	90		1	FC 56; PN 4
387–388	*De quantitate animae* Greatness of Soul	32, 1035–1080	89		5	FC 4; ACW 9
388–389	*De Genesi contra Manichaeos* On Genesis against the Manichees	34, 173–220				FC 84
388–395	*De libero arbitrio* On Free Choice	32, 1221–1310	74	29	6	FC 59; ACW 22
	De diversis quaestionibus octoginta tribus Eighty-three Different Questions	40, 11–100		44A	10	FC 70

AD		PL	CSEL	CCL	BA	English
c. 389	De magistro The Teacher	32, 1193–1220	77.1	29	6	FC 59; ACW 9
389–391	De vera religione True Religion	34, 121–172	77.2	32	8	LCC 6
c. 391	De utilitate credendi The Advantage of Believing	42, 65–92	25.1		8	LCC 6
392	Contra Fortunatum Manichaeum Debate with Fortunatus the Manichee	42, 111–130	25		17	
392–393	De duabus animabus contra Manichaeos On Two Souls, against the Manichees	42, 93–112	25		17	PN 4
393	De fide et symbolo Faith and the Creed	40, 181–196	41	46	9	FC 27; LCC 5
393–394	Psalmus contra partem Donati Song against the Donatist sect	43, 23–32	51		28	
	De Genesi ad litteram, imperfectus liber On the Literal Interpretation of Genesis, an unfinished book	34, 219–246 (added to, AD 426)	28.1			FC 84
	De sermone Domini in monte The Lord's Sermon on the Mount	34, 1229–1308		35		FC 11; ACW 5; PN 6
394	Contra Adimantum Against Adimantus the Manichee	42, 129–172	25		17	
394–395	Epistulae ad Galatas expositio Explanation: Epistle to the Galatians	35, 2105–2148	84			
	Epistulae ad Romanos expositio inchoata Incomplete Explanation: Epistle to the Romans	35, 2063–2088	84			SBL 23
	Expositio quarumdam propositionum	35, 2063–2088	84			

AD		PL	CSEL	CCL	BA	English
	epistulae ad Romanos; Explanation of a Passage from Epistle to the Romans					
395	*De continentia* Continence	40, 349–372	41		3	FC 16
	De mendacio Lying	40, 487–518	41		2	FC 16
396	*De diversis quaestionibus ad Simplicianum* Questions for Simplicianus (VII)	40, 101–148		44	10	LCC 6
	De agone Christiano Christian Struggle	40, 284–310	41		1	FC 2
	De doctrina Christiana (1–3.24) Christian Doctrine (3.25–end: AD 426)	34, 15–122	80	32	11	FC 2; PN 2
396	*Enarrationes in Psalmos* Explanations of the Psalms	36, 67–1029 / 37, 1033–1968		38/40		ACW 29/30; PN 8 (1–37)
397	*Contra epistulam quam vocant fundamenti* Against the Basic Letter of the Manichees	42, 173–206	25		17	Dods 5; PN 4
397–401	*Confessiones* Confessions	32, 659–868	33	27	13/14	FC 21; L 26/27
397–398	*Contra Faustum Manichaeum* Reply to Faustus the Manichee	42, 207–518	25			PN 4
	Contra Felicem Manichaeum Reply to Felix the Manichee	42, 519–552	25		17	
398	*Sermo de disciplina Christiana* Homily on Christian Discipline	40, 669–678		46		
c. 399	*Quaestiones Evangeliorum* Questions on the Gospels: Mt, Luke	35, 1321–1364		44B		
399	*De natura boni*	42, 551–572	25		1	LCC 6; PN 4

AD		PL	CSEL	CCL	BA	English
	The Nature of the Good					
	Contra Secundinum Manichaeum Reply to Secundinus the Manichee	42, 571–602	25		17	PN 4
399–419	*De Trinitate* The Trinity	42, 819–1098		50/50A	15/16	FC 45; AHI I.v.5; PN 3
400	*De fide rerum quae non videntur* Faith in Invisible Realities	40, 171–180		46	8	FC 4; PN 3
c. 400	*De consensu Evangelistarum* Consensus of the Evangelists	34, 1041–1230	43			
	Contra epistulam Parmeniani Against the letter of Parmenianus	43, 33–108	51		28	
	De opere monachorum The Work of Monks	40, 547–582	41		3	FC 16; PN 3
	De catechizandis rudibus On Instructing the Unlearned	40, 309–348		46	11.1	ACW 2; PN 3
	Adnotationes in Job Comments on Job	34, 825–886	28.2			
400–401	*De baptismo* Baptism	43, 107–244	51		29	PN 4
401	*De bono conjugali* The Good of Marriage	40, 373–396	41	29	2	FC 27; PN 3
	De sancta virginitate Holy Virginity	40, 397–428	41		3	FC 27; PN 3
401–405	*Contra litteras Petiliani* Reply to the letters of Petilianus	43, 245–383	52		30	Dods 3; PN 4
401–415	*De Genesi ad litteram* Literal Commentary on Genesis	34, 245–486	28.1		48/49	ACW 41/42
405	*De unitate Ecclesiae* The Unity of the Church	43, 391–446	52		28	
c. 406	*Contra Cresconium grammaticum* Reply to	43, 445–594	52		31	

AD		PL	CSEL	CCL	BA	English
	Cresconius, the grammarian					
406	De divinatione daemonum The Divination of Demons	40, 581–592	41		10	FC 27
c. 408–413	In Johannis evangelium tractatus Homilies on Gospel of John	35, 132–1976		36	71–74A	FC 78/79 (1–27); LCC 8; PN 7
410	De urbis Romae excidio The Destruction of the City of Rome	40, 715–724		46		
	De unico baptismo Only One Baptism	43, 595–614	53		31	PN 5
412	De peccatorum meritis et remissione et baptismo parvulorum Punishment and Forgiveness of Sins and Baptism of Infants	44, 109–200	60			
	Breviculus collationis cum Donatistis Brief Meeting with the Donatists	43, 613–650	53	149A	32	
	Ad Donatistas Against the Donatists	43, 651–690	53		32	
412–413	De fide et operibus Faith and Works	40, 197–230	41		8	FC 27; ACW 48; LCC 6; PN 3
412	De spiritu et littera The Spirit and the Letter	44, 201–246	60			LCC 8; PN 5
413–427	De civitate Dei City of God	41, 13–804	40.1 40.2	47/48	33–37	FC 8, 14, 24; PN 2
413–415	De natura et gratia Nature and Grace	44, 247–290	60		21	FC 86; PN 5
413–414	Tractatus in ep. Johannis ad Parthos Homilies on John's Epistle to the Parthi	35, 1977–2062		8		LCC 8; PN 7
414	De bono viduitatis The Good of Widowhood	40, 429–450	41		3	FC 16; PN 3
415	Contra Priscillianistas et Origenistas	42, 669–678		49		AHI I.v.15

AD		PL	CSEL	CCL	BA	English
	Reply to Priscillianists and Origenists					
	De origine animae	33	44		38	FC 44
	Letter 166 Origin of the Soul					
415/416	*De perfectione iustitiae*	44, 291–318	42		21	Dods 4; PN 5
	The Perfection of Human Justice					
417	*De gestis Pelagi*	44, 319–360	42		21	FC 86; Dods 1; PN 5
	Proceedings with Pelagius					
418	*Gesta cum Emerito*	43, 697–706	53		32	
	Proceedings with Emeritus					
	Ad Caesarienses	43, 689–698			32	
	Reply to the Caesarians					
	De gratia Christi et de peccato originali	44, 359–410	42		22	PN 5
	The Grace of Christ and Original Sin					
	De patientia	40, 611–626	41		2	FC 16; PN 5
	Patience					
418/419	*Contra sermonem Arianorum*	42, 683–708				
	Reply to an Arian Sermon					
c. 419	*De octo Quaestionibus ex veteri testamento*	35, 1374–1376		33		
	Eight Questions on the Old Testament					
419	*Locutiones in Heptateuchum*	34, 485–546	28.1	33		
	Discourses on the Heptateuch					
	Quaestiones in Heptateuchum	34, 547–824	28.2	33		
	Questions on the Heptateuch					
419/420	*De nuptiis et concupiscentia*	44, 413–474	42		23	PN 5; Dods 12
	Marriage and Concupiscence	40, 451–486	41		2	FC 27
	De coniugiis adulteris					
	Adulterous Marriage					
	Contra adversarium legis et prophetarum	42, 603–666		49		AHI I.v.15
	Against Adversaries					

AD		PL	CSEL	CCL	BA	English
	of the Law and the Prophets					
	Contra Gaudentium Donatistarum episcopum Against Gaudentius a Donatist bishop	43, 707–758	53		32	
419/421	*De anima et eius origine* The Soul and its Origin	44, 475–548	60		22	PN 5
420	*Contra duas epistulas Pelagianorum* Against Two Pelagian Letters	44, 549–638	60		23	PN 5
	Contra mendacium Against Lying	40, 517–548	41		2	FC 16; PN 3
420/422	*De cura pro mortuis* Care for the Dead	40, 591–610	41		2	FC 27; PN 3
421	*Contra Julianum* Against Julian	44, 641–874				FC 35
421/422	*Enchiridion ad Laurentium* Faith, Hope and Charity	40, 231–290		46	9	FC 2; ACW 3; PN 3
422/425	*De VIII Dulciti Quaestionibus* Questions from Dulcitius	40, 147–170		44A	10	FC 16
426/427	*De gratia et libero arbitrio* Grace and Free Choice	44, 881–912			24	FC 59; PN 5
	De correptione et gratia Admonition and Grace	44, 915–946			24	FC 2; PN 5
	Retractationes Retractations	32, 583–656	36	57	12	FC 60
	Speculum de Scriptura sacra Mirror of Holy Scripture	34, 887–1040	12			
427/428	*Collatio cum Maximino Arianorum episcopo* Discussion with Maximinus, Arian bishop	42, 709–742				AHI I.v.15
c. 428	*Contra Maximinum* Reply to Maximus	42, 743–814				AHI I.v.15

AD		PL	CSEL	CCL	BA	English
428/429	*De haeresibus* Heresies	42, 21–50		46		AHI I.v.15
	De praedestinatione *sanctorum* The Predestination of the Saints	44, 959–992			24	FC 86; Dods 3; PN 5
	De dono *perseverantiae* Gift of Perseverance	45, 993–1034			24	FC 86; Dods 3; PN 5
428/430	*Contra secundam* *Juliani:* *responsionem opus* *imperfectum* Unfinished Work against Julian	45, 1049–1608	85.1			
429/430?	*De utilitate ieiunii* The Advantage of Fasting	40, 669–678		46	2	FC 16
386–429	*Epistulae* Letters	33, 61–1162	34/44 57/58			FC 12; 18, 20, 30, 32; L 239; PN 1; Dods 6 & 13
	Epistulae 1*–29* (recently discovered)		88		46B	
393–430	*Sermones* Homilies	38/39; 46/47		41/46B		FC 81 FC 11 (some); ACW 15 (some); AHI III.v.1–4 (1–150)

Bibliography

A selection of books in English readily available for readers who wish to pursue in greater detail the topics discussed in this book.

James F. Anderson, *St Augustine and Being* (The Hague, 1965).
A. Hilary Armstrong, *Saint Augustine and Christian Platonism* (Villanova, PA, 1964).
(ed.), *The Cambridge History of Later Greek and Early Medieval Philosophy* (Cambridge, 1967).
William S. Babcock (ed.), *The Ethics of St Augustine* (Atlanta, GA, 1991).
H. J. Blumenthal and R. A. Markus, *Neoplatonism and Early Christianity* (London, 1981).
Gerald Bonner, *St Augustine of Hippo: Life, Controversies* (rev. edn, Philadelphia, PA, 1986).
God's Decree and Man's Destiny (Brookfield, VT, 1987).
Kari E. Borresen, *Subordination and Equivalence: The Nature and Role of Woman in Augustine and Thomas Aquinas* (Washington, DC, 1981).
Vernon Bourke, *Augustine's Quest of Wisdom* (Milwaukee, WI, 1945).
Augustine's View of Reality (Villanova, PA, 1964).
Wisdom from St Augustine (Houston, TX, 1984).
Augustine's Love of Wisdom (West Lafayette, IN, 1992).
Peter Brown, *Augustine of Hippo* (Berkeley, CA, 1967).
Religion and Society in the Age of St Augustine (London, 1972).
Bruce Bubacz, *St Augustine's Theory of Knowledge* (New York, 1981).
F. C. Burkitt, *The Religion of the Manichees* (Cambridge, 1925).
John Burnaby, *Amor Dei: Augustine on the Love of God as the Motive of Christian Life* (2nd edn, London, 1947).
J. Patout Burns, *The Development of Augustine's Doctrine of Operative Grace* (Paris, 1980).
Edward C. Butler, *Western Mysticism* (London, 1967).
Henry Chadwick, *Augustine* (Oxford, 1986).
Saint Augustine, Confessions (Oxford, 1991).
Mary T. Clark, *Augustine, Philosopher of Freedom* (New York, 1959).
Augustinian Personalism (Villanova, PA, 1970).
Augustine of Hippo, Classics of Western Spirituality (Ramsey, NJ, 1984).
Frederick Copleston, *A History of Philosophy* II (New York, 1962).
A. Dihle, *The Theory of Will in Classical Antiquity* (Berkeley, 1982).

John Dillon, *The Middle Platonists* (London, 1977).

Dorothy Donnelly, *De civitate Dei: An Annotated Bibliography of Modern Criticism, 1960–1990* (New York, 1991).

G. R. Evans, *Augustine on Evil* (London, 1982).

W. H. C. Frend, *The Donatist Church* (Oxford, 1952).

S. Gersh, *Middle Platonism and Neo-Platonism: The Latin Tradition* I (Notre Dame, IN, 1986).

Langdon Gilkey, *Reaping the Whirlwind* (New York, 1976).

Etienne Gilson, *The Christian Philosophy of Saint Augustine*, tr. L. E. M. Lynch (New York, 1960, 1983).

Peter Gorday, *Principles of Patristic Exegesis: Romans 9–11 in Origen, John Chrysostom, and Augustine* (New York, 1983).

Carol Harrison, *Beauty and Revelation in the Thought of St Augustine* (Oxford, 1992).

Paul Henry, *St Augustine on Personality* (New York, 1960).

The Path to Transcendence, tr. F. F. Burch (Pittsburgh, PA, 1981).

William J. Hill, *The Three-Personed God* (Washington, DC, 1982).

Ludger Holscher, *The Reality of the Mind* (London, 1986).

Christopher Kirwan, *Augustine: The Arguments of the Philosophers* (London, 1989 and 1991).

G. B. Ladner, *The Idea of Reform* (Cambridge, MA, 1959).

George Lawless, *Augustine of Hippo and His Monastic Rule* (Oxford, 1987).

John T. Lienhard, Earl Muller, and Roland Teske (eds), *Augustine: Presbyter factus sum* (New York, 1993).

Henri de Lubac, *Augustinianism and Modern Theology*, tr. L. Sheppard (London, 1969).

Alasdair MacIntyre, *Three Rival Versions of Moral Enquiry* (Notre Dame, IN, 1990).

M. J. McKeough, *The Meaning of the rationes seminales in St Augustine* (Washington, DC, 1926).

Robert Markus (ed.), *Augustine: Critical Essays* (Garden City, NY, 1972).

Saeculum: History and Society in the Theology of St Augustine (Cambridge, 1988).

Henri Marrou, *St Augustine and His Influence through the Ages* (New York, 1957).

The Resurrection and Saint Augustine's Theology of Human Values, tr. M. Consolata (Villanova, PA, 1966).

F. X. Martin and J. A. Richmond (eds), *From Augustine to Eriugena* (Washington, DC, 1991).

Margaret Miles, *Augustine on the Body* (Missoula, MT, 1979).

John Mourant, *Saint Augustine on Memory* (Villanova, PA, 1980).

Ronald H. Nash, *The Light of the Mind* (Lexington, KY, 1969).

Arthur Nock, *Conversion* (Lanham, MD, 1988; reissue).

Robert J. O'Connell, *St Augustine's Early Theory of Man* (Cambridge, MA, 1968).

Gerard J. P. O'Daly, *Augustine's Philosophy of Mind* (Berkeley, 1987).

James J. O'Donnell (ed.), *Augustine's Confessions*, 3 vols (text and commentary) (Oxford, 1992).

Oliver O'Donovan, *The Problem of Self-Love in St Augustine* (New Haven, 1980).

Dominic O'Meara, *Neoplatonism and Christian Thought* (Albany, 1982).

John J. O'Meara, *Porphyry's Philosophy from Oracles in Augustine* (Paris, 1959).

Charter of Christendom (New York, 1961).

The Young Augustine (London, 1980).

Studies in Augustine and Eriugena, ed. T. Halton (Washington, DC, 1992).

J. van Oort, *Jerusalem and Babylon* (Leiden, 1991).

C. J. O'Toole, *The Philosophy of Creation in the Writings of St Augustine* (Washington, DC, 1944).

Wolfhart Pannenberg, *Human Nature, Election, and History* (Philadelphia: The Westminster Press, 1977).

Lloyd Patterson, *God and History in Early Christian Thought* (New York, 1967).

Jaroslav Pelikan, *The Mystery of Continuity: Time and History, Memory and Eternity in the Thought of St Augustine* (Charlottesville, VA, 1986).

Michele Pelligrino, *The True Priest* (Villanova, PA, 1988).

Eugene Portalié, *A Guide to the Thought of St Augustine*, tr. R. J. Bastian (Westport, CT, 1975).

Possidius, *The Life of Saint Augustine*, ed. J. E. Rotelle (Villanova, PA, 1988).

Mary C. Preus, *Eloquence and Ignorance in Augustine's On the Nature and Origin of the Soul* (Atlanta, GA, 1985).

Paul Rigby, *Original Sin in Augustine's Confessions* (Ottawa, 1987).

John M. Rist, *Platonism and Its Christian Heritage* (London, 1985).

Caroline Schuetzinger, *The German Controversy on Augustine's Illumination Theory* (New York, 1960).

Colin Starnes, *Augustine's Conversion* (Waterloo, Ontario, 1990).

William R. Stevenson, *Christian Love and Just War* (Macon, GA, 1987).

Eugene TeSelle, *Augustine the Theologian* (New York, 1970).

T. J. Van Bavel, *The Rule of St Augustine*, trans. R. Canning (London, 1984).

F. Van der Meer, *Augustine the Bishop*, tr. B. Battershaw (London, 1961).

Luc Verheijen, *Saint Augustine's Monasticism in the Light of Acts 4:32-35* (Villanova, PA, 1979).

Marthinus Versfeld, *St Augustine's Confessions and City of God* (Cape Town, 1990).

Benedict Viviano, *The Kingdom of God in History* (Wilmington, DE, 1988).

Graham Walker, *Moral Foundations of Constitutional Thought* (Princeton, NJ, 1990).

Emilie Zum Brunn, *St Augustine: Being and Nothingness*, tr. R. Namad (New York, 1988).

Adolar Zumkeller, *Augustine's Ideal of the Religious Life*, tr. E. Colledge (New York, 1986).

Augustine's Rule, tr. M. J. O'Connell (Villanova, PA, 1987).

Abbreviations

Works of Augustine

C	*Confessiones*
CA	*Contra Academicos*
CD	*Contra duas epistolas Pelagianorum ad Bonifacium Papam*
CEM	*Contra epistulam Manichaei quam vocant fundamenti*
CEP	*Contra epistulam Parmeniani*
CF	*Contra Faustum*
CJ	*Contra Julianum haeresis Pelagianorum defensorem*
CLP	*Contra litteras Petiliani Donatistae*
DAO	*De anima et eius origine*
DB	*De baptismo contra Donatistas*
DBC	*De bono conjugali*
DBe	*De beata vita*
DCD	*De civitate Dei*
DCG	*De correptione et gratia*
DD7	*De diversis quaestionibus VII ad Simplicianum*
DD83	*De diversis quaestionibus LXXXIII*
DDoC	*De doctrina christiana*
DDoP	*De dono perseverantiae*
DGnI	*De Genesi ad litteram liber imperfectus*
DGnL	*De Genesi ad litteram libri XII*
DGnM	*De Genesi contra Manichaeos*
DGrC	*De gratia Christi et peccato originali*
DGrL	*De gratia et libero arbitrio*
DH	*De haeresibus*
DLA	*De libero arbitrio*
DMa	*De magistro*
DME	*De moribus ecclesiae catholicae et de moribus Manichaeorum*
DMu	*De musica*
DNB	*De natura boni contra Manichaeos*
DNG	*De natura et gratia*
DNu	*De nuptiis et concupiscentia*
DOR	*De ordine*
DPS	*De praedestinatione sanctorum*
DQ	*De quantitate animae*

DSL	*De spiritu et littera*
DSD	*De sermone Domini in monte*
DT	*De Trinitate*
DUC	*De utilitate credendi*
DVR	*De vera religione*
E	*Epistulae*
En	*Enchiridion ad Laurentium de fide, spe, caritate*
EnP	*Enarrationes in Psalmos*
ExG	*Expositio Epistulae ad Galatas*
J	*In Epistulam Joannis ad Parthos tractatus X*
JE	*In Joannis evangelium tractatus CXXIV*
OJ	*Opus imperfectum contra Julianum*
R	*Retractationes*
S	*Sermones*
SO	*Soliloquia*

Other abbreviations

Latin texts

PL	Migne, *Patrologia Latina*, vols 32–46 (Paris, 1841–42)
CSEL	*Corpus Scriptorum Ecclesiasticorum Latinorum* (Vienna, 1965–)
CCL	*Corpus Christianorum, latina* (Brepols, 1953–)
BA	*Bibliothèque Augustinienne* (Paris, 1947– ; Latin text, French translation and notes)

English translations

ACW	Ancient Christian Writers (Westminster, MD, and Longmans, London, 1946; available: New Jersey: Paulist Press)
AHI	Augustinian Historical Institute (Villanova, PA: *Works of St Augustine. A Translation for the 21st Century*, 1992–)
Dods	Marcus Dods (ed.), *The Works of Aurelius Augustinus*, 15 vols (Edinburgh, 1871–76)
FC	Fathers of the Church (New York and Washington: Catholic University of America Press, 1947–)
L	Loeb Classical Library (Cambridge, MA: Harvard University Press)
LCC	Library of Christian Classics (London and Philadelphia: Westminster Press, 1953–)
PN	Select Library of Nicene and Post-Nicene Fathers of the Church (1887–1902; reprint: Grand Rapids, MI: Eerdmans, 1956)
SBL	Society for Biblical Literature: Early Christian Literature Series (Chico, CA: Scholars Press)

1

Genesis of a Christian thinker

Since Augustine's thought is deeply related to experience, we may profit-ably begin this survey of his teachings with assistance from both his auto-biography, the *Confessions* (397–401), and the biography authored by Possidius, his archivist and friend who became the Bishop of Calama.[1]

Augustine was born (AD 354) and died (AD 430) within the Roman world of North Africa, where he lived for 71 of the 76 years of his life.

In Thagaste (now Souk-Ahras), in the province of Numidia, in a low mountainous region of eastern Algeria, not too far from Tunisia, he was born into the Latin-speaking family of Patricius, a pagan, and Monica, a Christian, whose Berber ancestors had been naturalized. The name 'Berber' was thought to have been given to some of the natives of North Africa by the Romans, and might have signified 'barbarian'. The natives were also called Libyans or Numidians (nomads) or Moors. They differed by geographical location, not by race. Berbers were prob-ably no darker than the Romans. Although Augustine's father, Patricius, was not wealthy, he owned some property and was a *decurio*, a member of the Town Council. It is said that a *decurio* was expected to contribute money for public projects, and this may have reduced the funds available for household needs. The family nevertheless belonged to the middle class and aimed to educate Augustine for a legal career. From birth he was a Roman citizen; from birth also he became a Christian catechumen when 'signed with the sign of the cross and seasoned with salt' (C I.11.77) as he came from his mother's womb. From Monica he learned to cherish the name of Christ (C III.4.8).

After attending the local school at Thagaste, Augustine went fifteen miles south to Madaura where he completed his secondary studies in preparation for a professional education at Carthage. But his father had more ambition for his son's future than funds to make it possible. So at the age of sixteen Augustine found himself with a year's leisure, which he used to amuse himself and to delve into sensual pleasures of all kinds until he put himself under a sort of addiction to them. Later he seemed to blame his mother for her permissiveness regarding this youthful sensuality, and for her postponing his baptism. In his day

1

Christians were often not baptized until after adolescence so that the sins of their youth might be forgiven by baptism. John O'Meara thinks that in comparison with pagan behaviour in fourth-century Africa, Augustine's actions may not have been as sinful as he portrays them; but judged by the Christian standards of the Bishop of Hippo who wrote the *Confessions*, he was justified in speaking of 'so small a boy, so great a sinner'. During this time at home in his sixteenth year, his father became a catechumen (C II.3.6). Monica prayed unceasingly for this unfaithful husband with his quick temper as well as for her wayward son.

The next year, with financial support from Romanianus, a family friend, Augustine departed for Carthage, the second greatest Latin city. There he studied the poets, Virgil (70–19 BC) and Terence (195–159 BC); historians such as Sallust (86–34 BC), orators, especially Cicero (106–43 BC). Virgil and Cicero often speak out from the pages of the later Augustine, giving the impression that he had committed them to memory.

He was now seventeen and found himself immersed in the daily activities of Carthaginian youth. He frequented the enormous baths in the Forum (the foundations of these can still be seen by visitors to Carthage today). They were used as a meeting place for discussions and gymnastics. He attended the theatre. He visited the amphitheatre where the martyrs had been tortured and where gladiators now struggled with wild animals. The temptations of this city exceeded those of Thagaste and were not completely resisted by Augustine. He formed a liaison with a young African woman who became his concubine for thirteen years and bore him a son, Adeodatus (C IX.6.14).

His studies, however, were not neglected. He soon distinguished himself in the school of Rhetoric. In his nineteenth year he read Cicero's *Hortensius*, an exhortation to philosophy not unlike that in the dialogue *On Philosophy* by Aristotle (384–322 BC). The *Hortensius* is a lost text but fragments of it can be found in Augustine's writings. In it happiness was linked to the quest for wisdom, which is life according to what is highest in man, the mind. This text enkindled in Augustine a burning desire for truth and made him feel that all his worldly ambitions were misplaced. He was troubled, however, that the name of Christ was not there. For in the midst of his waywardness he remained a Christian catechumen and attended church now and then. Prompted by this new zeal for truth, he turned to the Scriptures only to feel dissatisfied with their lack of style and clarity as well as with the portrayal of God in the Old Testament as emotional. Then, he tells God, 'I fell among men whose mouths were the snare of the devil, lined with the mixture of the syllables of your name, and of our Lord Jesus Christ. They cried out "Truth, Truth", and spoke much thereof to me' (C III.6.10). These men were called Manichees and belonged to a gnostic religious group founded by Mani (AD 216–276) of Babylonia. They claimed to offer the true version of Christ's religion by rejecting the Old Testament which, they said, gave a false picture of God as human, and unfavourably described the patriarchs and prophets while even containing contradictions of the New Testament. These Manichees looked with special favour on the epistles of St Paul.

The Manichee emphasis on Christ and their stress on purity of life appealed to Augustine. The Manichees also offered a mythical explanation of evil, a problem deeply troubling to him. Their trump card was their assurance that reason alone, not faith, was needed for salvation (DUC 1.2); this coincided with Augustine's new allegiance to philosophy. The Manichees influenced him to associate 'authority' in the Church with the superstitious behaviour of some of its North African members. His confidence in Catholic Christianity became greatly weakened.

Soon after joining the Manichees as an auditor Augustine returned to Thagaste to begin a teaching career. His father had died, but not before having been baptized. In less than a year the death of his closest friend saddened him so deeply that the desire to escape from the constant reminders of their times together sent him back to Carthage (AD 374). There he became a teacher of rhetoric, the kind of teacher whose students became his friends – some lifelong like Alypius (CVI.7.11). Monica refused to live with Augustine in Carthage until a dream assured her that he would give up his heresy.

Augustine's association with the Manichees at Carthage increased. So did his zeal in bringing as many friends as possible into the Manichee sect. Meanwhile he engaged in oratorical contests and gained influential friends like Flaccianus, a future proconsul of Africa in AD 393, and Symmachus, a proconsul at Carthage in AD 373, and the current proconsul, Vindicianus, who crowned Augustine victor in an oratorical contest. Now at the age of 26 Augustine wrote his first work, *On the Beautiful and the Fitting*, a lost work which he summarizes in the *Confessions* (IV.13.20 – 15.28). It was dedicated to the Syrian, Hierius, a contemporary orator in Rome; Augustine admired him for his reputation and wanted to become known by him. This work is important for revealing Augustine's early thoughts on beauty before he read *Ennead* I.6 'On Beauty' by Plotinus (AD 205–270), who was the founder of Neoplatonism, which was considered a revival of Plato's teaching. Augustine's aesthetic theory emphasized integrity and composition, but this first book was also a public expression of his belief in Manichee doctrine, especially that the soul is a particle of the divine substance. This led Augustine at this point to identify the human soul with the ultimate good, a kind of basis for his belief that human reason sufficed in the search for truth.

Augustine was obviously proud of his intellectual capacity. He boasted that he could understand the most difficult works without any interpreter. One such work was the *Categories* of Aristotle (C IV.16.28). He also read many of the physical theories of the philosophers as reported by Apuleius (*c.* AD 124) and Varro (116–27 BC) and began to contrast these with the mythical explanation of the planets and stars put forward by the Manichees. This made him raise some questions with Manichee friends concerning astronomy. They had no answers but promised that when their bishop Faustus came to Carthage, he would have answers. Only when Faustus came and admitted his inability to answer these questions did Augustine begin to free himself mentally from Manichee doctrine, although he did not publicly break with the sect. Mani's lack of credibility in this area led Augustine to mistrust him in religious matters. The link with this sect also weakened when he heard a Christian, Helpidius, argue with a Manichee in a most convincing way.

Since the Manichees emphasized both astrology and the role of demons in the world, Augustine frequently indulged in horoscope reading and the placating of demons to ensure success for himself. These activities gradually stopped through the influence of friends like Vindicianus, Firminus and others (C VII.6.8). Augustine remained a Manichee for nine years, AD 373–382 (DME I.18.34; II.19.68; C IV.1.1).

In AD 383 he sailed to Rome where, so he had heard, the students were more disciplined. He lived in the house of a Manichee auditor, and at first was overcome by illness. He did not ask for baptism, as he had done when ill as an adolescent. When he recovered, the Manichees helped him open a school of Rhetoric. The students were better behaved but less good in paying their fees. His own state of mind was not a happy one. Disillusioned with those who had assured him that they possessed the truth about God and man and the moral struggle, he was reluctant to think of truth as a realizable goal. And so in AD 384 at the age of 30 he separated from the Manichee sect and adopted the sceptical position of those who were described in Cicero's *Academica* as successors of the Platonists of the original Academy at Athens. Their school was called the New Academy (to distinguish it from Plato's Academy where philosophic doctrines had been taught as true conclusions). 'There began to arise in me the thought that those philosophers whom they call Academics, were wiser than others for holding that men should doubt everything and that no truth can be perceived by men' (C V.10.19). He thereupon lowered his sails and settled for what was *probably* true, imitating Cicero's position. Paradoxically, he did accept one theory as true, as taught by both the Stoics (adherents of the philosophy of Zeno, a teacher around 310 BC) and the Manichees, namely, that anything real was corporeal. This included God and the soul, although 'matter' in their case was of a very refined kind. So, he went on thinking of God as he always had, as a bodily substance extended everywhere, like an infinite space (C VII.1.1–2).

After a year of teaching at Rome, Augustine applied at the suggestion of Manichee friends for the position of public rhetor (teacher of Rhetoric) in the imperial city of Milan. This was obtained through the pagan Symmachus who recommended Augustine to Bauto the proconsul, a powerful personage. In the latter's honour Augustine delivered a panegyric on the occasion of Bauto's tenth anniversary as proconsul (AD 385); later in the same year he gave a panegyric honouring the young emperor, Valentinian II. Ambrose (c. AD 339–397) was Bishop of Milan, and to him Augustine introduced himself and was impressed by the bishop's kind welcome. After all, the new public rhetor, as far as Ambrose knew, still belonged to the heretical Manichee sect outlawed by the government.[2] Ambrose was to be indirectly extremely influential in Augustine's conversion. The newcomer listened eagerly to this preacher's explanation of the word of God in his homilies.[3]

Monica came to Milan that very summer and learned from her son that he was no longer a Manichee. She expressed no great surprise, and also noted that this son now had his step well placed on the traditional ladder to success. From the rank of rhetor, political leaders frequently arose. Augustine could hope for a governorship and a life of social prominence. But money was needed to make the ascent, since a Roman custom existed of gifts being offered to the powerful for favours received. A wife with a large dowry could provide such money. An appropriate marriage was arranged by Monica. This necessitated sending Adeodatus's mother back to Africa. This appals modern readers of the *Confessions*, but fourth-century readers would have known that under Roman law concubines could not be married legally. The general acceptance of this did not prevent Augustine from feeling the pangs of separation. 'My heart so deeply attached to her was cut and wounded . . . she returned to Africa vowing that she would never go with another man' (C VI.15.25). But the proposed fiancée was too young for immediate marriage, and, during the waiting period, Augustine took a mistress.

Even in the midst of this worldly manipulating the search for truth never abated. At Milan he once again entertained the hope for truth as he listened to the sermons of Ambrose and read some writings of Neoplatonists (philosophers who gave a metaphysical and spiritual interpretation of the doctrine of Plato, beginning with Plotinus, whose *Enneads* were edited by Porphyry [AD 232–303], his student).

Bishop Ambrose was an educated and eloquent speaker, and Augustine the orator at first attended his sermons to enjoy the eloquence. But he also learned from Ambrose. His spiritual and allegorical interpretation of Scripture enabled Augustine to recognize the error of the Manichee rejection of the Old Testament through their over-literal interpretation. Ambrose often quoted the passage: 'The letter killeth, but the spirit giveth life' (2 Cor 3:6). In explaining the meaning of 'And he said: "Let us make man to our image and likeness"' (Gen 1.16), the Manichees had taught that since a man is corporeal, this means that God is corporeal. Ambrose explained that the text referred to an image and likeness in soul rather than in body. Its purpose was not to teach that God was corporeal, but that human persons have spiritual capacities which open them to knowing and loving God. Ambrose was quite possibly the one who freed Augustine from blaming moral evil upon a struggle between a Prince of Light and a Prince of Darkness, both operating within the soul, as taught by the Manichees. Augustine reported in the *Confessions* (VII.3.5) that he deeply considered what he had heard, namely, that one's own free will is the cause of moral evil. Through Ambrose, Augustine experienced the presence of truth. In listening to his eloquence, 'there also entered no less the truth he affirmed, though only gradually. At first what he said was apparently defensible, and I did not now think it imprudent to affirm the Catholic faith which I had thought defenceless against the Manichee critics' (C V.14.24).

All this propelled Augustine into deciding to abandon Manichee doctrines, which he had grown to disbelieve, and to accept his status as a catechumen, which he had abandoned in his nineteenth year. 'I therefore made the decision for the present to be a catechumen in the Catholic Church, which the tradition of my parents recommended to me, until some clear light should come by which I could direct my course' (C V.14.25).

Some philosophical roadblocks, however, prevented him from fully accepting all the statements of Ambrose. It was almost impossible for Augustine to conceive of anything real as incorporeal (C VII.1.1–2). He also found it difficult to rid himself of the left-over belief from his Manichee days that evil occurred within him rather than by him.

Just at this time someone loaned him 'certain Platonist books' translated from Greek into Latin by Marius Victorinus, a fourth-century African rhetor who had reached prominence in Rome. They are thought by some scholars to have been writings of Plotinus and Porphyry, perhaps a few treatises from the *Enneads* of Plotinus and perhaps the *Sentences* as well as the *Return of the Soul* of Porphyry. From his response in the *Confessions* it seems that these writings removed some of his philosophical roadblocks. He read there of a triad of spiritual hypostases and of an intellectual ascent to God. He was liberated from the Manichee idea of a corporeal God.

In those books the spiritual aspects of human beings were examined seriously and completely in relation to the end of all human striving — union with a transcendent God. As a Catholic catechumen he knew of God as a trinity and at first identified the Christian Trinity with the three hypostases of Plotinus, not attending at that time to the inferiority to the One of the last two Plotinian hypostases — Nous (Intelligence) and All-Soul (C VII.9.13 – 10.16). If at that time (AD 386) he read Porphyry's work *Return of the Soul* (*De regressu animae*), he learned of how necessary asceticism is, the discipline of the body, as a preparation for the contemplation of the One, God. He attempted an ascent to the One through mental effort as advocated by Plotinus, and some think he attained it. The weight of his sensual habits, however, pulled him earthward (C VI.18.24 and 20.26). Nevertheless, the hope for wisdom, awakened by his reading of Cicero's *Hortensius*, returned now in greater strength with the reading of these books of the Platonists. They lifted his spirits and in an elated mood he yearned to embark upon a philosophic community of friends to foster the pursuit of wisdom. The plan was opposed, however, by wives and fiancées.

Plotinus had given centrality to the intellect on the journey to happiness. True life for human beings must therefore be the life of intelligence, but lo and behold: a body has been added to the human being. It seemed necessary then to withdraw one's attention from bodily things to attend to the inner life and thereby prepare for the mystical experience of the One. After Augustine failed to maintain his fleeting experience of transcendence (C VI.12.24), in disappointment he turned to the epistles of the apostle Paul to see whether he agreed with the Neoplatonists. Paul emphasized the one true Mediator, Christ Incarnate, as necessary for union with God (C VII.21.27). Augustine then realized that Neoplatonism and Manichee doctrine were both opposed to the human incarnation of God and to his real death on the cross. In this pride they were alike. But his early impression of the Platonic doctrines was that they harmonized with the Christian mysteries and showed the inner unity of reason and faith (CA II.1.1; III.20.43; DOR II.5.16; DBe I.4).

Neoplatonism, although directly encountered by Augustine only at this time, was already known to the Christian intellectuals at Milan. Ambrose had taken from Origen (c. 185–254) and the Alexandrines (theologians of the early Church at Alexandria influenced by the Platonists) a Christian Neoplatonic expression of the faith, and the sermons of Ambrose contain literal quotations from Plato and Plotinus.[4] A dedicated priest who had baptized Ambrose and who became Bishop of Milan in 397, Simplicianus, told Augustine how much he admired Platonism. This he said when Augustine visited him shortly after reading the books of the Platonists. In addition, Simplicianus had known Victorinus, the translator, in Rome and recounted the story of his extraordinary conversion from a learned rhetor, whose statue had already been erected in Trajan's Forum, to a humble Christian, from a defensive pagan to a theologian of the Christian Trinity. And what was Augustine's reaction? 'As soon as your servant Simplicianus told me this story about Victorinus, I was eager to follow his example' (C VIII.5.10). This longing to follow Victorinus did not enable him to do so. Years later he wrote: 'The law of sin is the violence of habit by which even the unwilling mind is dragged down and held, as it deserves to be, since by its own choice it slipped into the habit' (C VIII.5.12). And he went on to say whence comes release: 'Wretched man that I was, who would deliver me from this body of death except your grace through Jesus Christ our Lord?' (Rom 7:24–25).

Grace was not then given. Soon thereafter an African friend, Ponticianus, visited Augustine and discovered that the book Augustine had been reading was by the apostle Paul. When Augustine admitted that he was giving much serious study to Scripture, his visitor told the story of Antony, the Egyptian hermit of whom Augustine and Alypius had never heard. Whereupon Ponticianus, seeing their interest, began telling them of the monasteries being built and of the hermits in the desert. Recently, while he was on official business in Trier, there was a necessary delay. So two of his colleagues, civil servants of the emperor, had gone for a walk and entered a monastic house, where they found a book on the life of Antony. When they read about his leaving all things to follow Christ more closely, they were on fire to do likewise and resigned their posts to become monks. Their generosity and the immediacy of their surrender to God aroused Augustine to face himself. He was appalled by the sight of his vices. In the *Confessions* he acknowledged his procrastination in seeking for the wisdom he longed for. 'But I was an unhappy young man, wretched as at the beginning of my adolescence

7

when I prayed to you for chastity and said: "Grant me chastity and continence but not yet"' (C VIII.7.17).

This story of Antony, who had championed the vocation to chastity for himself and his disciples, occasioned a moral crisis for Augustine. He expressed his excruciating experience of alienation and powerlessness in the language of the epistles to the Galatians and the Romans (C VIII.5.11–12). In the garden of his Milan house he was praying fiercely for divine help when he heard a child's voice singing *tolle lege*, 'Take and read'. He felt this as a call to imitate Antony by opening the Scriptures to find a message from God. He opened the epistle to the Romans at 13:13–14 where he was exhorted to put on Christ and let go of all vices. A 'light of certainty' enveloped him and 'all shadow of doubt disappeared' (C VIII.12.29).

It was AD 386 and Augustine was 33 years of age. Cicero's scepticism had been ousted by Paul. Personal interiority and transcendence became for Augustine more real than his sense-dominated imagination. This double movement of conversion to interiority and self-transcendence became the model of the Augustinian journey to God. Augustine was enabled to commit himself to the truth of the Catholic Church as instituted by Christ for the giving of the grace that saves.

He did not immediately resign from his career but waited until the vintage vacation and then retired to a country villa at Cassiciacum, thought to have been part of the present town of Cassago near Milan. He submitted his name for baptism to Ambrose, along with the names of Alypius and Adeodatus, and asked Ambrose what he should read in preparation. Ambrose advised him to read the Book of Isaiah, but Augustine did not find it helpful. There in the villa with his mother, brother, son, cousins, Alypius, Evodius and two young pupils they did the daily housework, discussed Cicero and Virgil, prayed the psalms. Four of Augustine's dialogues were produced there, the first three resulting from daily discussions: *Against Scepticism*, *The Happy Life*, *On Order* and the *Soliloquies*.

At last Augustine fully embarked upon the quest for wisdom, and in that quest he opened his mind to philosophic reason and to the authority that calls for faith. Much in these early dialogues is borrowed from Neoplatonism, but it is far from being the dominant concern. Truth is the main object of the discussions, and what reason can offer to confirm revealed teachings is gratefully accepted. It is a period when Augustine is more conscious of the harmony between Neoplatonism and Christianity than he ever will be in the future. He knows already, however, that the incarnation of Christ is essential and central to Christianity, whereas it is scornfully rejected by Porphyry, and passed over in silence by Plotinus. Although both reason and authority are praised, priority is given to authority. 'Therefore in nothing shall I depart from the authority of Christ, and reason will find truth with the Platonists, and this will not oppose our sacred mysteries' (CA III.41–43).

Before Lent in AD 387 Augustine went to Milan to prepare for baptism by taking instructions given by the bishop. At the Easter Vigil he was baptized, and he remained in Milan for almost a year, long enough to produce a book, the *Immortality of the Soul*. In earnest he began to write a kind of reading programme to prepare souls to make contact with the intelligible realm. These were to be texts on the liberal disciplines. Five chapters of a book *On Music* were written and a text *On Grammar* was begun. Augustine and his friends decided that they would form a community for contemplation and for the service of God and neighbour in North Africa. So they made their way to Rome and to the seaport, Ostia. There Monica and Augustine, standing near a window overlooking a garden and discussing eternal life, found themselves uplifted beyond all corporeal objects, beyond all human word and thought until they, panting after wisdom, 'touched it in some small degree by a moment of total concentration of the heart' (C IX.10.24).

Perhaps it was this foretaste of heaven which led Monica to tell Augustine that she was now content to die: 'The one reason why I wanted to stay longer in this life was my desire to see you a Catholic Christian before I die. My God has granted this in a way more than I had hoped. For I see you despising this world's success to become his servant' (C IX.10.26). Within five days she contracted a fever and died (C IX.11.27–28). There at Ostia Monica was buried; later, her bones were taken to St Augustine's Church in Rome where they rest in a tomb beneath the side altar. Augustine was overcome by the kind words of praise his mother had for him on her deathbed, knowing, as he did, how much anxiety he had caused her. For him her life had always been a beacon light shining in the darkness of a pagan environment. Her religious spirit created a home atmosphere devoid of the quarrelling which marked many African households. With unusual singleheartedness she constantly kept in contact with her wandering son and never lost hope that goodness would make its appeal to him. Augustine recalled 'her holy and considerate treatment of us' (C IX.12.33) and although he refrained from weeping at the funeral, he was heavy with sadness and pain, so that finally as he prayed to God for her, his tears flowed freely for her and for himself (C IX.12.33). Augustine asked all the readers of the *Confessions* to remember at the altar Monica and Patricius 'through whose physical bond' God had brought him into life without his knowing how (C IX.13.37).

Augustine and the group now around him were unable to sail immediately to Africa, prevented by a blockade of the port. So they returned to Rome where they remained for more than a year. There Augustine began his work *On Free Choice* I and II, a work he took up again only in AD 395, completing it in 396 at Hippo.

At this time also he wrote the treatise *On Greatness of Soul* and prepared short answers to questions raised by friends, answers that eventually would appear in the work *Eighty-three Different Questions* along with other answers given while living at Thagaste and Hippo. His former persuasion of colleagues to join the Manichees weighed heavily on his heart, so at Rome he began the first of many anti-Manichee writings, this one entitled *The Catholic and the Manichee Way of Life*, completed in AD 390 at Thagaste.

Finally in the autumn of 388 they set sail for Carthage and went on to Thagaste where together with friends they set up a lay monastery in Augustine's former house. Most of the family property was sold and the money given to the poor. They settled upon a regular order of day so that they could devote themselves to the contemplative life. Intellectual work was part of this life. Reading and discussion went on. Augustine wrote a work *On the Teacher*, a dialogue with his son, Adeodatus. This included an investigation into the nature of words and of the causes of learning. Augustine praised Adeodatus for his brilliant answers — this son who died shortly thereafter at the age of seventeen (C IX.6.14).

The sixth chapter of the text *On Music* was completed at Thagaste and the liberal arts series given up. Quite possibly the urgency he felt to argue persuasively for the Catholic faith against the Manichees led him to take up and finish the work, *The Catholic and the Manichee Way of Life*. This was followed by *True Religion*, dedicated to his patron, Romanianus, who had followed him into the snares of the Manichees. With an ardent desire to liberate this friend he writes an appreciative account of the Catholic doctrines of the Trinity and the Incarnation and speaks of the asset in having an institutional authority, the Church which, far from denying the value of reason, respects it, uses it, and goes beyond it in offering truths open only to faith. He also discusses the need for faith in reference to historical facts that must be reported by others who have experienced them, as in Scripture. In comparing philosophical religion with revealed religion he concluded that the Platonists knew God but did not worship him as God, joining as they did in rituals and magic of popular religion. (This indicates his awareness of Porphyry's works.) The first of five commentaries on Genesis was written in this monastic setting in AD 389: *On Genesis against the Manichees*.

In AD 391 on a visit to Hippo Regius (now called Annaba in Algeria, 45 miles from Thagaste) to confer with someone considering monastic life, and in search of a new location for a monastery, Augustine entered the local church. On seeing him, Valerius, a Greek-speaking Bishop of Hippo from Sicily, called out his need for an assistant priest. This way of obtaining priests was not uncommon in the fourth century. The congregation responded by citing Augustine's name. And with reluctance he consented.[5] He agreed to be ordained presbyter with the proviso that he could live in a monastery in the garden close to the Hippo church (S 355.1.2). Some companions from Thagaste also came, while others from Hippo joined them. It is unclear whether or not the monastery at Thagaste continued.

When asked by Valerius, not at ease in speaking Latin and unable to understand the Punic dialect, to preach in church — a task usually reserved for bishops — Augustine became aware of his need to study Scripture and asked for six months to continue his biblical education (E 21). His work *On Free Choice* now taken up and completed (end of II, all of III) reveals a deepened awareness of Catholic teaching on redemption and grace. In 393 he delivered at the Synod of Hippo a lecture *On Faith and the Creed* and in the same year began the *Literal Commentary on Genesis* which was never completed. This work raises philosophical questions concerning the created world.

Sermons and letters at this period show an intellectual involvement with the theology of the Incarnation of Christ, and of the redemption of humankind. It was also a time for Augustine of greater penetration into the epistles of St Paul. He completed the *Exposition of Eighty-four Propositions on the Epistle to the Romans*, a *Commentary on the Epistle to the Galatians*, and left incomplete a *Commentary on the Epistle to the Romans*. Later works during the Hippo period can be found in the bibliography: works pastoral and polemical, against Donatists and Pelagians, whose teachings will appear in later chapters.

In AD 395 Valerius wrote to the Bishop of Carthage, the episcopal primate, to ask that Augustine become coadjutor bishop. The answer was affirmative. In addition to that request being an unusual one, as not provided by Canon Law, it pertained to a priest not entirely trusted by Megalius, Bishop of Calama and primate of Numidia. He, along with some others, was more aware of Augustine the Manichee than of Augustine the Catholic Christian. This means that some were not convinced of the sincerity of Augustine's conversion. The Donatists, it has been suggested, may also have taunted the Catholics with having a priest once publicly noted for heresy and pagan sexual behaviour. After all, Augustine's baptism had taken place in Milan. Valerius felt that he had to seek the intervention of the Bishop of Carthage to ensure Augustine's consecration. The controversy over his sincerity which emerged at this time may have been a deciding factor in his writing the *Confessions* (397–401): a prose-poem of penitence for his past and of praise for God's loving providence. In its own way it is an apologia for his present sincerity. The occasion for the work might also have been Alypius's appeal to Augustine to write the story of Alypius's spiritual journey in response to a request from Paulinus of Nola who had inquired about the extent of Ambrose's influence on Alypius. Alypius was apparently too modest to fulfil the request and may have asked his friend, Augustine, to do it for him. Alypius also sent five books of Augustine to Paulinus. The latter may have asked Augustine to write his own story. This he did in such a way as to include the story of Alypius (C VI.7.11 – 10.16).

In any case, Possidius has told us that Augustine wanted to write the *Confessions* so that 'no one would believe or think him otherwise than he really was or greater than rumour made him'.[6]

In AD 395 Valerius ordained Augustine as auxiliary bishop; in 396 he became Bishop of Hippo upon the death of Valerius. For 35 years he remained there and converted the bishop's residence into a monastic household of clerics. Ten future bishops in Africa came from this monastic centre.[7]

In addition to his writing, his pastoral teaching and ministry at

Hippo, Augustine had to make almost fifty journeys to Carthage, a trip taking about nine days by the inland route.[8] Much of his time continued to be spent on debates and writings to defend Christian teaching against those who were putting forth opposing doctrines: the Manichees, the Donatists, the pagans, the Arians, the Pelagians. The details of these arguments will be examined in later chapters. Extant works of Augustine include treatises, letters, sermons, as well as commentaries on Scripture.

In AD 426 Heraclius was chosen by Augustine to be his successor, and to assist him in the episcopal ministry. With more time at his disposal, Augustine was able to review all his writings, to explain their purposes, and, where necessary, to make corrections. The Latin title is *Retractationes*, one best translated, according to Henry Chadwick, as *Reconsiderations*, because the book 'is almost as much a positive defence as a withdrawal of indiscretions'.[9]

The debate with Pelagianism (the theory that grace was not necessary for saving actions) was ongoing. When Augustine died in AD 430, he had not completed his refutation of a Pelagian, Julian of Eclanum (*c*. 386–454). The Vandals had begun a fourteen-month siege of the city of Hippo. In the third month of the siege Augustine died. He spent the last ten days of his life in constant prayer. He had the penitential psalms of David copied and placed on the wall, where he read them with abundant tears.

The Vandals, finally entering the city, burned it. Augustine's library was preserved by Possidius. At some point in time Augustine's body is said to have been taken to Sardinia, and in AD 724 ransomed 'by its weight in gold' by Count Liutprand, King of Lombardy, who wished to be buried near Augustine and Boethius. The bones were taken to Pavia in Italy where the sculpture at the main altar in St Peter's Church of the Golden Sky depicts high points in the life and deeds of Augustine, declared a saint by popular acclaim. On 28 August each year the Church celebrates the heroic virtues of this theologian and bishop who celebrated in his *Confessions* the merciful grace of God as source of all salvation and of all virtue.

Notes

1 Possidius, 'Life of St Augustine' in *Early Christian Biographies*, tr. R. J. Defarrari (Fathers of the Church 15; Washington, DC: The Catholic University of America Press, 1952), 12.
2 Ibid.
3 Ibid., 1.
4 P. Courcelle, *Les Lettres Grecques en Occident* (Paris: E. de Boccard, 1950) and *Recherches sur les Confessions de Saint Augustin* (Paris: E. de Boccard, 1950); P. Henry, *Plotin et l'Occident* (Louvain: Spicilegium Sacrum Lovaniense, 1934).
5 Possidius, op. cit., 4.
6 Ibid., Preface.
7 Ibid., 11.
8 Cf. O. Perler, *Les voyages de saint Augustin* (Paris: Etudes Augustiniennes, 1969).
9 H. Chadwick, *Augustine* (Oxford: Oxford University Press. 1986), p. 35.

2

Search for truth

In his nineteenth year Augustine was studying the books of rhetoric at Carthage in order to become an orator. Among the books was one written by Cicero, a book called *Hortensius*. This book related the high joys of a life devoted to wisdom. It was both an invitation to and introduction to philosophy, a discipline as yet unknown to Augustine. It made him realize the lack of this kind of joy in the life he was leading, and it inflamed him with a desire for truth. He turned to the Scriptures only to find them 'unworthy of comparison with the grand style of Cicero' (C III.5). Among his acquaintances at this time were some teachers of the doctrine of Mani, a Mesopotamian who had claimed that the Holy Spirit was made present in him. These Manichees called themselves Christians because they revered Christ, but they denied that he had a real human body, because their creation theory entailed matter coming from an evil Principle. They assured Augustine that reason alone can give access to truth. Other features of their doctrine also appealed to him. They accepted most of the New Testament. They rejected the genealogies and the infancy narratives, the Acts of the Apostles (because it described the Holy Spirit as having come at Pentecost), and passages from St Paul which disagreed with Manichean teaching. They repudiated the Old Testament as a bundle of absurdities. They interpreted evil as something occurring in someone rather than what someone did. To his religious sect Mani had taught that the universe had two principles: Light and Darkness or God and evil, both bodily. In the conflict between the Principle of Light and the Principle of Darkness, some of the divine being, light, was stolen by demons who gave it to the Principle of Darkness or the devil. The bodily world was created by God out of a mixture of the good and evil natures and is therefore evil. In human beings certain portions of light are present and account for an inner conflict of opposing forces. In view of this doctrine Augustine could exonerate himself from any moral blame for his actions. He began to approve of whatever the Manichees told him because he wanted it to be true. Encouraged by them, he used his eloquence in arguing with Catholics against the Catholic faith. This Manicheism shared the common Stoic assumption that everything is corporeal and thus did not help Augustine to think of God as anything other than a vast body; for a time it also quieted his urge to seek the origin of evil.

During his nine years as a Manichee Augustine read all the books available to him in the liberal arts as well as the *Categories* of Aristotle. These readings raised questions for him about the nature of the universe, questions which the Manichees told him could be answered by their Bishop, Faustus of Milevis. But when Faustus came to Carthage he proved unable to answer such questions. The Manichees lost credibility in Augustine's eyes and he began to regret that through his arguments many of his friends had been deceived. During this period he was accustomed to consult astrologers to give him some assurance of progress in his career. His friends assured him that any accurate prediction by astrologers was by chance, but he gave up on them when Nebridius pointed out that they gave opposite predictions concerning two infants born at exactly the same time and that the predictions were governed by what the astrologers knew of the family circumstances of each child (C IV.3.2 – VII.6.8).

Disillusioned with the false religion of the Manichees, Augustine nevertheless remained alienated from the Catholic faith because the Manichees had completely misrepresented it to him. After leaving for Rome he entered a twilight zone of disbelief in the human capacity for attaining truth, a position he learned about from Cicero, who wrote about the ancient sceptical philosophers called the Academics because they taught in the Academy where Plato had taught.

Augustine's release from misrepresentations of the Catholic religion began when, after accepting a post as public rhetor at Milan, he heard Bishop Ambrose giving explanations of Old Testament passages which the Manichees had read too literally and dismissed as absurd. One great obstacle remained, however, to any final liberation from Manicheism. That was Augustine's inability to conceive of anything real as being other than corporeal. Yet he found the philosophers' statements about physical elements and natural substances and the heavenly bodies more intelligible than the myths and fables concocted by the Manichees to explain natural events. He felt obliged to separate himself from them and he decided to remain a catechumen in the Catholic Church until he could find the light by which to steer his course.

Two events let in more light. One was the continued preaching of Ambrose; the other was his sudden reading of some books of the Platonists. Both experiences helped to remove the obstacle of materialism left over from Manicheism and present in Stoicism, a philosophy held by many Romans. Of Ambrose he wrote:

> Yet every Sunday I listened to him rightly preaching to the people the word of truth, and I became more and more sure that all those knots of cunning calumny which in their attacks on the holy books, my deceivers had tied could be unravelled ... I blushed to think of how for all these years I had been barking not against the Catholic faith but against figments of carnal imaginations. And indeed I had been rash and impious; for I had spoken in

condemnation of things which I ought to have taken the trouble to investigate (C VI.3.4).

The final stage in his intellectual liberation from Manichean materialism came when he read some books written by Platonists and translated from Greek into Latin by Marius Victorinus, a Roman orator. 'But then, after reading these books of the Platonists which taught me to seek for a truth which was incorporeal, I came to see your invisible things, understood by those things which are made' (C VII.9.13).

Augustine was now not only certain that God existed. He was also certain that God was infinite, 'yet not in the sense of being diffused through space' (C VII.20.26). Too morally weak to be able to enjoy God, Augustine felt inspired once again to read the Scriptures, especially the letters of Paul. He spoke of them as 'taming' him, disposing him to accept Christ the Saviour as the way to God. He learned that through these Scriptures one is 'not only instructed so as to know You who are the same forever, but also so as to grow strong enough to lay hold on You' (C VII.21). Although Augustine never denied the philosophical formation he received from the Platonists, the ten years which intervened between that event and his present life as a Catholic bishop had brought increased awareness of the limitations of philosophic reason in regard to happiness. As Bishop of Hippo he wrote of the 'presumption' of the philosophers who know their goal without knowing the way to it: Christ, the incarnate Word.

When Augustine told Simplicianus, Ambrose's assistant priest, that the books of the Platonists had removed some of his intellectual difficulties, the priest rejoiced because 'in the Platonists God and his Word are everywhere implied' (C VII.2.3). It is paradoxical that the man whose translation of the Platonic books had given Augustine a certain access to philosophic truth through reason also assisted him to receive faith in Christ and thus to receive Truth itself, source of all truths. This man was Victorinus. After having publicly praised the Roman gods as a professional orator he realized through reading the Scriptures and Christian writings that they were false gods. This fellow-African and renowned orator, whose statue had already been erected in Trajan's forum, humbly asked for Christian baptism and declared openly his salvation in front of the whole congregation (C VIII.2.4). On hearing this Augustine was on fire to have his courage. Shortly after this, another fellow-African visited him and told of Antony's life in the desert and of two young men in the emperor's service who left all to become like Antony as hermits.

These stories immediately preceded Augustine's own conversion as a response to St Paul's exhortation to follow Christ (Rom 13:13–15).

In awaiting baptism Augustine spent several months outside Milan in a villa at Cassiciacum. This was a period of concentrated philosophical exploration of questions relating to human capacity and human destiny. Surrounded by a few students and some relatives, he led these philosophical discussions. They became the point of departure for his theory of knowledge, his theory of happiness, and his theory of human and divine reality.

The first investigation concerned the possibility of attaining truth. If the sceptics were right and knowledge is impossible, Augustine would be wasting his time philosophizing about man and God. The roadblock of Academic Scepticism had to be removed before he could continue his journey in the pursuit of truth. After all, for some time he himself had adopted the cautious attitude of the sceptic who suspended judgement as to what is really true while accepting a probably true opinion in order to act. Some of his friends whom he had led into Manicheism did not follow him out of that sect but remained within it while unconvinced of its truth or the possibility of truth. One such friend was Romanianus. To him Augustine dedicated the dialogue called *Against the Academics* (AD 386).

Two needs compelled these early discussions. The first was the urgent need to determine whether there could be human access to truth because of what is at stake, namely, 'our life, our morals, our soul' (CA II.9.22). The second need was to manifest to others what he had come to realize: that philosophic reason, contrary to the teaching of the Manichees, was insufficient to open one to the truth that saves.

Augustine began by discussing the trustworthiness of the senses and the status of intellectual judgements. In later efforts to account for intellectual knowledge he formulated doctrines of the Divine Ideas and of illumination, but his beliefs concerning these are not altogether absent from the early writings.

SENSE KNOWLEDGE

Sense illusions were often cited as cause for disbelief in the objectivity of knowledge coming through the senses. Augustine cited the illusion of an oar when, within water, it is perceived as broken. He defended the eyes, however, for having reported what appears to be the case. Those who know the laws of the refraction of light are able to make a correct judgement that the oar is not broken.

In later writings he explained how sense knowledge occurs. Sensations are reliable reports of events occurring in the five senses. Perception of the sensible object, however, which arouses the sensations takes place because the human soul is vitally attentive to everything affecting the body, primarily for the purpose of preserving its life and health (E 122.2). Awareness of sensible things comes, therefore, through reports by the senses. But it becomes structured as knowledge by the imaginal and intellective functions of the soul. An image of the sensible object is fixed in the memory. This is Augustine's theory of active sensation. The soul is active even in the earliest stage of sense knowledge. Although the sensation comes from a sensible object, the sensation is produced by the soul which perceives the object after structuring it into an image. A sensible thing, a sense, a bodily and imaginal vision — all are needed but it is the soul which acts in them. Augustine defined perception as 'an action upon the body not hid from the soul' (DQ 24). The material aspects of sensation are not denied as necessary conditions, only as sufficient ones. There is a difference between looking at something and seeing something (DQ 27.53). The mind's eye is formed from that which the memory retains (DT XI.3.6). Therefore memory is more than a storehouse of past impressions; it is actively involved in mediating between perception and understanding (DT XI.8.14). Those who say that the oar seen in water is broken are misjudging through ignorance of the laws of light rather than from the unreliability of the senses.

INTELLECTUAL KNOWLEDGE

We know things intellectually, according to Augustine, indirectly through our senses, and directly through intellectual activity. The impossibility of having intellectual knowledge was the main contention of the Sceptics. When they settled for probability instead of certainty they spoke of the 'probable' as truth-like. Augustine responded: 'If someone who had never seen your father said, on seeing your brother, that he was like your father, you would consider him a madman or fool' (CA II.7.16). And to this he added: 'Likewise, the Academics are ridiculous in saying that in daily life they follow what is truth-like although they do not know what the truth is' (CA II.7.19).

Accepting the challenge to produce statements that cannot be taken as false, Augustine cites disjunctive statements such as: there is one world or many worlds. Equally true and obviously so is the expression of the law of contradiction: a thing cannot be both true and not true at the same time and in the same respect. Mathematical propositions are likewise recognizable as eternally true. In later writings he said: *si fallor, sum* (DLA II.37), if I am deceived, it is nevertheless true that I exist. Even if we doubt anything or everything, it is certain that while we are doubting we exist (DVR 73; DCD XI.26). To these he will add in later works the certainty that human self-awareness provides: 'Hence you know that you exist; you know you live; you know you understand' (SO II.1.1; DBe II.7: DT X.10.14). This self-awareness which is present during every human action is an habitual experience of truth and is distinguishable from self-reflection. Augustine calls the former *se nosse*, a self-presence; he calls the latter *se cogitare*, to reflect on one's knowledge (DT X.3.5). And finally, the Sceptics' categorical denial that true knowledge is possible is stated as a *truth* that all are invited to accept.

The exploration into all facets of human access to truth continued throughout Augustine's life. Two early treatises — *On the Teacher* and *On Free Choice* — dealt with the objectivity of knowledge and the transcendence of truth with respect to the human mind. In the former, a dialogue with Adeodatus, his son, there is stress on the priority of knowledge to words. Words are signs which signify thoughts. As a sign, a word points to a reality beyond itself. Thus the word indicates rather than represents. The subordination of words to thoughts is recognizable in the fact that unless one knows the reality that a word signifies, it does not function as a sign; it does not point to anything beyond itself (DMa 26). In Augustine's view, words can signify external objects or thoughts or intentions. Christopher Kirwan is critical of this view and asks: do words really signify thoughts or are they the subject matter of those thoughts? He asserts that groups of words rather than single words convey thought. But he also points out that Wittgenstein's insights regarding ostensive definition are in harmony with passages in the treatise *On the Teacher*.[1]

Since truth is immutable, whereas the human mind is mutable, Augustine concluded that the truth of thought must arise from the presence of a participated light shining within the mind. He uses this metaphor of 'illumination' as early as the work *On the Teacher*, but he explains it more fully in later writings; yet it is never sufficiently clarified in my opinion. All one can do is to let the reader hear Augustine explaining it. 'But when things are spoken of which we perceive through the mind, that is, through intellect and reason, we are talking about things which, being present, we see in that inner light by which he himself who is called the inner man is illuminated, and in which he delights' (DMa xii. 40). He seems to indicate that the mind is naturally empowered to know truth because, in being created to the image of God who is truth, there is present here a certain connaturality. The Creator never withdraws from his creation. Since human beings are created through the Word or Wisdom of God, Augustine tells Adeodatus that Christ is the interior teacher through whom all have access to truth. This is made explicit in a later work: 'For our illumination is participation in the Word, namely, in that life that is the light of humankind' (DT IV.4; C IV.25; DCD X.2). The truth lives in the Wisdom of the Son so that 'The Son *qua* Word of God can be called God's creative plan' (JE I.9).

In the treatise *On Free Choice* (395), begun in Rome and completed in Hippo, Augustine again presents evidence for truth in the form of *a priori* judgements, mathematical propositions, and moral norms. He notes that whereas human truths are qualified by objectivity and immutability, the mutable aspect of temporal existence is obvious in the ascending scale of existing, living, knowing (*esse, vivere, intelligere*). Therefore, the source of objective and immutable truth has to transcend the human mind. The mutually contradictory properties of immutability/mutability entail radically different realities. The experience of truth has to be an experience of eternal being. This truth, above the human mind, and illuminating man's natural acts of judging and apprehending essences, is an immutable Wisdom identifiable with God. This Wisdom is the fourth step in the ascending scale of being, living, knowing. Such Wisdom is the Good, sought by all. To understand that God is the Good and to judge all goods in relation to it is human wisdom, the object of the philosopher's quest. Because truth is superior to the human mind, characterized as it is by immutability and eternity, it is not subject to the mind; it is not constructible by it. Wisdom is the highest truth and is 'the Selfsame' (*idipsum*). To participate in Wisdom is to be in contact with eternal Being (C IV.25; DT IV.4; DCD X.2). In disagreement with Plato and Plotinus, but in agreement with the Middle Platonists, Augustine taught that the archetypes or forms or ideas of all realities are primordial forms in the mind of God in accord with which he creates.

DIVINE IDEAS

In Question 46 of *Eighty-three Different Questions* Augustine discusses at length the divine ideas, the forms of things through which they receive their ontological truth. This 'intelligible world' is identified with the Word of God through whom the world was created by the divine Trinity. These divine ideas are creating and ordering principles. But in no way are they additions to the divine Being (DT IV.3). A passage in the *City of God* confirms this, while simultaneously attributing to Plato what was really the teaching of the Middle Platonists. 'And God, as Plato constantly reminds us, held in his eternal understanding the forms, not only of the entire universe, but also of all animate beings. Forms are in the Son of God *qua* Word' (DCD XII.27). These divine ideas are the standards by which judgements concerning temporal realities are made, and the mind has access to them by illumination (DGnL XII.24).

DIVINE ILLUMINATION

Augustine's theory of divine illumination is intimately linked with the divine ideas. He wrote: 'These ideas are present to the gaze of the mind in a certain incorporeal light of its own kind' (DT XII.15.24). There is also a natural link between these ideas and created realities which accounts for the understanding of an idea and a knowledge of what participates in it. Illumination is entailed by the human experience of knowing whatever is true. What we today call self-evidence in the experience of an intrinsically intelligible truth is quite like the experience which Augustine calls illumination. The experience which we might call 'insight', the seeing of something as necessarily true, is also suggestive of illumination. Since neither the mutable mind nor the material senses can be the complete source of true intellectual judgements, human beings must, Augustine thinks, participate in truth through a shining down of the Ideas of God (DLA II.12.33; III.1.1). Etienne Gilson says that it is by closeness to God that the rational soul is illumined by God with the incorporeal light through which it knows the 'eternal reasons' by its own intelligence.[2] Ronald Nash explains that the illumination occurs because there is a natural harmony between the created world and the human mind.[3] The human mind is aware of eternal truths, at least virtually, and uses them to pass judgement on the created things patterned after them.

In his book entitled *The Light of the Mind*, Nash reduces the numerous interpretations of divine illumination to four kinds which he calls the Thomistic, the Franciscan, the Formal, and the Ontological. In his review of this book, E. L. Fortin summarized Nash's discussion in this way:

The first and least acceptable of these, defended by Boyer, identifies the divine light of which Augustine speaks with the agent intellect and falsely ascribes to Augustine a theory of abstraction analogous to that of Aristotle. The second, to which the name of Portalié is attached, argues that the ideas are impressed on the human mind by God himself but leaves the mind with only a passive role to play in the act of knowing. The third, which finds its chief proponents in Gilson, DeWulf, Copleston, and Kaelin, sees the role of illumination as that of imparting a quality of certitude or necessity to the ideas but is unable to account for their content. There remains the ontological interpretation, hitherto shunned by most historians, which alone would do full justice to the complexity of Augustine's thought and which combines among other things the benefits of conceptualism and realism. In essence, it postulates an immediate awareness of the eternal truths on the part of the human mind. This statement is not to be taken to mean that man sees all things in God, as Malebranche later contended, but that man's reason has been so structured by God as to be capable of knowing the ideas in the divine mind as well as the creation that is patterned on them. Only by having recourse to such an isomorphism, Nash suggests, is it possible to resolve what he calls the three great paradoxes with which any account of Augustine's views must come to grips and explain; namely, how the human intellect is both active and passive, how the archetypal forms are at once distinct and not distinct from the mind itself, and how the mind is and is not at the same time the light that makes knowledge possible. A brief synthesis of the most pertinent Augustinian texts accordingly reveals (1) that the ideas in the mind are *a priori*, that is to say, not derived from experience, (2) that they are *virtual* or not always actually thought, and (3) that they constitute the necessary *precondition of science*.

Diverse interpretations have been made because there are texts which seem to indicate that God is the direct illuminator in human knowing. Yet there are also texts which are most explicit in saying that there is no direct intervention of God himself in the act of knowing. One such is this: 'the nature of the intellectual mind is so formed as to see those things which, according to the disposition of the Creator, are subjoined to intelligible things in the natural order, in a sort of incorporeal light of its own kind, as the eye of the flesh sees things that lie about it in this corporeal light, of which light it is made to be receptive and to which it is adapted' (DT XII.15.24). And again: 'illumined by Him with light, intelligible light, the soul discerns — not with physical eyes, but with *its own highest part in which lies its excellence, i.e. with its intelligence* those reasons whose vision brings to it full blessedness'.

This illumination of the mind is a metaphor related to the fact that one needs light in order to see a sensible object, yet the light does not do the seeing. The existence of Absolute Truth is like the sun which makes possible a human person's knowing of partial truths. Augustine clearly teaches that in this life no one sees God, and yet he teaches that because there are divine ideas we are able to make true judgements. And so God, being one with the ideas through which he has created the world, is the ultimate source of human knowing. Because of God's existence, the mind judges truly just as the senses having power to see sensible things can do so only in the light of the sun or its substitute (S 1.12). By his illumination theory he does not intend to deny that 'knowing' is a natural human activity, but he is affirming that since truth has divine characteristics (immutability, eternity) rather than human ones (mutability, temporality), any true human knowledge witnesses to an affinity with God.

A recent and unsuccessful interpretation of this illumination theory has been made by Alasdair MacIntyre in his Gifford lectures where he gives an account of Aquinas's work as the culmination and integration of the Augustinian and Aristotelian traditions. In describing how a child first learns a name by a teacher pointing at something, he writes:

> The mind thus has to find within itself that which points it towards a source of intelligibility beyond itself, one which will provide what ostension by itself cannot; guided towards that source it discovers within itself an apprehension of timeless standards, of forms, an apprehension which is itself possible only in the light afforded by a source of intelligibility beyond the mind.[4]

MacIntyre seems to be going aside from Augustine's own teaching when, after saying that 'the analogical use of the concept of light, with its assimilation of the intelligible to the visible is essential to the Augustinian epistemology', he adds: 'So God is present to every human mind, albeit often unrecognized, in every act of apprehension and judgement, and present not only as omnipresent creator but *as constituting that act of apprehension and judgement*'.[5] It is true that Augustine left unstated just how the human intellect is related to the divine ideas (later, Aquinas will say that it is through the essence abstracted from material things that there is coincidence between human ideas and divine ideas). But Augustine does not specify God as constituting human apprehension and judgement. Illumination as a grace for understanding what one believes is distinct from natural illumination enabling the intellect to have insight regarding *a priori* truths. Thus, *pace* MacIntyre, human beings in a state of nature do not, according to Augustine, lack understanding altogether.[6]

Nor is it the case that the Augustinian theory supposes that 'all intellectual error is rooted in moral defect'.[7] Indeed in the *City of God* Augustine cites the errors of many philosophers whom he never accuses of moral fault. He does say that humility is needed to accept authority; therefore, it is needed for faith, which prepares for the understanding of revealed Christian doctrine. On the other hand, in his work *On the Trinity* Augustine speaks of the soul as

21

... reminded that it should turn to the Lord as to that light by which it was touched in some way, even when it was turned away from Him. For hence it is that even the godless think of eternity, and rightly condemn and rightly praise many things in the moral conduct of men. By what rules, pray, do they judge these things if not by those in which they see how each one ought to live, even though they themselves do not live in the same manner? Where do they see them? For they do not see them in their own nature, since these things are doubtless in the mind, and their minds are admittedly changeable; but it sees these rules as unchangeable ... where are these rules written in which even the unjust man recognizes what is just, and in which he perceives that he ought to have what he does not have. Where, then, are they written except in the book of that light which is called Truth. From thence every just law is transcribed and transferred to the heart of the man who works justice, not by wandering to it but being, as it were, impressed upon it ... But he who does not work justice, and yet sees what is to be worked, he it is who is turned away from this light but is still touched by it (DT XIV.15.21; R I.4.2).

When MacIntyre asserts that the totality of Augustine's thought must be believed to understand any part of it, is he implying that there is no distinction within Augustine's total teaching of what can be known by human reason and what must be accepted on faith? Surely his first and foremost task as a Christian thinker was to defend the possibility of acquiring truth through human reason. Could he have accepted as much as he did from previous philosophers if he had claimed 'that it is only through an initial commitment to one specific type of Christian belief that rational enquiry can be developed'?[8] On the contrary, he praised the Platonists for intellectually discovering the goal of human aspirations. It is only the way (the incarnate Word, Jesus of history) to the goal which concerns salvation and requires faith in a trusted authority: the Christ of Scriptures.

Surely Question 48 of *Eighty-three Different Questions* could have saved MacIntyre from his unwarranted generalization. There Augustine raises the question of what can be believed.

Three classes of things are objects of belief. First, there are those things which always are believed and never understood, e.g., history, which deals with events both temporal and human. Second, there are those things which are understood as soon as they are believed, e.g. all human reasonings either in mathematics or in any of the sciences. Third, there are those things which are first believed and afterwards understood [Is 7:9 S]. Of such a character is that which cannot be understood of divine things except by those who are pure in heart. This understanding is achieved through observing those commandments which concern virtuous living.

It is obvious that MacIntyre subsumes all knowledge under the third category, namely, truths pertaining to salvation. Augustine often referred to *a priori* truths as being in the memory. He feared, however, that the word 'memory' might too closely link his illumination theory with the recollection theory of Plato. Plato's theory entailed the soul's pre-existence in an intelligible world where the Forms or Ideas had been seen and subsequently forgotten through earthly embodiment. Although

Augustine sometimes mentioned the pre-existence theory he tried to guard himself against being interpreted as favouring the soul's pre-existence. In reviewing the early work *Against the Sceptics*, he referred to what he had written of the soul there (II.3.7): 'It will return the more safely into heaven.' 'But I would have been safer in saying "will go" rather than "will return" because of those who think that human souls, having fallen from or having been driven out of heaven in punishment for their sins, are thrust into bodies here below' (R I.1.3). In his work *On the Trinity* Augustine mentions Plato's theory of recollection and distances himself from it. 'But we should rather believe that the nature of the intellectual mind is so formed, that, joined by the Creator's plan to intelligible objects in a natural order, it sees these objects in a kind of incorporeal light of a special kind, just as the eye of the flesh sees objects in its immediate vicinity in the bodily light, for it has been created receptive to, and compatible with, it' (DT XII.24).

For the most part, one's awareness of the divine light is mediated through the experience of any human knowledge. But some philosophers, according to Augustine, had a mystical experience by contact with the Light. They 'have been able to penetrate with their mind's eye beyond all created things and to touch, although it be ever so small a part, the light of the unchangeable Truth' (DT IV.15.20; C IX.24).

Undoubtedly, Augustine's illumination theory shows the influence of certain passages in the *Enneads* of Plotinus (V.3.17; V.5.7; VI.7.23). An acknowledgement of this can be found in the *City of God*. But there we also read that this Platonic theory found favour with Augustine because it agreed with the Gospel which speaks of John the baptizer as a witness to the Light 'which enlightens every man who comes into the world' (John 1:6–9); 'He was not that Light', 'a distinction', Augustine said, 'which sufficiently proves that the rational or intellectual soul such as John cannot be its own light, but needs illumination from another, the true Light' (DCD X.2). The fact that all receive illumination indicates that human knowledge is a natural process, not reserved to those having grace. Rather than explaining how human knowledge actually takes place Augustine seems more interested, with the Neoplatonists, in maintaining that the human soul can transcend the mutable world.

Nevertheless, Christ the Light of the world is, for Augustine, the interior teacher who makes possible not merely the illumination of minds to know partial truths but the very seeing of God. This Light shone in darkness, and darkness did not comprehend it. Through Adam's sin his posterity fell into darkness and lost the clear vision of God. To restore hope for this vision, Christ offered the light of faith as a step toward the fullness of truth by 'understanding' now and 'vision' later. 'Thus he became a man whom men could see, so that, healed by faith, they might afterwards see what then they could not see' (E 140.3.7). In a recent work Carol Harrison has given a full development of Augustine's growing appreciation of the role and value of sensible reality in restoring to human beings that awareness of God lost through Adam's sin. She claims that Augustine taught that the appreciation of beauty in the created world, in history, in human persons, in the Incarnate Son stimulated 'faith in their divine source, hope for vision of it, and love which moves towards it'.[9]

In the need to argue against Scepticism, Augustine emphasized in his early writings the power of human reason. But human reason itself does not explain the *quest* for knowledge. As an essential activity of the soul, the will is operative in knowing, above all in seeking knowledge. In many of his works Augustine teaches that 'human knowledge is formed by the purpose of thought' (SO I.13; DT X.11; XV.43).[10]

But to attain to certain objects there is something more needed than intellect and will. Lest his statements on behalf of reason might seem an apologia for the Manichean position that the rational mind can know all that is necessary for happiness and thereby reinforce the allegiance for Romanianus and others to that sect, Augustine also stressed the role of authority and faith in knowing one's Christian destiny. He advocated, as eminently reasonable, the use of faith to promote understanding of Christian doctrines. Faith, he held, is a reasonable attitude in the search for truth which transcends the natural powers of knowing. Confidence in the possibility of arriving at the truth which saves is generated by the Gospel invocation: 'Seek and you shall find.' The finding of truth that gives eternal joy comes through the gift of faith, offered to all (DDoC II.12.17; E 120.2; JE VII.29.6).

What Augustine taught concerning the spirituality of human knowing has never been more deeply nor more extensively explored than it has been within recent years. Through his introspective method Augustine made observations and analyses that can enrich contemporary philosophy of mind. In bringing to the surface for philosophers the inner data of human knowledge concealed in Augustine's metaphors, Bruce Bubacz has demonstrated that Augustine is an important epistemologist who showed the mind's activity and capability in his unified account of knowledge.[11]

The present day discussion of the body–mind problem has stimulated Ludger Holscher to search the texts of Augustine for his estimate of the non-material aspects of human activities. Holscher concludes that by such activities 'man is capable . . . of transcending himself and entering into meaningful cognitive contact with the world and other persons, of acting on the world freely and in a morally responsible way, of knowing and determining *himself* in a fully awakened conscious manner . . . As such a conscious, spiritual, personal being each man is also absolutely unique and irreplaceable.[12] After agreeing with Augustine that the analysis of knowledge demonstrates the substantiality of the human soul (DT XII.1; II.8.14), Holscher refers to those properties that belong neither to the soul alone nor to the body alone, but only to a psychophysical being. For man to be this 'one concrete being essentially presupposes the distinctness of its two components, body and soul'.[13] This concrete being, a psycho-physical unity, is a person; it is so, however, primarily in virtue of its spiritual soul. After elaborating on Augustine's analyses of human activities, Holscher enters into critical dialogue with the materialistic anthropologies directly addressed by Augustine and with those that have succeeded them, namely, epiphenomenalism, mind–brain identity theory, Marxism, and others.

Another scholar who has done research on Augustine's philosophy of mind, Gerard O'Daly, wants to stress the fact that 'a chronological approach reveals no substantial development, still less any fundamental change . . . The main lines of Augustine's approach to problems of the soul and mind are established by 386.'[14] He concludes that the Neoplatonic theories of intellection and the forms did not influence the structure of Augustine's theory although it was affected by some of their terminological features. He admits, however, that Augustine adapted one of the hypostases − Nous (mind) − to his account of the states of the angelic order and its cognition, especially in its conversion to God as Truth.[15]

Notes

1 Christopher Kirwan, *Augustine* (London: Routledge, 1989), p. 53.
2 E. Gilson, *The Christian Philosophy of St Augustine* (New York: Scribners, 1960), pp. 66–111.
3 R. H. Nash, *The Light of the Mind* (Lexington, KY: The University Press of Kentucky, 1969). Review by E. Fortin, *The Thomist*, V.34 (1970), pp. 692–5.
4 A. MacIntyre, *Three Rival Versions of Moral Enquiry* (Notre Dame, IN: University of Notre Dame Press, 1990), p. 84.
5 Ibid., p. 100.
6 Ibid., p. 101.
7 Ibid., p. 110.
8 Ibid., p. 102.
9 C. Harrison, *Beauty and Revelation in the Thought of Augustine* (Oxford: Clarendon Press, 1992), p. 46.
10 G. O'Daly, *Augustine's Philosophy of Mind* (Berkeley: University of California Press, 1987), p. 211.
11 B. Bubacz, *St Augustine's Theory of Knowledge* (New York: The Edwin Mellen Press, 1981).
12 L. Holscher, *The Reality of Mind* (New York: Routledge & Kegan Paul, 1986), p. 209.
13 Ibid., p. 217.
14 O'Daly, op. cit., pp. 4–5.
15 Ibid., p. 196.

3

Happiness and human existence

On reading the *Confessions* one realizes that the young Augustine sought happiness in a variety of ways, chiefly among perishable things. The first seven chapters tell the story of an unhappy child, a confused youth, a miserable man. His first clue that there were pleasures in intellectual activities directed towards stable realities came, as we have seen, through Cicero, and later through Plotinus and Porphyry. Hence the urgency of his defence of the human access to truth, which began with his dialogue *Against the Sceptics* and developed, as noted, into a theory of knowledge entailing divine ideas and illumination.

The first question raised, however, in this dialogue was whether happiness comes from the possession of truth or the mere quest of it. Clearly any answer must be related to the nature of happiness. Therefore, Augustine interrupted the dialogue on his thirty-second birthday, 13 November 386, to begin another on *The Happy Life*. This dialogue lasted three days and became the first completed work since his conversion. It was followed by the second part of the interrupted discussion on the possibility of attaining truth.

The Happy Life opened with a general agreement that the desire for happiness is a universal one. This position was not so much an assumption on Augustine's part as a legacy from the philosophers to Greek and Roman culture. In Cicero's *Hortensius* there was a strong assertion of the intrinsic connection between philosophic activity and happiness, a decidedly Aristotelian notion expressed in the *Nicomachean Ethics* (1099a15). It is found also with Plato in *Phaedrus* (248b) and *Symposium* (210a), and above all with Plotinus (*Ennead* I.4.3.). Plotinus added to the commonly accepted notion that all men desire happiness the affirmation that some men achieve it in temporal life. They do so through contemplation of the highest reality, the One (VI.9.11.32). Thus the happy life is within human reach (I.4.3.39). It is reached by becoming like the One who is the Good and the source of beauty (I.6.8.16), a likeness demanding discipline of the senses and self-identity: the reclaiming of one's intellectual orientation toward the One (V.3.17.38).

With this philosophical background it is not surprising that Augustine begins his formal investigation into the nature of happiness by discussing his hazardous voyage to the *port of philosophy* 'from which one enters the hinterland of the happy life' (DBe I.1). The participants in the discussion were his mother, Monica, his brother, Navigius, his son, Adeodatus, two African students, Trygetius and Licentius, and two relatives, Lastidianus and Rusticus.

The first question raised was whether happiness consists in having what one desires. To this they agreed, but Monica added: only if one desires good things. And Augustine added: the reality desired must be something permanent, 'neither dependent on fate nor subject to any mishap'. When Trygetius suggested that some people favoured by fortune considered themselves happy, Augustine responded that as long as some misfortune could occur, there was fear of losing what they had; such fear would eliminate happiness. Therefore, anyone desiring happiness must obtain that which cannot be snatched away.

In this way the desire for happiness is connected with the desire for truth. Thus Augustine related their discussion to the question of Scepticism. No one, he said, does not wish to possess what he desires. Since the Sceptics, in only searching for the truth, do not possess it, they cannot be happy. But no one is wise if he is not happy. Therefore, the Academic is not wise (II.14). In this move Augustine implied that the innate desire for happiness is an innate desire for truth. This view is related to the previous observation that being in need constitutes misery which cannot exist simultaneously with happiness. Referring to a man of great riches, he had suggested that this man might not be considered miserable. Whereupon Monica said: 'he still was in need of wisdom, since he entertained the fear of losing what he possessed. Are we going to consider him in need, if he is without silver and gold and not in need if he should lack wisdom?' (DBe I.4).

Augustine expressed 'delight because it was she who had uttered that truth which, as gleaned from the books of the philosophers, I had intended to bring forward as an imposing final argument' (I.4). And so they conclude that happiness is nothing other than not to be in need, that is, to be wise. The wise soul is characterized by moderation and temperance, keeping its balance between extremes. When this soul devotes itself to the wisdom that is God, it possesses moderation and is happy.

> We have heard through divine Authority that the Son of God is nothing but the wisdom of God, and the Son of God is truly God. Thus everyone possessing God is happy . . . But do you believe that Wisdom is different from Truth? For it has been said: 'I am the Truth' (John 14:6). The Supreme Measure of truth is God the Father. Whoever attains the Supreme Measure, through the Truth, is happy. This means, to have God within the soul, that is, to enjoy God (IV.33–34).

In his last remarks Augustine says that, while still seeking, one is not yet wise nor fully happy. But he adds that Christ is the Way, the Truth, and the Life, and to recognize this is the happy life (IV.35). Monica has the last word in saying that the Trinity is the true happy life 'which we

27

must assume that we can attain soon by a well-founded faith, a joyful hope, and an ardent love' (IV.35).

This discussion of happiness and other treatments of it in the dialogues indicate that with Augustine's embracing of philosophy came a conviction at first that happiness is attainable in this life. Several authors have recorded a radical change in his attitude as his knowledge of Scripture increased.[1]

Throughout his life the theme of happiness was rarely absent from any of his writings. We have seen that, helped by Plotinus, he discovered that God is the goal of the search for happiness. The harmony of this goal with the natural functioning of the human soul is presented in great detail in Book XIX of the *City of God*. There Augustine reviews Varro's description on 288 schools of philosophy differentiated by their definitions of the highest good, and therefore, of happiness. This is not an argument against the universal desire for happiness, but it indicates that all do not understand happiness in the same sense. Augustine himself had entertained some doubt regarding the universality of this desire, asking 'How can I search for what I have not yet known?' (C X.20.29). It occurred to him that there might be some dim memory of happiness in the human race through its descent from Adam, who had been created in happiness. But he came to realize that the experience of truth is implicitly an involvement with something permanent and very satisfying.

The early insight arrived at in *The Happy Life*, namely, that fear and happiness are mutually exclusive, eventually led Augustine to realize that complete happiness is possible only when the human person is permanently united to God, the Truth, after the resurrection of the body. Indeed, in *The Trinity* Augustine gives a proof for the immortality of the soul from the universal desire for happiness, a desire that cannot be completely satisfied in this life (XIII.8.11). The list of disasters that have occurred and can occur in earthly life, as noted in Book XIX of the *City of God*, is no evidence of pessimism. It is a realistic assessment of happiness as a participation in eternity rather than an experience in time. Happiness is available in hope (DDoC I.22.20; DT IX.1.1; XIII.7.10; C X.20.29; DCD II.29; XIX.4.10; XXII.30; DME I.11.18). The fulfilment of that hope, based on Christ's promises, will be an eternal peace where the highest activity of the human spirit is enjoying the vision of God (R I.2.). This happiness is described as far as it can be in the last book of the *City of God*. 'And this is nothing else than what God has promised — that he will give eternal happiness to souls joined to their own bodies' (XXII.27).

Following his method of taking from the philosophers whatever they taught that was true and completing their insights with truths revealed by God (that is, walking two paths to wisdom: reason and faith), Augustine developed a more adequate theory of happiness than that with which he began. In the *Confessions* he maintains what he concluded in *The Happy Life*, praying: 'Thou Thyself art joy. And this is the happy life, to rejoice unto Thee ... and there is none other' (C X.22.32). Happiness is therefore not to be located in a person's subjective feelings, nor even in the virtues adorning the human being. There is no true human perfection apart from God; the vision of God will be the true fulfilment of the human person. The philosophers pointed to the goal but not to the way to it. Christ who opens the soul to faith, hope and charity is the Way. Those who do not know him but live well by obeying the eternal law available to all persons through conscience are on the road to happiness. But those who turn within, and find both the unchanging being above the mind and their relationship with the divine ideas, already participate in the truth that generates happiness. God uses the structure of the mind which he has created to make his presence known. Is Augustine not more concerned with this divine illuminating presence than with any analysis of precisely how thought-formation takes place?

Augustine's proof for God's existence, for illumination, in the dialogue *On Free Choice* provides the philosophical underpinning for the search for happiness. God is always with the human being, but is the human being with God? Augustine thinks that the Plotinian experience of God which is not a vision of him but an ineffable union has to be but a fleeting experience. If sustained it would be the beatific vision (C IX.10.25). Augustine has come to the conclusion that the happiness of knowing God in this life, of being with him, should have as much constancy as possible in approximation to the permanence of the future beatific vision of God. Awareness of the presence of God in intellectual activity is a first step toward possessing him, being with him by love.

Through his understanding of God as a trinity of Father, Son and Holy Spirit, with the Holy Spirit as *caritas* (love), given to the human soul at baptism, he discovered that the love of God both promoted the knowledge of God here on earth and was the fruit of that knowledge. Just as Father, Son and Spirit are mutually implied, so too is their image in the human soul: the memory-mind, knowledge and love (DT IX.4.7; X.1.3).

This stress on love as a response to God's love revealed in Christ Jesus and making possible the possession of God here and now radically transformed the way to happiness opened to Augustine by the philosophers. To possess God is to love God (DME I.34; XIV.25). Philosophers can become aware of his reality through introspection and an analysis of knowledge; Christ made known the reality of God's love to all.

Under the influence of the incarnation and the resurrection of the body of Christ, Augustine expanded his theory to include happiness, not only for the soul, but for the body through the soul. With the philosophers he sees, as they did, the need for immortality, but not of the soul alone. The incarnation of Christ has affected both the concept of the nature of happiness as the fulfilment of both body and soul, and of the way to happiness as faith in Christ who opens one to grace, a participation in divine life. Such grace can only be given to intellectual souls whose spiritual activity gives them a likeness to God (DT XIII.19.24; DME VII.2; DCD IX.17). In reviewing *The Happy Life* at the end of his life, Augustine regretted that he had in some respects accepted the opinions of the philosophers that happiness can be achieved in this life, 'yet the Apostle Paul hopes for a perfect knowledge of God, the greatest that man can have, in the life to come (1 Cor 13:12–13), for that alone should be called a happy life where the incorruptible and immortal body will be subject to its spirit without any vexation or resistance' (R I.2). But indeed the transformation of what the philosophers had contributed to Greek and Roman culture, great as it was, had already begun, as we noted, even before the dialogue *On the Happy Life* ended. Moreover, it might be more aptly called a completion of what they taught.

Because of the centrality of happiness in the thought of Augustine he is usually and rightly called a *eudaimonist*. A eudaimonist is one who sees happiness as the end or purpose of ethical action. When this is taken as signifying one who seeks his own happiness in everything he does, it can be, and often is, repudiated as selfishness. However, in teaching (as will be seen in the chapter on morality) that the love of God is happiness and that Christ clearly taught that the love of God cannot be separated from the love of neighbour, the Augustinian version of *eudaimonism* involves constant concern for others and generosity.

HUMAN REALITY

Augustine's view of humanity originated under the pressure of his search for the true meaning of happiness. At first he repeated the common definition presented in school logic books, namely: man is a rational mortal being (DOR II.31; DMa 24). He also spoke in Platonic fashion of the soul using the body (DME I.27.52; DQ 13.22). For the most part he referred to man rather than human person because these two expressions signified for him the same reality, a human being. This is apparent in the statement: 'The soul with a body does not make two persons, but one man' (JE XIX.15). Augustine's later theory of human reality was related to his view of the world as created and to his view of human knowledge. In an early letter to Nebridius, and also in the *Confessions* (X.10.17), he suggests three aspects of any reality: whether it is, what it is, and to what is it ordered. In Letter 140.2.3 he classifies reality hierarchically as divine, psychic and bodily. On the divine level God dwells in eternity; within the divine mind are the eternal truths (*rationes aeternae*), like Platonic forms, but now modified as the divine knowledge, one with the divine Being. These divine Ideas, as we saw above, are the eternal patterns for all created things. This is the level of immutability. On the lowest level are material things, mutable in space and time. In this region is constant change regulated by *rationes seminales*, hidden forms like seeds, created within matter in the beginning by God for the sake of the future development of the world. This sensible level is inferior to the psychic level and to the divine level, but it is in no way evil. All natures are intrinsically good as physical realities (DNB). Evil is not a nature; it is a corruption of the good will, a deflection from its end, and in this way could be called an event. It is the privation or absence of a perfection which ought *to be present*, but *is not present* (DD7 I.2.8).

Between God and purely bodily things there is the human soul, mutable in time but not in place. To account for this mutability Augustine attributed 'spiritual matter' to the soul. He spoke of God as having created spiritual and corporeal prime matter (DGnM I.5; DGnL VII.7; XII.32; E 120.2; *Ennead* II.43). Along with previous thinkers, he cited composition in the soul as distinguishing it from the utter simplicity of God. Without the notion of the composition of essence and existence in created things, a notion used by St Thomas Aquinas, the notion of spiritual matter denoted the difference between the soul and pure Spirit, God. Spiritual matter did not possess the characteristics of physical matter (EnP 145.4). The soul's consciousness implies its superiority to any body. The soul's possession of ideas, its activities of perceiving, understanding, willing, its self-awareness and self-reflection were an assurance to Augustine of its spirituality. For this reason he placed the soul on the intermediate level of reality, although well aware that, on earth, souls do not exist apart from bodies.

In addition to his hierarchy of natures, Augustine presents a hierarchy of created activities: being, living, sensing, remembering, understanding (DQ 33). We have seen that in his theory of knowledge he regarded sensing as an activity of the soul by its attentiveness to the sense organs. Since the body belongs to a lower level, it cannot act upon the soul. Remembering, understanding and willing are acts of the human soul which come directly from the soul itself, assisted by illumination through the soul's mysterious kinship with the divine Ideas.

Within this intellectual soul Augustine recognizes another hierarchy, starting from discursive reasoning and moving to reflecting on good actions, to doing the good, to desiring the highest contemplation, and finally to contemplating God. The soul is present in all these activities; Augustine does not refer to powers as intervening between the soul and its activities. He attributes to the soul three kinds of vision: bodily, imaginal (*spiritalis*) and intellectual (DGnL XII.6–14).

After having radically distinguished the kind of reality that body is from the kind that soul is, Augustine nevertheless taught that human nature included both. He noted, with Varro's help, that some philosophers placed the supreme good in the soul, some in the body, and some in both (DCD XIX.3). Varro opted for both and therefore thought that happiness, made up of bodily and spiritual goods, is possible in this life for the virtuous man. Augustine, as previously explained, regarded human vulnerability to change and loss of every kind as incompatible with that perfect happy life which must lack all fear. He saw the life of virtue as demanding vigilance and fortitude in the midst of temptations and dangers. Those who live rightly will attain the happiness of eternal life. Eternity is an essential mark of happiness, as Augustine sees it. 'There we shall enjoy the gifts of nature, that is, all that God the Creator of all natures has bestowed upon ours — gifts not only good but eternal — not only of the spirit, healed now by Wisdom, but also of the body, renewed by the resurrection' (DCD XIX.10). Eternal life in peace is the supreme good of the City of God, which is the community of all those who love God with their whole mind, heart and soul, and who love their neighbours as themselves. Those who live their temporal life in reference to eternal life are happy not in fullness but in hope (DCD XIX.20). Such is the peace now enjoyed through faith that generates hope, later to be enjoyed through vision. The risen body of the human individual will be his or her very own body, though spiritualized, as was Christ's risen body. 'Take away death, the last enemy, and my own flesh will be my dear friend throughout eternity' (S 155.15).

In his view of human reality Augustine does not go along with a Platonic identification of man with the soul. Numerous are the statements testifying to this. 'A soul united to a body does not make two persons but one' (JE XIX.5.). 'For man is not a body alone nor a soul alone but a being composed of both' (DCD XIII.24). And again: 'Anyone who wishes to separate the body from the soul is stupid' (DAO IV.2.2). In fact, human beings should be instructed about the way to love themselves, 'how to love their bodies so that they may take care of them reasonably and wisely' (DDoC I.25.26; R II.41).

Nevertheless, just how the soul, a spiritual substance, is united to the body, a bodily one, was for Augustine a puzzling problem. He considered it a greater mystery than the union of the divine and human natures in the incarnate Christ. Augustine does not explain this union as that of matter and form. Plotinus had rejected this Aristotelian distinction, as well as the Stoic interpretation of the whole human reality as bodily. In welcoming the Platonic view of the soul and body as two substances, Plotinus nevertheless gave an original account of their union. He said:

> ... none of the ways of a thing's being in anything which are currently spoken of fits the relationship of the soul to the body, but it is also said that the soul is in the body as the steersman is in the ship; this is a good comparison as far as the soul's ability to be separate from the body goes, but would not supply very satisfactorily the manner of its presence, which is what we ourselves are investigating (*Ennead* IV.3.21).

After investigating all the inadequacies of the Platonic metaphor to explain the union of body and soul, Plotinus asked if we may say that the soul is present to the body as fire is present to air? For fire, i.e. light,

> ... like soul ... is present throughout the whole and mixed with none of it, and stays still itself while the air flows past; and when the air goes outside the space where the light is, it departs without retaining anything of it, but while it is under the light, it is illuminated, so that one can rightly say here too that the air is in the light rather than the light in the air (*Ennead* IV.3.22).

Then in his customary way Plotinus put this under the authority of Plato by referring to *Timaeus* (36d9–e3), where Plato does not put the soul in the body when speaking of the universe.[2] He also says that 'there is a part of the soul in which body is and part in which there is no body, clearly the powers of the soul of which the body has no need. And the same principle clearly applies to the other souls' (*Ennead* IV.3.22). This explanation, whether Augustine learned it directly from Plotinus or through Porphyry's discussion of mixtures, as some maintain,[3] enabled him to view body and soul as closely united while also distinct, without confusion of one with the other. He thought it paralleled by the coming together of the divine and human natures in the Person of Christ, a togetherness which did not, like ordinary human mixtures, lead to the diminishment of either nature. Just as he never made up his mind on the origin of the human soul, so he also continued to think that 'the manner in which spirits are united to bodies ... is marvellous, and exceeds the understanding of man' (DCD XXI.10; E 137.3.11). He was not disturbed by his own hesitations regarding the soul's origin since it is more necessary to know the soul's destiny than its origin. In like manner, he did not think that to be united to body is the most important function of the soul. In a tract on St John's Gospel, he wrote: 'Expand your soul beyond yourself' (JE XX.12). The ontological relationship of the creature to the Creator is the basis for this self-transcendence, so evident in the mutable soul's experience of immutable truth. The soul's most important function is to make contact with the source of truth and finally arrive through love at a personal union with God. This is the happy life seen from afar by philosophers and brought within reach by Christ the Mediator (DT X.3-5; C X.23-33; DBe III.18).

From his reflections on the words of Genesis (2.7), 'Let us make man to *our* image and likeness', said by God, whose very being as Trinity is a dynamic relating in self-communication and receptivity, Augustine taught that human persons are distinguished more by their likeness to God than by their difference from animals. Consequently the value of human reality comes, not only from rationality, but from relationality, that is, from a capacity for friendship with Father, Son and Spirit, and with human persons. Christ is the Mediator who makes this capacity for friendship an actuality, through the grace of faith, hope and love. As the perfect image of the Father, Christ manifests self-communicating love. The human person, made to the Image, has the destiny of returning to its source by likeness to the Image, through the self-transcendence of love. In the final analysis, faith in the incarnate Word is for Augustine the necessary condition for understanding human existence and the nature of happiness.

Notes

1 F. van Fleteren, 'Augustine's ascent of the soul: a reconsideration', *Augustinian Studies*, 5 (1974), p. 59.
2 This is a reference to Plato's cosmic soul which Augustine once considered possible but then dropped as implausible, lacking any support in Scripture. Cf. V. Bourke, 'St Augustine and the Cosmic Soul', *Giornale di Metafisica* 9 (1954), pp. 431-40.
3 E. L. Fortin, 'Saint Augustin et la doctrine néoplatonicienne de l'âme', *Augustinus Magister* 3 (1954), pp. 371-80.

4

God and creation

It is well known that Augustine took to heart whatever he read in Scripture. This was strikingly the case with the passage he read in Isaiah (7:9): 'Unless you believe you will not understand'. He interpreted this as referring to that which pertains to salvation (E 120). If understanding flows from faith, it is one of the gifts of the Holy Spirit. And yet such understanding can provide for the human mind certain affirmations which the mind can then see for itself to be true. Understanding through faith that God exists and that he has created the world are two such affirmations.

We have seen that Augustine realized through reason and faith that only God could bring the happiness desired by all persons. When such happiness is attained, at least in hope, through love of God, there is entailed a craving for a better knowledge of the one loved. Augustine sought to know as much as possible about God, opening his mind to God's self-revelation, but also questioning the visible things on earth: the bodily world, human beings, especially the human soul.

Although he had been liberated from two rival versions of how the world came to be — the Manichean and the Plotinian — he felt a responsibility to show that the Christian version was reasonable. As prologue, the arguments against the other versions were necessary. He brought forward the argument given by Nebridius against the Manichean dualism of good and evil principles, light and darkness. Nebridius asked what the nation of darkness would have done to God, the principle of light, if he had been unwilling to fight against it. If it could have harmed God, then God, if capable of suffering corruption, would not really be God. If it were admitted that it could do no harm to God, then there would be no reason for a battle and, likewise, no portions of the divine substance would be mixed with earthly things 'formed from the mixture of good and evil that was produced when these two natures fought each other' (DH 46). So, if the Manichees taught that God was corruptible, this teaching is obviously false; if they acknowledged that he had to be incorruptible, then their theories were impossible (C VII.2.3).

Although Plotinus provided Augustine with the concept of spiritual reality, it was from Scripture that he came to know of creation *ex nihilo*.

He seems not to have identified Plotinus with emanationism. In fact, he uses the word 'create' in respect of the soul of the world and intellectual souls (DCD X.2). He never attributed the notion of creation out of nothing to Plato or Plotinus. He referred to the Plotinian One as the author of the world from which reality flows. But he specifically rejected emanationism as explicitly taught by Manichees and Gnostics (E 166). Augustine considered that if the world emerged from the substance of God, then part of God is subjected to finitude and to change. But 'the nature and the substance of God ... is absolutely unchangeable' (DGnL VII.2).

In contrast to two (for him) contemporary positions, Augustine argued for the creation of the world out of nothing (*ex nihilo*). 'You made heaven and earth, not out of yourself. For then they would have been equal to your Only-begotten, and through this equal to You. There was nothing beyond You from which you might make them, O God, one Trinity, and trinal Unity' (C XII.7.7). As for the eternal existence of matter to which forms were sent, that too was rejected by Augustine. 'For if something that He had not made helped him to make those things He wanted to make, He would not be omnipotent' (DGnI I.6). As previously noted, Augustine pondered long and hard over the question of when God created the human soul, and he considered all the theories available in the culture. He was quite certain, however, that the human soul was created by God.

> With regard to the soul, which God breathed into the face of man, I have no firm position except to say that it is from God in such a way that it is not the substance of God; that it is incorporeal, that is, not a body but a spirit; that it is not born of God's substance and does not proceed from God's substance, but is made by God; that it is not made by the conversion of a body or an irrational soul into it; and hence it is made from nothing. And I hold that it is immortal in view of the nature of the life that it has, which it cannot possibly lose; but that in view of a kind of mutability that it has, making it possible to change for the better or worse, it can be rightly considered as mortal also [as compared with God's immortality] (DGnL VII.28.43).

He continued to argue that there was nothing in the world that emerged from God, and that nothing existed there without having been willed to exist by God. Because God alone is absolute Being, he alone can give existence to things (C XI.5.7). 'God makes to be whatever in any way is, in so far as it is, for unless he did so, it would not be such and such, nay, rather, it could not be at all' (DCD XII.25). As pure Being, God is eternal, with no before or after (C XI.17; DCD XII.1). Time is one of the creatures which, according to Scripture as Augustine reads it, had a beginning (Gen 1:1). There was no time before the world existed, and the world is not co-eternal with God. The past and the future of human time are reducible to present memory and anticipation, but the present, an indivisible moment, quickly departs for the coming of another (C XI). It is through a distension of the soul, Augustine holds, that the past and future can exist together in the present and allow for the measurement of time.

The words 'before' and 'after' derive their meaning from human consciousness. With an eternal mind there is no before or after. The cause of the creation which God looked upon and saw to be very good could be nothing other than the goodness of God as love (DCD XI.21). 'Your creation subsists out of the fullness of your goodness' (C XIII.2.2).

The road followed by Augustine to arrive at knowledge of God led him from the discovery of the reality of truth to the eternal and absolute Being of God, and thus to his immutability (DLA II.12–15). He found the creative role of God described in the book of Ecclesiasticus (Sirach) (18:1). There it says that God created heaven and earth together, that is, simultaneously. Heaven was interpreted by Augustine as meaning the spiritual creatures; earth was taken to mean visible things. 'But we must not suppose that unformed matter is prior in time to things that are formed; both the thing made and the matter from which it was made were created together' (DGnL I.15.29). The unformed matter which never exists apart from forms is quasi-non-being; the form is a participation in the divine Ideas. In one act God gives being to a formless matter tending to nothingness, and he converts this matter to himself by informing it. In understanding what faith reveals concerning creation, Augustine expressed that understanding in relation to the cultural context of his age, appreciative as it was of the philosophical culture of the Greek world. His understanding of the created world was expressed in the light of Aristotelian form–matter theory as he came to know it through the Neoplatonists, of Platonic participation in the world of Ideas theory, and of Heraclitus's stress on mutability.

Having declared that God, according to the Scriptures, created and formed all things simultaneously, Augustine had to distinguish between the things which appeared in the beginning and those which appeared later. He said: 'For through Wisdom all things were made, and the change we now see in creatures, measured by the lapse of time, as each one fulfils its proper function, comes to creatures from those causal reasons implanted in them, which God scattered as seeds at the moment of creation when *He spoke and they were made, He commanded and they were created*' (Ps 32:9; DGnL IV.33.51). 'We must conclude, then, that these reasons were created to exercise their causality in either one way or the other: by providing for the ordinary development of new creatures in appropriate periods of time, or by providing for the rare occurrence of a miraculous production of a creature, in accordance with what God wills as proper for the occasion' (DGnL VI.14.25). These *rationes seminales* are not tangible seeds but seedlike powers causing things to appear later according to God's plan. J. H. Taylor, who translated Augustine's *The Literal Meaning of Genesis*, has pointed out that Augustine, 'not having any inkling of the distinction between the priestly tradition and the Yahwist tradition as seen in Genesis by modern criticism . . . is concerned about harmonizing the first account of creation (Gen 1:1 – 2.4) with the second (Gen 2:5–25)'.[1] Augustine was concerned to explain just how creation could have been completed when heaven and earth were created if new things did indeed make their appearance in the world (DT III.9.6).

The fact that it was said in Genesis that God rested on the seventh day did not mean, according to Augustine, that the created world is completely on its own (DGnL IV.12.22). God preserves all beings in existence, rules them through their archetypal forms in the divine mind, and brings to development the seeds (*rationes seminales*) he has scattered throughout the universe.

Yet Augustine's doctrine of the simultaneous creation of all things (Sir 18:1) made the Genesis account of the creation of man difficult to interpret. In Genesis 1:26–7 we read that God created man and woman on the sixth day, whereas in Genesis 2:7 we read that, after God rested on the seventh day, he formed man from the slime of the earth and formed Eve from the rib of Adam. Augustine therefore interprets the two texts as referring to the two parts of the human being. Both parts, soul and body, were created on the same day. The soul was *fully* formed on the first day 'in its own proper being' (DGnL VII.24.35) and hidden until breathed into the body. The body was created as a seminal reason (DGnL VI.9.16) so that the second text refers to God's development of the bodies of Adam and Eve, his continued creative activity whereby he works to bring the world to its perfection. Augustine long entertained the notion that there might be a world-soul acting as God's providence over nature. But he was never fully convinced that such a soul existed as Plotinus taught (DCD XIII.16 and 17).

The intelligibility of the universe, as previously noted, is based for Augustine upon its direct creation by God according to the divine Ideas. Each created thing by virtue of what Thomists call its essence is similar to a divine Idea, and each creature has more or less being according to an hierarchical arrangement of essences. The Ideas are aptly called the uncreated archetypes. Things participate more or less fully in being according to the divine ideas which they resemble. Few scholars today would attribute efficient causality to Plato's form of the Good. Therefore, even though Augustine did not distinguish his creation doctrine in this technical way, it is true to say that, for him, God's creativity is both an efficient and an exemplary (extrinsic form) causality, whereas Platonic participation is merely a formal one (C VII.11.17; DCD XII.2; DNB I and III).

But the Word of God is the perfect resemblance of the Father. A thing not only imitates a divine Idea by virtue of its essence, and thus images in a special way the divine reality. It also participates in the divine likeness, the Word of God, the Father's perfect resemblance through whom all has been created. So, the Word of God is the source of the unity, the reality, and the beauty of the creature (DMu VI.7.56; E 18.2; DVR 36.66).

Guided by faith seeking understanding, Augustine realized that in addition to the likeness to God as one, creatures must show traces of God as Trinity. There are traces of the triune God in the act of sensation: the object seen, the image of it, and the seeing through the soul's attention (DT XI.2.5). But such a comparison with Father, Son and Spirit is not wholly accurate. Augustine wrote of many triadic aspects of physical nature, but the unity aspect seemed lost. He therefore sought the image of God in the spiritual part of man. Insofar as it is said in Genesis 1:26: 'Let us make man to our image and likeness', it is being said that in man one can find an image of the Trinity. Augustine looked to the soul as more like to God in its spirituality, and he discussed its likeness to the real consubstantiality of the three Persons of the Trinity. As an image of God he first proposed the mind, knowledge and love (DT IX.2.2 – 5.8); then the memory, understanding, and love of self (DT X.11.17 – 12.19); and finally, remembering, understanding and loving God (DT XIV.8.11–12; XV.27.49). In this effort to find in the soul an image of the Trinity, Augustine emphasized the consubstantiality of the mental acts he cited, and he ruled out any real distinction between the soul and its functions, retaining only a distinction among the functions by relationship (DT IX.4.7; X.11.18). He argued that the soul's knowledge and love of itself was precisely equal to the soul. Such love and knowledge are the very substance of the soul, and so the three terms are a consubstantial trinity. This image is not actualized, however, until other things are known and loved. In the final image (remembering, knowing, willing), remembering refers to the functioning mind as always possessed but not always thought about. When the mind does think about itself, it is said to recognize itself as we do when remembering. If the mind, so recognized, acts in the light of the eternal reasons, it expresses itself in a 'word' of true self-knowledge; this images the Son's generation from the Father. Thus the act of conceiving truth images the Word's conception by the Father (DT IX.7.12; JE I.8). Love for self causes the generation of true self-knowledge, and, when this is generated, there is joy in loving it. The mind and the word are bonded by love, a perfect equality (DT IX.7.12–13; IX.10.15; IX.11.16; XV.21.41). Note the reciprocal implication of the three terms: no remembering (mind) without knowing; no willing (love) without knowing.

The soul, however, does not really find itself as a true image of the Trinity until God is recognized as the one who is remembered, known and loved. For in the eternal Trinity, it is God who is Love, and therefore no one is an actual image of the Trinity without loving God. To know oneself as one really is, namely, an image of God, is to recall God as he expresses and loves himself. This is Wisdom, an actualized participation in the Word of God who represents the Father's self-knowledge and self-love (DT IX.12.18; XI.7.11; XI.8.15; XIV.22.42).

Augustine admits that the lack of absolute simplicity in the human soul prevents any perfect imaging of the Divine Being. It is more possible to see in the human soul an analogy of the Trinity rather than one of the divine Unity (DT XV.5.7; 7.11; 9.16; 22.42). 'We admire his marvellous simplicity because in the nature of God being is not different from knowing or anything else we might say of him' (E 169).

To speak of God as a single substance is to speak of him as a single Essentia (essence) which is derived from Esse (to be) and refers to divine existence as we learn from God's naming of himself to Moses as 'I am Who Am' (Exod 3:4). In this sense Augustine spoke of God the Creator as one essence and three persons, and he said that by this formula we are only saying that the Father is *not* the Son, the Son is *not* the Father, the Holy Spirit is *neither* the Father nor the Son because they are opposed as relations intrinsic to the Being that is God (DT V.2.3; V.9.10; VII.4.7).

In discussing the soul as an image of God Augustine frequently calls it beautiful. Although in his theory of knowledge Augustine offers no explicit statements regarding transcendental ideas (those that transcend the Aristotelian categories and are applicable to all things in varying degrees), such as being, unity, truth, goodness, beauty, he frequently affirms the transcendentals of God in an absolute sense. Just as God is Existence itself, so also is he Unity, Truth, Goodness and Beauty. God as Truth is the very foundation of the Augustinian theory of knowledge. God as Goodness is the ground of Augustine's theory of happiness. And God as Beauty and Creator of the sensible world is the source of his theory of aesthetics. Thus beautiful things in the temporal world have positive value in the joy they arouse and in the role they can play in leading the percipient to be mindful of the source of their beauty. In a recent work Carol Harrison has assembled many texts which show that Augustine appreciated sensible beauty for itself and for what it contributes to the regaining of the human person's original beauty as God's 'icon'.[2] She defends Augustine against all classification of his aesthetics as so overly Neoplatonic as to make him blind to sensible beauty. Such classification is not an accurate portrayal of Neoplatonism. On the contrary, Harrison argues, created realities (the temporal revelations of God) have the magnificent mission of reconverting human beings to God by evoking love for the beautiful. Because sensible beauty can distract humanity from its source and lead to sin, Augustine was aware of its ambivalence and of the need for faith to understand its full significance as a sign of far greater Beauty in its Maker. Augustine agreed that 'the beauty of the creation is not set aside as a seductive snare for carnal men, but as the [revelation] of a Supreme Artist'.[3] He warned, however, against missing the reconversion to God which the experience of beauty can foster. 'Let not that which has been made by Him detain your affections so that you should lose Him by whom you yourself were also made' (EnP 39.7). Augustine himself eventually ascended from beautiful things to the 'Beauty so ancient and so new'. This ascent involves both the senses and the intellect, as well as the will responding to grace.

All things which are beautiful to the senses, whether they are produced by nature or by the arts, have a spatial or temporal beauty, as for example, the body and its movements. But the equality and unity which are known only by the mind, and according to which the mind judges of corporeal beauty by the intermediary of the senses, are not extended in space nor unstable in time (DVR 30.56).

In presenting Augustine's view on beauty as a theological aesthetics, Harrison is being faithful to Augustine's way of not separating what he thinks by reason and what he understands by faith. She rightly argues that the doctrine of creation *ex nihilo*, of the incarnation of God's Son, of an historical revelation, and the doctrine of the resurrection of the body, all had the effect of influencing Augustine to view the beauty of the temporal realm in a very positive way.

Many of Augustine's philosophical views were indeed stimulated by his reading of the Scriptures. His reading of Exodus 3:14, where to Moses God revealed his name as 'I AM who AM', promoted much reflection as to what this meant regarding what was most basic to God. He concluded that it had to be: True Being. In this way his faith in the words of Scripture led to a metaphysical understanding of God's nature. All aspects of God would have to be grounded in what is most basic, namely, existence or being. Perfect Being is immutable in the sense that no change is needed to perfect it. Augustine speaks of God as *essentia*, but his explanation of this word, as well as the fact that he does not distinguish essence from existence as potency from act, clearly shows that *essentia* denotes the fullness of divine existence. In a passage on how to think about God, he wrote:

> Doubtless, He is substance, or if this is a better word, essence (*essentia*), what the Greeks call *ousia*. For as wisdom (*sapientia*) is from what it is to be wise (*ab eo quod est sapere*), and as knowledge (*scientia*) is from what it is to know (*scire*), so is essence (*essentia*) derived from what it is to be (*ab eo quod est esse*) (DT V.2.3).[4]

Essence for Augustine therefore means to-be-ness or be-ing. And in fact, according to Augustine, 'perhaps God alone should be called essence. For He alone truly is, since He is immutable' (DT VII.5.10). As Vernon Bourke well argues, the only contrary that Augustine admits for *essentia* is *non-esse*, non-being. And Bourke rightly concludes: 'If we call Augustine an essentialist, we must understand essence as he did, completely one with *esse*.'

> Thou art my God . . . and Thou dost cry out from afar: yea, verily, I am who am. And I heard it as one hears something in the heart, and there was no reason for me to doubt. It would have been easier for me to doubt that I am alive than that there is no Truth that is clearly seen being understood through the things that are made.
> And I looked closely at the other things below Thee and saw that they are not wholly existent, nor are they wholly non-existent. Indeed, they do not exist because they are not what Thou art. That truly exists which abides immutably (C VII.10.16 – 11.17).[5]

In citing 'existence' as primary, Augustine is distancing himself from Platonic and Neoplatonic metaphysicians who place the Good above the Forms, or the One, or first principle, above being (DCD XII.2; EnP 6.3; 7.7; DT V.2.3; JE XXXVIII.8.10; DDoC I.32). Nor should the fact that he constantly associates immutability with true being lead one to infer that he has made it an attribute more fundamental than being. James Anderson has carefully studied the relevant texts and has concluded that the phrase 'because He is immutable' may 'not entail a formal inference, merely a factual connection'.[6] Indeed, if this is not the case, Augustine would be contradicting himself, since in some places he says 'that because God is, and supremely is, He is immutable' (DCD XII.2). So anyone inclined to classify Augustine as a metaphysical essentialist should first read the texts collected by Anderson. These manifest an explicit existential interpretation of the Exodus passage, and they bring forward the adverbs used to show that God alone is *Esse*: adverbs such as 'truly being', 'properly being', 'primarily being', 'absolutely being', and 'supremely being'. Anderson asserts that 'in treating of the divine Ideas, Augustine expressly concludes to their immutability and eternity from the fact that they are . . . one with the divine Esse' (DD83 46.2), and elsewhere states that for God, to be is to subsist (DT VII.4.9).

Augustine's immutability/mutability distinction, so often used by him, was surely a legacy from the Platonists whom he praised for being sensitive to the mutability of things in contrast to the immutability of the intelligible world. But he was also encouraged to accept it by the word of the Psalmist: 'You shall change them, and they shall be changed; but You are always the Selfsame' (EnP 101.27–28). Moreover, since immutability is an attribute of God, it, like all the attributes, falls under Augustine's statement: 'that which He has He also is, and all these are one' (DCD XI.10.3).[7] While Anderson admits that Augustine did not assert any 'real distinction' in created things of existence and essence as principles of created being, yet 'his distinction between *esse* and *non-esse* plays the analogous part of the Thomist "real distinction" in that for Augustine as well as for Thomas, *esse* in all things except God is really limited or measured'.[8]

There is in Augustine's thought-world the basis for reasoning analogically from finite existents to the Supreme Existent ('I am who am'), from good things to the Supreme Good (doctrine of creation), and from beautiful realities to that 'Beauty, ever ancient, ever new'. Yet he himself reasoned from the experience of intellectual knowledge to the existence of transcendent Truth, Perfect Being and the creative source, through love, of all beings. The conviction of God's omnipresence throughout his creation and most especially in the human soul, preserving existence and ordering it to its destiny, influenced Augustine's philosophy to be essentially theocentric.

Notes

1 St Augustine, *The Literal Meaning of Genesis* I, tr. J. H. Taylor (New York: The Newman Press, 1982), p. 253.
2 C. Harrison, *Beauty and Revelation in the Thought of Saint Augustine* (Oxford: Clarendon Press, 1992).
3 Ibid., p. 136.
4 As quoted in V. Bourke, *Augustine's View of Reality* (Villanova, PA: Villanova Press, 1964).
5 Ibid.
6 J. F. Anderson, *St Augustine and Being* (The Hague: Martinus Nijhoff, 1965), pp. 12–18.
7 As quoted ibid., p. 33.
8 Ibid., p. 51.

5

Morality, grace and freedom

The moral theory of Augustine was both like and unlike that of the Greek philosophers. It was like Greek moral theory in placing happiness as the end of all human striving, and it was like the Neoplatonic philosophy in relating human goodness to a choice of greater over lesser goods, with God as the true source of happiness. Unlike the Greeks, who emphasized knowledge and self-sufficiency, Augustine taught that the human person reaches union with God with God's help by loving him in response to his love. This is not to say that love was ignored by the Greeks. With them, however, it seemed to function as a minor chord in their doctrinal symphony; in Augustine's, it was a major chord. Whole-hearted love included all the positive human emotions under the guidance of a mind in touch with truth. He emphasized right will in addition to true knowledge as the way to the happiness of being united with God in the bond of friendship. 'When the will ... cleaves to the immutable God ... men find therein the happy life' (DLA II.19.52). Such is the vocation of human beings. To the pride of the philosophers Augustine opposed humility. All are called to return to their source by humility in accepting the gift of faith in the word of Christ. When such a faith-conversion leads to baptism, they are gifted with the Holy Spirit dwelling within them and pouring into their hearts the gift of charity (*caritas*), which empowers them to love God. Thus Augustine developed a Christian ethics with emphasis on humility, faith, truth and love.

It is readily seen that Augustine's moral theory deals with the historical reality of the human person's vocation to participate in the Trinitarian life of truth and love. In his work *On the Trinity* he called the human person *capax Dei*, open to God.

His theory of morality therefore transcends any natural ethic without excluding it. Christ's command to love God with one's whole heart, one's whole soul, and one's whole mind, and one's neighbour as oneself, is the main Augustinian moral imperative. It is a command that brings with it the promise of divine assistance to obey it. 'Give what you command and command what you will' was the prayer he made to entreat God for that fire of love needed to consume the desires which could alienate him

42

from God (C X.29). This prayer referred to that central commandment which is inclusive of all natural ethical directives. 'Ethics are here, since a good and honest life is not formed otherwise than by loving as they should be loved those realities which we ought to love, namely, God and our neighbour' (E 137.5.17).

Augustine attributes to all human persons, baptized or not, a natural foundation for morality because of their ontological link with their Creator. Not only do they experience a yearning for a good to satisfy the infinite capacity of the will (C I.1), but they also possess an awareness of what is right and wrong. Every human person

> ... remembers the Lord its God. For He always is ... And He is whole everywhere, and for that reason people live, move, and have their being in Him (Acts 17:28), and therefore can remember Him ... [and] are reminded that they should turn to the Lord as to that light by which they were touched in some way, even when they were turned away from Him. For hence it is that even the godless think of eternity, and rightly condemn and praise many things in the moral conduct of men (DT XIV.21).

So the basic laws of morality are present to human consciousness. The light of truth never ceases shining upon human minds to provide the rules which follow from the nature of God and the relationship of human beings to God. Many who do not act justly are nevertheless touched by the light and realize that what they are doing is wrong. Others are heedless of the moral law they could know by reflection, and they transgress the law. 'But even such a one is sometimes touched by the splendour of Truth that is present everywhere when, upon being admonished, he confesses his sin' (DT XIV.15.21).

This awareness of the moral good with the freedom to choose it or turn from it is synonymous with the virtue of prudence and is the basis of moral obligation. 'And what shall I say of the virtue which is called prudence? Is not its complete care devoted to discerning goods from evils, so that no mistake may intrude concerning the obligation to desire the former and to avoid the latter?' (DCD XIX.4.4). Moral obligation includes an awareness of God as the source of moral law and as the one who determined the purpose of human creatures.

The human person is free to obey or to disobey the moral law, but not free from the obligation to obey it. This means that one may not eliminate or change the laws stated explicitly by the revealing God and known implicitly by those with an upright conscience. This also means that one cannot change the fact that people are created by God for an end above their natural powers of attainment, but not beyond attainment when, with natural free will, they co-operate with God's grace to put order into their love.

The central role given to love in Augustine's moral doctrine led him to think deeply about the various objects of love. He distinguished between loving realities because they are useful for the attainment of final happiness and loving them because they are intrinsically enjoyable. This implies that one will be able to enjoy the intrinsically enjoyable even in the next life. In making an early statement that only God is intrinsically enjoyable, Augustine seemed to look upon the love of neighbour as merely instrumental to the love of God. The immediate reaction to this is horror at the apparent devaluation of the human person. It is usually contrasted with the moral imperative of the eighteenth-century German philosopher, Immanuel Kant: treat humanity in every case as an end, never as a means only. Oliver O'Donovan has emphasized that Augustine's discussion of love takes place within the setting of the creation story.[1] His view of the love that is owed to other human persons has its source in Genesis 1:26, which Augustine took as a statement about the ontological value of human persons — that is to say, that their value derives from the fact that they are images of God, who is of absolute worth.

As the highest good, God is to be enjoyed. This enjoyment, engaging one's whole soul, heart and mind, is wrongly experienced when transferred to a created value to which one cannot in truth subordinate oneself (DLA I.15.33).

Human regression and self-destruction occur by a bad using and a bad enjoying amounting to abuse and idolatry. Augustine speaks of 'perverse people who wish to enjoy money but to use God; they do not spend their money for God's sake but cultivate God for money's sake' (DCD XI.25).

The biblical dedication of the self to God establishes the right order of love. Since the love (*caritas*) poured into the hearts of the faithful at baptism is not merely a desire for the highest happiness but a participation in God's generous love as manifested in the Trinitarian processions and in creation and in the incarnation of the Word of God, this love is directed toward that which is love-worthy — God, first of all, for his own sake (SO I.13.22; DO 83.35), and then the self and neighbour as so dear to God as to have been made in his image and likeness. Human persons are not viewed realistically if they are viewed apart from their ontological relationship to God and God's personal relationship to them. The former relationship is grounded in creation; the latter is grounded in the grace of friendship into which the first man was created and into which baptism in its various forms introduces persons after Adam. Their created and redeemed status ontologically makes human reality love-worthy. That is why in the love of one's friend the friend is being loved for his or her own great value (something Aristotle also held), and God is simultaneously being enjoyed. And in the enjoyment of God, one's friend is likewise being enjoyed. Thus the love of neighbour as one to be enjoyed is the right use of neighbour; subordinating non-human realities to oneself by loving them as instruments is the right use of material things. The 'right use' of one's neighbour consists in not 'making use' of him or her as a stepping stone to obtain one's happiness by progressing in the love of God.

So Augustine tells us that an ordered love will require a right judgement about the intrinsic value of things. The right love of persons will include a desire for them to love God. This is the right use of neighbours, a loving of them that brings them closer to their final happiness. This parallels what Augustine calls God's use of human beings. 'That use which God is said to make of us is made not to his utility but to ours, and insofar as He is concerned, refers only to his goodness' (DDoC I.32.35).

Insofar as the term 'use' carries a definite sense of the 'instrumental', Augustine turned away from it in his later writings when discussing the love of human persons.[2] In doing so he was understanding better what his faith told him: that there is an indissoluble connection between the love of God and the love of neighbour, with both God and neighbour respected as 'ends' of great intrinsic value, never to be used as means for self-profit. So we find Augustine saying in a very late work:

> Since every creature is either equal or inferior to us, the inferior is to be used for God but the equal [one's neighbour] is to be enjoyed as you ought to take joy in yourself, not focusing on self but on Him who made you, so also should it be in regard to the other person that you love as you do yourself. Thus we may take joy in ourselves and in our brethren, but as related to the Lord (DT IX.8.13).

GRACE

Augustine's doctrine of grace was not developed quickly. It was based on both his own experience of powerlessness to do the truth in love prior to his conversion, and to his continual study of Scripture assisted by authoritative interpretations. At first he thought that the consent to believe which brought justification by faith was only a matter of one's own free will but that only the power to do the good now and consistently came from the grace (gift) of God. After meditating on the words of Jesus (John 15:5) 'Without me you can do nothing', and his words in John 6:44, 'No one can come to me unless he is drawn by the Father who sent me', and Romans 9 he developed his teaching (AD 396) on 'prevenient grace', whereby God gives power to those not willing to believe to make them willing to believe (DD7 I.11.2, 5 and 10). He speaks of this prevenient grace in the work on *Faith, Hope and Charity* chapter 32, probably written about AD 420. In the *Retractations* I.22, in speaking of an earlier writing, he said:

> And what I said shortly afterwards: 'For it is ours to believe and will, but His to give to those who believe and will, the power of doing good 'through the Holy Spirit' through whom 'charity is poured forth in our hearts' (Rom 5.5) is indeed true; but by virtue of this rule ['The same God . . . works all in all'], both are His, because He Himself prepares the will (Prov 8:35), and ours also because we do only what we will.

This passage taken from a work written only several years before Augustine's death is important for his constant position that grace does not eliminate free will but increases its freedom by promoting, although never compelling, the choice of the good. In his work on the theological virtues he cited Paul's words to the Philippians (2:13): *'For it is God who works in you, both to will and to accomplish according to his good will'*, and to the Romans (9:16): *'So then it is not of him that wills, nor of him that sins, but of God that shows mercy'*. Lest one interpret this as meaning that the human agent does nothing, Augustine wrote:

> On the other hand, when a man is old enough to use his reason, beyond doubt he cannot believe or hope or love unless he wills to do so, nor obtain the palm of God's heavenly calling unless he decides to run for it. In what sense then is it *not of him that wills, nor of him that runs, but of God that shows mercy*, unless it be that the *will* itself, as Scripture says, is made ready beforehand by the Lord (Prov 8:35)? Otherwise, if *it is not of him that wills, nor of him that runs, but of God that shows mercy* was said because the action is from both, that is, from the will of man and from the mercy of God, then we accept that saying, *it is not of him that wills, nor of him that runs, but of God that shows mercy* as if it meant: The will of man alone does not suffice if the mercy of God be not also present.

But then neither does the mercy of God alone suffice if the will of man is not also active (En 32).

The latter passage is important for showing that Augustine considered grace not as some external compulsion placed upon the human will but as a helpful interior energy assisting people to will to believe in Christ as the giver of salvation. Such grace is often called sufficient for conversion to God. It is offered to all and given to all who desire it. God does not overpower anyone to bring them to do good or evil. After the will has been stimulated to do an act leading to salvation by 'prevenient grace' the will is assisted in its actions by 'co-operating grace'. Both are actual graces, that is to say, an illumination of the mind and a strengthening of the will to do actions meritorious of salvation. To the semi-Pelagians who thought, as Augustine once did, that the human will could bring faith, he said: 'For what hast thou that thou hast not received? And if thou hast received it, why do you boast as if you had not received it? (1 Cor 4:7). And it was chiefly by this testimony that I myself also was convinced when I was in a similar error, and thinking that faith whereby we believe in God is not God's gift, but that it is in us from ourselves' (DPS III.7).

With baptism comes the indwelling of the Holy Spirit (Rom 5:5) who unites the believer in love to Christ so that he or she becomes an adopted child of God the Father, able to enjoy the divine happiness of the triune love. This Gift which is the Holy Spirit is called by later theologians 'uncreated grace'. What Augustine calls the grace of *caritas* is called sanctifying or habitual grace in late theology. All sins are forgiven at baptism, that is to say, original sin and actual sins if the believer has committed them. (Original sin will be discussed below in reference to the objection of Pelagius.) All who retain the grace received at baptism will merit eternal life.

Augustine spoke of this deification in a homily on Psalm 50:2:

> See in the same Psalm those to whom he says: I have said, you are gods, and children of the Highest all (Ps 81:6–7). It is evident then that He has called men gods, that are deified by his grace, not born of his substance. For he justifies, who is just through his own self, and not of another; and he deifies who is God through himself, not by the partaking of another. But he that justifies does himself deify, in that by justifying, he makes sons of God. For he has given them power to become the sons of God (John 1:12). If we have been made sons of God, we have also been made gods: but this is the effect of grace adopting, not of nature generating. For the only Son of God, God, and one God with the Father, Our Lord and Saviour Jesus Christ, was in the beginning the Word, and the Word with God, the Word was God. The rest that are made gods, are made by his own grace, are not born of his substance, that they should be the same as he, but that by favour they should come to him, and be fellow-heirs with Christ. For so great is the love in him the heir that he has willed to have fellow-heirs . . . 'See', says the Apostle, 'what love God has bestowed upon us that we should be called, and be, the sons of God!' (1 John 3:2).

The grace by which one is deified by participating in the very communal life of the triune God, the life of love (*caritas*) can be lost by freely choosing to do gravely sinful actions. On the other hand, the *grace of perseverance*, the power of remaining in grace until the end of one's life may be obtained by asking God for it in prayer.

> There are some who either do not pray at all, or pray coldly, because from the Lord's words, they have learned that God knows what is necessary for us before we ask it of him. Must the truth of this declaration be given up, or shall we think that it should be erased from the gospel on account of such people? No, since it is clear that God has prepared some things to be given even to those who do not pray for them, such as the beginning of faith, and other things not to be given except to those who pray for them, such as perseverance even unto the end, certainly he who thinks that he has this latter from himself does not pray to have it. Therefore we must take care lest, while we are afraid of exhortation growing lukewarm, prayer should be stifled and arrogance stimulated (DDoP XVI.39).

What Augustine taught concerning the need for grace to do actions that make one a participant in the Kingdom or City of God he claimed to have learned from the traditional teaching of the Doctors of the Church who drew it from Scripture. In his work *On the Gift of Perseverance* he refers to Cyprian (d. 258), Ambrose and Gregory of Nazianzus (329–389) and he says:

> Such doctors, and so great as these, when they say that there is nothing of which we may boast as though it were our own which God has not given to us, [such as] that we honour God and receive Christ, that from undevout people we are made devout and religious, that we believe in the Trinity itself, certainly attribute all these things to God's grace, acknowledge them as God's gifts and testify that they come to us from him, and are not from ourselves (DDoP XIX.50).

The need for such a defence of Augustine's doctrine of grace arose because of a certain British, or at least Celtic, Christian layman named Pelagius (350–c. 425). He resided in Rome among Christians, living among Manichees, who considered that the human body and other material bodies were the product of an evil principle so that human beings often did wrong. He became an ardent defender of the goodness of God's creation and of the obligation to use the great human powers given by God. As a spiritual director to many Christians he urged a disciplined (almost Stoic) way of life to imitate Christ. When he read Augustine's *Confessions* he decided that the many statements attributing the conversion to the mercy of God would undermine the moral effort of Christians. He publicized his belief that the human nature in which men and women are created is God's gift of grace, because rationality makes one an image of God and gives dominion over fish and fowl and all living things. He denied that the original sin of Adam and Eve affected human nature; for Pelagius, original sin consists in an 'imitation' of Adam and can be eliminated by an 'imitation' of Christ. He therefore taught that baptism was not needed for the remission of any 'original' guilt. The gift of faith can be received in adult baptism by those who choose it in the power of their own free wills. Against all this Augustine argued that actions which bring eternal life with God are beyond the capacity of the human will and require God's grace.

Augustine's first formal response to Pelagius was an indirect one. A follower of Pelagius, Celestius, like many Romans after the fall of Rome, fled to Carthage. There he expressed the Pelagian view on the non-necessity for infant baptism. When he applied to become a priest, he was asked by the Synod of bishops to explain his views. Because they were Pelagian he was excommunicated. Later he went to Ephesus and became a priest there. The imperial commissioner, Marcellinus, was intellectually concerned and wrote to Augustine for some instruction. Augustine responded with a treatise *On the Consequences of Sins and their Forgiveness* in which he spoke of results like death and concupiscence (uncontrolled desire) following upon the sin of Adam, the father of the human race. As an offence against God, sin can be forgiven and remedied only by God. All the moral effort in the world will not heal wounded humanity and elevate it to the state of friendship with God enjoyed in Paradise. Augustine focused on St Paul's letter to the Romans 5:12: 'Through one man sin entered the world, and through sin death, and thus death has spread through the whole human race because everyone has sinned.' Around AD 394 Augustine made an intensive analysis of St Paul's epistles to the Romans and the Galatians. It is commonly held that he was influenced by the interpretations of Ambrosiaster and of Tyconius (d. c. 400). Ambrosiaster was the name given by Erasmus to an unknown commentator (PL XVII); Tyconius was an African Donatist lay theologian whom Augustine respected.[3]

It has to be remembered, however, that Augustine's own experience led him to resonate with St Paul's words in Romans 7:19–25:

For the good which I will, I do not; but the evil which I will not, that I do. Now if I do that which I will not, it is no more I that do it, but sin that dwells in me. I find then a law, that when I have a will to do good, evil is present within me. For I am delighted with the law of God, according to the inward man. But I see another law in my members, fighting against the law of my mind, and captivating me in the law of sin, that is in my members. Unhappy man that I am, who shall deliver me from the body of this death? The grace of God by Jesus Christ our Lord.

Both Augustine and Pelagius read this same word 'grace'. Pelagius interpreted it as meaning that Christ gave *knowledge* of how human life should be lived, which is indeed a grace (favour); moreover, God created human beings with free will and the free will is his gift (grace). God gives forgiveness to those who misuse their free will to offend him by sinning as Adam did, but no further gift is needed for them to do good actions. Augustine had known the law but found himself willing to follow it yet unable to do so. St Paul was ratifying this experience. Therefore Augustine interpreted the Pauline word 'grace' in this context as a divine enablement, a power to do what one sees is the right thing to do. This is something added to free choice which, as an inalienable human capacity, was not lost by Adam's sin. The graced will for Augustine, therefore, is more than free choice; it is freedom (*libertas*). For Augustine's use of the terms 'operative', 'co-operating' and 'prevenient grace', read *On Grace and Free Choice*, 33 and 38.

FREEDOM

What does Augustine understand by *libertas*? When the human free will receives a divine empowerment, the good action can be done spontaneously and with pleasure or delight. The natural power of free choice remains intact under grace and it operates in the doing of meritorious actions; it can also exercise its power to do actions against the will of God.

Augustine taught that in the original state of creation human beings were graced to love God with ease and delight, and to use their wills according to the order of love; that which is higher in being should be loved more than that which is lower. This was a state of habitual grace. Through free choice Adam and Eve disobeyed God and broke their loving relationship to him. On their own they could use their will for all natural purposes, but not so as to attain salvation through an intimate relationship to God. They no longer lived as friends of God nor experienced the freedom (*libertas*) of acting according to the divine will. Augustine taught that to restore such freedom to human beings the Son of God became man. He forgave their sin, but also saved them from sinning in the future by empowering them to do good out of love for God and thus to merit eternal happiness with him.

The grace of Christ was to heal concupiscence (uncontrolled desires) and ignorance, resulting from the sin of the parents of the human race, and to enable human actions to have eternal value. The sacrifice of Christ was saving and redemptive. Humanity was ransomed from its state of punishment through God's forgiveness. To fall from grace can occur by an act of the human will alone; to rise to grace can happen only by God's assisting the human will. Neither human regret nor the Mosaic Law could absolve man from sin. Since grace never destroys nature but perfects it, the empowerment it gives the will does not make the will less free but more free. Only a view of freedom as irrational, as a negative rather than a positive freedom, can sustain the position that grace reduces freedom. The view of freedom as something positive, a power for obtaining what the will naturally desires – the unlimited Good or God – is reconcilable with a grace that enables the human will to choose precisely that for which it was created. This enhancement of free will Augustine calls *libertas* in contrast to *liberum arbitrium*, the natural capacity for free choice. Grace renews the will to be itself, delighting in the good rather than in evil (DGrL IV.7; DD7 I.1.11). The grace of *libertas* is not the reward of human effort. As the free gift of God, the terms of its giving cannot be fathomed by human creatures (ExG 49). The prevalence of sin in the world witnesses not to the lack of free choice but to the lack of freedom (*libertas*). The law of liberty is the law of love (JE XLI.8.8; DGrL XV.31). God is love and this love which confers freedom upon the human will can be given only by God himself. The freedom it actualizes does not belong to the natural will by right as Pelagius claimed.

Augustine taught that the grace to love God was lost in Paradise; since human nature was not corrupted by Adam's sin, free choice was not lost, as has been claimed in a recent work where Augustine's statements on Adam's loss of freedom have been interpreted very differently.[4]

Augustine can defend himself from this recent interpretation in his own words:

> Now who among us would say that because of the sin of the first man, freedom of choice was lost to the human race? True, freedom (*libertas*) was lost through sin, that freedom, namely, which existed in paradise – the freedom of having complete justice with immortality. As a consequence human nature needs divine aid, in accord with those words of Our Lord: 'If the Son has freed you, then truly you are free' (John 8:36) free, to be sure, to live rightly and justly (CD I.25).

In the latter part of his life Augustine defended this view of a graced freedom against Julian of Eclanum, who lived for many years in southern Italy, where he attempted to lead a faction of bishops against the condemnation of Pelagius.

Julian charged that although Augustine in his early work *On Free Choice* had highlighted free choice as equivalent to the will possessed by all human beings and had shown against the Manichees that moral evil came from free will, at this later time Augustine's teaching on the need for grace was a relapse into Manichee fatalism. The Catholics in praising virginity were also accused by Julian of accepting the Manichee view of marriage as evil.

Julian's charge of Manicheism is chiefly related to its position that there is an evil principle at war against the good principle. He objected to Augustine's doctrine of original sin as implying that all are born under the power of the devil and have to be re-born in Christ (DLA III.20). The charge of fatalism was made because of Augustine's maintaining the absolute freedom of God's gift of grace, and because of his attributing foreknowledge and predestination to God. In writing the third book of *On Free Choice of the Will* Augustine had already agreed that God's foreknowledge of human acts did not make them unfree, because his knowledge was in harmony with the nature of the known. Necessary things were therefore foreknown as necessary; free actions were foreknown as free (DLA III.2). As to predestination, it refers to God's knowing those who will respond to his call and therefore preparing their wills by providing the motives that will enable them to choose the good they truly want. Augustine drew this teaching by reflecting on St. Matthew's words: 'Many are called but few are chosen.' 22:24 Etienne Gilson thinks that the problem is not to find out 'why God justifies this one rather than that, but to see how it happens that some of those God calls do not answer his call . . . Actually, if God wanted to do so, he could call all men in such a way that none would refused to answer his call.'[5]

For Augustine 'grace can be irresistible without being constraining, because it is either suited to the free choice of those it has decided to save, or, by transforming from within the will to which it is applied, it causes it to delight freely in things which it would otherwise find repugnant'.[6] Gilson concludes that 'divine predestination then, is but the infallible prevision of future works whereby God arranges circumstances and saving graces for his elect'.[7] Augustine confesses that all this seems unjust to the human intelligence, but is the work of perfect divine justice, a mystery he cannot penetrate (DD7 I.2.16; DPS VIII.14; E 194.6, 23; E 214.6–7). Yet in his work *On the Gift of Perseverance* Augustine speaks of what predestination is:

> . . . that no one comes to Christ unless it is given to him, and that it is given to those who are chosen in Him before the foundation of the world . . . and yet this predestination, which is plainly enough unfolded even by the words of the gospel, did not prevent the Lord's saying as well in respect of the commencement, what I have a little before mentioned, 'Believe in God, believe also in me', as in respect of perseverance, 'A man ought always to pray, and not to faint' (Luke 18:1) (XIV.35).

Predestination is an ordination to grace and glory. Augustine in later life did not relate it to God preparing wills by providing motives for good actions. Predestined persons were spoken of as God's 'Elect'. Those not elected were not predestined to damnation; God foreknew their evil acts which were freely done by them and entailed no will for salvation. The Bible was the source for this theory.[8]

The Council of Orange (529), which condemned Pelagianism, agreed with Augustine that God initiated conversion (prevenient grace) and gifted individuals with faith without regard to their merits. But it said nothing of the election of special individuals to glory by the grace of perseverance.

Although Augustine did not teach predestination to damnation, he was so interpreted by a ninth-century monk, Gottschalk, whose doctrine of a double predestination to eternal life and eternal death was condemned by the Synod of Quiercy in 849. Gottschalk's doctrine was revived by the Jansenists and was erroneously called 'Augustinian'.[9]

For Augustine the human will is never held 'in bondage' as it is for Calvin and the Protestant reformers. It is possible to point to texts verifying this. In a commentary on Genesis he said: By grace 'all men can be saved if they wish it' (DGnM I.3.6). And in the homilies on the Psalms the people are urged to desire the grace of God. 'You have received the power to take your place on the right hand of the Lord, that is, to become a son of God' (EnP 120.11). 'Not knowing whether you are predestined, struggle as if you were'; and 'Who are the elect? You, if you wish' (EnP 73.5). These remarks imply, of course, that prevenient grace has been offered to all. For what is the significance of this teaching in Augustine's eyes? He tells us: 'By this preaching of predestination only that most pernicious error is overthrown whereby it is said that the grace of God is given according to our merits' (DDoP XVII.42). All those who co-operate with grace are saved.[10]

Pelagianism was condemned at the Council of Carthage (AD 412); in July 415 Bishop John of Jerusalem met with some advisers and recommended that the accusations against Pelagius brought by Orosius (priest and friend of Augustine, sent by him to Palestine to support Jerome in his struggle against Pelagianism) be adjudicated in the Latin Church. At Lydda Pelagius distanced himself from Celestius, and the Synod granted him communion. Pelagianism, however, was condemned at the Synod of Carthage (416), where a letter was sent to Pope Innocent I asking for condemnation; at the Synod of Rome (417), where Pope Innocent I confirmed condemnation of Pelagius and Celestius; at the Council of Carthage (417/418), which resulted in Pope Zosimus, successor of Innocent I, condemning Pelagius after having exonerated him; at the General Council of Ephesus (431) and finally at the Council of Orange (529).

Augustine confessed that he did not know in what way the punishment for Adam's sin was transmitted to the human race, but he was certain that the effects of the sin were experienced by Adam's progeny. As Martin D'Arcy so aptly noted, 'he never succeeded in hitting upon an explanation of the origin of the soul that did justice to the doctrine of original sin'.[11] In his two letters which comprise the Treatise *On the Soul and its Origin* he warns against thinking that souls emanate from the Godhead as both the Manichees and Neoplatonists taught (for the Manichees, God was a material principle; for the Neoplatonists, the One was spiritual). He likewise warned against thinking that souls pre-existed their entrance into bodies, as Origen taught, and as the result of some sin fell into bodies as a punishment. He was certain that the necessity for baptism, which was the teaching of Scripture and adhered to by the Christian tradition, signified that a moral disease was inherited and that inclusion in the human race brought with it an inheritance of the debt to God incurred by the head of the human race. Since sin takes place only by rational choice, a bodily descent from Adam cannot account for its transmission. Yet souls cannot be derived from Adam's soul nor the souls of one's parents, since this would imply their materiality and extension, whereas they are spiritual and simple. Only through later souls coming forth from the first created soul, namely, by 'spiritual traducianism', can the transmission of original sin become evident. Augustine leaned toward Traducianism, but he knew it to be contrary to the nature of soul, and therefore he never embraced it. As Martin D'Arcy saw:

> ... in the *De Libero Arbitrio* (*On Free Choice of the Will*) he offers four hypotheses: either every soul issues by God's act from the first soul created by God, or God creates a special soul for each individual, or all souls pre-exist in God and are sent at the appointed time to govern a body, or lastly they descend into a body of their own accord. In the case of the two latter alternatives the soul can have no memory of its pre-existent state. This uncertainty shown by St. Augustine is, however, only a penumbra round what is shiningly clear, to wit, that the soul is not a part of God, but created by Him and of an immortal texture.[12]

It is notable that Augustine did not entertain the notion that pre-existent souls 'fell' into bodies for punishment of an original sin in the intelligible world (DCD XI.23; CJ IV.78; IV.83). That was gnostic teaching, and Origen's teaching (*On Principles* 11.23), with a possible hint toward this to be found in the *Enneads* of Plotinus (*Ennead* IV.3.9–16; IV.8.1–5). Despite the fact that it made the explanation of original sin very difficult, Augustine explicitly stated in *On the Soul and its Origin* that the soul was created by God (I.4.4). He remained undecided, however, about when and how the soul originated:[13] whether all souls were created in and propagated from the soul of the first man, Adam, and subsequently from parents to their offspring (Traducianism) or whether a soul is given to each individual as to Adam without propagation (Creationism). In his *Retractations* written four years before his death, Augustine said: 'Moreover, in all these books while I was discussing numerous pertinent points, I defended my uncertainty about the origin of the souls which are given to individual men' (R II.82). Of this hesitation Frederick Copleston has noted: 'He seems to have *toyed* with some form of the Platonic pre-existence theory while refusing to allow that the soul was put into the body as a punishment for faults committed in a pre-earthly condition'.[14]

When accused of inventing the doctrine of original sin Augustine responded: 'My instructor is Cyprian ... my instructor is Ambrose, whose books I have read, and whose words I have heard from his own lips, and through whom I received the washing of regeneration' (OJ VI.21). And he could have added that Jerome (*c*. 342–420), who had written a work against the Pelagians (*Liber adversus Pelaganos* AD 415), wrote to ask for his help in driving 'this baneful heresy from the churches' (E 172).

Augustine had a herculean task. He had to uphold the existence of free choice as the source of evil against the Manichees who attributed evil to an extrinsic principle. He had to defend against Pelagius the need for grace in the doing of saving actions while maintaining that grace did not eliminate the need for the will to adhere to God. As late as AD 427 he wrote to a young monk, 'you would have persevered in that which you had heard and believed, if your will had remained the same' (DCG VII.11).

With the help of the Neoplatonic notion of evil as privation of the good (and therefore of 'being'), Augustine taught that moral evil is the will's turning away from the total good for which it was made. This is a privation of right order, the order of love. The will is good but the one using it against its natural orientation toward the good is responsible for the evil that he or she originates. There is a turning from God in every evil act; the act is real and so the moral agent is real. But since the act is defective, Augustine speaks of such an agent as a deficient rather than efficient cause of evil (DCD XII.7). In having made the love of God the centre of morality as directed by Scripture, the indwelling of the Holy Spirit (habitual grace) is required for human beings to share in that love of God called *caritas*. As an ethic of the love of God, Augustine's moral theory is concerned with the historical creation of all human persons toward their fulfilment by union with God. This brought obligation and implied free will and grace. Augustine had worked out this moral theory before he heard of Pelagius. God who gave existence to human beings did not forsake them in the moral actions needed to perfect that existence. This view can be found expressed as early as AD 397 in a commentary on chapter nine of the epistle to the Romans (DD7 I.2). Anyone who wishes to read one work in which Augustine makes his clearest presentation of his religious views on Christian moral life is well advised to read *On the Grace of Christ and Original Sin* (AD 418).

The later anti-Pelagian works were written out of pastoral concern for the preservation of the faith of persons exposed to the opinion of Pelagius and his followers. Augustine argued long and constantly that to confuse grace with fate is to misunderstand the nature of love. Love is always voluntary and, at its best, in harmony with the deepest longings of human beings. Grace acts internally, not externally, and through the gift of love (*caritas*) it is the perfection of freedom (DSL 30). The most positive ideals to which the human race has always aspired are realizable only through the acceptance of grace.

> For we assert that the human will is so far assisted by divine aid in the accomplishment of justice that, over and above the fact that man is created with the power of voluntary self-determination, over and above the teaching from which he derives precepts as to how he ought to live, he also receives the Holy Spirit, whereby there is engendered in his mind the love for and delight in that supreme and immutable good which is God, even now while

he still walks by faith and not yet by sight, that, this being given to him as a free offering, he may be inflamed with desire to participate in that True Light (DSL 5).

Because of his emphasis on God's governance in human affairs (*On Nature and Grace*, c. 415), in response to Pelagian self-reliance, the older Augustine has recently been called an 'ethical voluntarist'.[15] But is there any evidence that he gave up the view of moral actions as perfecting human persons, or the view that the objects of love determine the quality of love?

The criticism just noted suggests that Augustine substituted divine law for the natural law which he cited in his early days. This means that there would be no cognitive approach to what justice requires. Augustine did not use the expression 'natural law' but he did refer to the laws of conduct rooted in nature. 'In the *De libero arbitrio* (*On Free Choice*) I.6.15, he speaks of a law called the highest reason to which temporal laws are subject, which is impressed on us ... that whereby all things are perfectly ordered so that the right thing is done.'[16]

In *Confessions* III.8.15, Augustine cites the universality of the duty to love God, asking: 'Can it be wrong for any of us at any time or in any place to love God with his whole heart, and with his whole soul, and with his whole mind, and to love his neighbour as himself?' He implies that this obligation can be acknowledged by human reason, and that whatever is opposed to this fundamental law of the love of God and neighbour is intrinsically evil. He goes on to say that the chief evils spring from lust for power, from the eyes, or from sensuality (C III.8.16). The virtue which makes possible an obedience to the law of God is humility. That is why Augustine interprets Adam's sin and that of Eve as a sin of pride which externalized itself in disobedience.[17] Sin does not arise from the body's assault upon the soul: bodily insubordination follows from the soul's insubordination to God.

After commenting that 'it is a general law of human society to obey their rulers', Augustine concludes: 'how much more must God, ruler of all creation, be obeyed without hesitation in whatever he imposes upon it' (C III.8.16). If this is divine command morality, it is already there in 397! But is it? It is one thing to uphold against Pelagian naturalism and rationalism the omnipotence of God and the need for actual grace in actions meritorious of eternal life. It is quite another thing to divorce God's decrees and commands from the 'eternal reasons' so as to embrace an ethical voluntarism. Augustine did the former, not the latter.

He never stopped teaching that God guides the world to its fulfilment through his eternal reasons to which spiritual creatures have access in some way. These ideas provide guidance toward a true knowledge of the diverse values of created things. In their own way they adumbrate eternal law. Humans participate in the eternal law and experience it primarily, as noted, as a law of love of the supreme Good, a right estimate of other goods, and appropriate responses to them. Among the other goods is the human self who properly loves himself or herself when he or she prefers the supreme good, God, to the self and to all others. In doing this a human person subordinates the satisfaction of sense life to that of the soul. In this task the virtues of prudence, justice, fortitude and temperance are called into action to safeguard the obligatory love of God above all things. For those who have lost awareness of the light of truth shining upon their created intellect, those whose minds are darkened by the legacy of Adam's sin, there are explicit precepts in Scripture and in Church teaching to guide human action, namely, the ten commandments. These commandments are not arbitrary. They are in harmony with the law of nature and with the eternal reasons according to which God created the world and provided for its fulfilment. Entailed in God's creative activity is his supreme authority which governs the universe according to wisdom. Obedience to his commands promotes the moral goodness of human creatures; it is *enlightened* rather than *blind* obedience.

For a Christian, natural law does not suffice. One will want to study the Scriptures to discover the nature of the Trinitarian God in whose image human creatures have been created. Philosophers can argue to the existence of God, but knowledge of God as the Trinity of Father, Son and Spirit, subsistent truth and goodness, is known through Christ's revelation. The purpose of ethical teachings is to bring about a greater likeness of human persons to the Trinity, a likeness achieved through actions coming from a 'right love'. Love is right when it is guided by truth, a conviction possessed by Augustine when he was writing the *Contra Academicos* (*Against the Sceptics*) and never relinquished.

Consequently, Augustine subsumes philosophical ethical principles within Christian morality. He does not deny that moral norms can be discovered by reason, but he holds that the Christian motive for observing them is the love of God and neighbour. Grace brings integrity to the soul by its healing power so that the soul is strengthened to do what is right. Moreover, Christ expressed God's will regarding human actions in the Sermon on the Mount, so Christian moral norms were added to natural law requirements. Augustine in later life neither denied the existence of natural law nor demoted the value of reason in moral discernment. But he came to offer a new insistence on Christian prudence — the spontaneous taking of joy in responding to God by doing the moral action he has willed. Rather than repudiating reason, he came to a greater emphasis on the will as the personal power of self-surrender to God whose will was never separated from his wisdom.

Notes

1 O. O'Donovan, '*Usus* and *fructio* in Augustine', *Journal of Theological Studies* 33 (1982), pp. 361–97.
2 Ibid.
3 For a thorough treatment of Augustine's developing understanding of grace, cf. E. TeSelle, *Augustine the Theologian* (New York: Herder & Herder, 1970), pp. 156–65.
4 E. Pagels, *Adam, Eve, and the Serpent* (New York: Random House, 1988). This work

completely ignores Augustine's distinction between *liberum arbitrium* and *libertas*. The political framework imposed upon his theology is an anachronism, and tends to be misleading.

5 E. Gilson, *The Christian Philosophy of Saint Augustine*, tr. L. E. M. Lynch (New York: Random House, 1960), p. 153.

6 Ibid.

7 Ibid.

8 Gen 25:19ff., God's favouring of Jacob over Esau; Dan 12:1; Ps 69:29; Rom 8:28–30; Eph 1:3–4; 2 Tim 1:29; Jn 6:44–55; 10:29; Mt 20:23.

9 F. L. Cross and E. A. Livingstone, 'Gottschalk' in *The Oxford Dictionary of the Christian Church* (revised edn, 1983), pp. 584–5.

10 The thinking of Pelagius was presented in his *Expositions of the Epistles of St Paul* (B. Altaner, *Patrologie* (4th edn, Freiburg, 1960), 439), and in his work *On Nature*.

11 M. D'Arcy, 'The philosophy of St Augustine' in *A Monument to St Augustine* (New York: The Dial Press, 1930), pp. 172–3.

12 Ibid.

13 G. J. P. O'Daly, 'Did St. Augustine ever believe in the soul's pre-existence?', *Augustinian Studies* 5 (1974), pp. 227–35. Cf. Augustine, *Retractations* I.1.3, on *Contra Academicos* 1.22.

14 F. Copleston, *A History of Philosophy* II (New York: Doubleday, 1962), pp. 94–5.

15 V. Bourke, *Augustine's Love of Wisdom* (West Lafayette, Indiana: Purdue University Press, 1992), p. 47. Cf. G. Fasso, *Storia della filosofia del dritto* (Bologna: Il Mulino, 1966), pp. 196–200. Cf. Bourke, *Wisdom from St Augustine*, pp. 136–56.

16 V. Bourke, *Augustine's Love of Wisdom*, p. 46; he also refers to at least one use of the expression 'natural law' in *Exposition of Psalm 118.4. Lex ista naturalis*.

17 J. P. Burns, 'Augustine on the origin and progress of evil' in W. S. Babcock (ed.), *The Ethics of St Augustine* (Atlanta, 1991). See also his *The Development of Augustine's Doctrine of Operative Grace* (Paris, 1980).

6

Christ and Trinity

The first formal treatise 'On the Incarnation of the Word' was written by Athanasius (c. AD 295–373), Bishop of Alexandria, who while still a deacon attended the Imperial Council of Nicaea (AD 325). By the creed resulting from this Council both Arianism, the doctrine that the Son of God was *created* by the Father, and Origenism, the position that the Son of God was *inferior* to God the father (as Plotinus described the Nous [divine intellect] with reference to the One), were condemned. Athanasius attributed the false Trinitarian theology of the Arians to their speculating on the Trinity before trying to understand what Scripture said of the divinity of Christ and its necessary relation to the economy of salvation. Christ should be approached as an historical human being and the divine Saviour of humankind — rather than through the cosmological theories of the Gnostics and Hellenistic thinkers who considered 'body' unworthy of being joined to a transcendent God. Whether or not Augustine read Athanasius's treatises against the Arians, he strove for greater clarity in what he had received through Ambrose with regard to an understanding of Christ and of the Trinity. Like Athanasius, he learned from Scripture to reverence the human body as Christ's chosen vehicle to enter into a new covenant with human persons. The Incarnation of Christ became for Augustine a paradigm for understanding the union of the human soul and body and for appreciating in Christ the deepest possibilities of being human.

He first learned of Christ from his mother, and as an adult he pondered greatly on the role of Christ as described in the Prologue of St John's Gospel. This accounts for his disappointment, first with the description of wisdom given by Cicero in the *Hortensius* (C III.4) and, second, with the account of the soul's ascent to the One as given by Plotinus in the *Enneads* (I.6). The name of Christ was missing from both writings. Truth, life and union with God seemed impossible to Augustine without Christ whom he had heard of as the one and only mediator. In later life he spoke feelingly of this:

... one Mediator, the uncreated Word of God, by whom all things were made, and in partaking of whom we are blessed ... By his humanity He shows us that, in order to obtain that blessed and beatific good, we need not seek other mediators to lead us through the successive steps of this attainment, but that the blessed and beatific God, having Himself become a partaker of our humanity, has offered us ready access to the participation of His divinity ... at once the way of life on earth and life itself in heaven (DCD IX.15).

He admonished Porphyry, the devoted student of Plotinus and editor of his *Enneads*, who expressed the futility of seeking any universal way to God, that this way is discoverable in Christ (DCD X.321).

It took Augustine some time to discover this for himself. Although he had heard of and read of Christ, he took seriously his human actions as described in the Scriptures and therefore thought of Christ 'simply as a man of the very highest wisdom, whom no one could equal; and in particular it seemed that his miraculous birth from a virgin ... showed such divine care for us that he deserved full authority over us as a master' (C VII.19.25). 'But', said Augustine, 'I had not the faintest notion of the mystery contained in "The Word was made flesh."' Yet it was only by the mediation of Christ that Augustine could gain the strength to commune with the God for whom he longed more ardently after reading of the mystical experience described in the books of the Platonists. Years later he reflected on this experience and commented: 'I tried to find a way of gaining the strength necessary for enjoying you, and I could not find it until I embraced that Mediator between God and man calling to me and saying, "I am the Way, the Truth, and the Life", and mingling with our flesh that food which I lacked strength to take ...' (C VII.18.24). Augustine found that way in surrendering to Christ when in the moment of grace in the Milan garden he picked up the letter to the Romans and was taught by St Paul to put on the Lord Jesus Christ (Rom 13:13). Between that time and AD 388 he came to believe in Christ as both divine and human. This was doubtless assisted by the instructions given by Ambrose to the catechumens in the spring of AD 387. By the time he wrote the treatise *On True Religion* he both stated the doctrine of the incarnation of God's Son and named the Arians and Photinians as holding heretical positions on it (DVR V.9):

To heal souls God adopts all kinds of means suitable to the times which are ordered by his marvellous wisdom ... But in no way did he show greater loving-kindness in his dealings with the human race for its good, than when the Wisdom of God, his only Son, co-eternal and consubstantial with the Father, deigned to assume human nature when the Word became flesh and dwelt among us. For thus he showed to carnal people, given over to bodily sense and unable with the mind to behold the truth, how lofty a place among creatures belonged to human nature, in that He appeared to men not merely visibly — for he could have done that in some ethereal body adapted to our weak powers of vision — but as a true man. The assuming of our nature was to be also its liberation. And that no one should perchance suppose that the creator of sex despised sex, he became a man born of a woman (DVR XVI.30).

Nevertheless, Ambrose had been better at stating the doctrine of the incarnation of God the Son than at speculating on the manner of the union of God and humanity. Augustine experienced his own inability to explain that union and admittedly grew in the power to do so through argumentation with opposing views.

When in AD 391 as a presbyter (priest) he assumed the role of teacher of the faithful, he found it necessary to argue, first, against those who denied full humanity to Christ, and secondly against those who denied full divinity to him. In doing so he faced the problem of showing how it was possible that in one person there could be two natures without any diminishment in either one, as usually occurs in a physical mixture. His solution exhibits the way he made use of Neoplatonic philosophy as a rational support for scriptural teachings. He found in Scripture that Christ was Son of Man and Son of God; in Neoplatonic philosophy he found two realities — body and soul — united with diminishment to neither one.

Among those who denied a full humanity to Christ were the Docetists (an early Church group) and the Apollinarists (followers of Apollinarius (c. 310–c. 390)). The Docetists, named from the Greek word *dokēsis* (appearance), denied a real body to Christ. They maintained that his body was an illusion. They considered the crucifixion to be beneath the dignity and power of God. Gnostic sects who drew a sharp dichotomy between spirit and matter were delighted with the Docetic position. In his work *On Christian Combat* Augustine argued that Christ had a real human body. He also argued for the presence of a rational soul in the human nature of Christ. The Apollinarists had argued that in Christ the divine Logos had replaced the human soul or, if he had a soul as a natural principle of life, it was not a rational soul. In his letter to Dardanus Augustine referred to this error:

> At this point I inquire, or rather I recognize, in what way you understand Christ as man. Surely not as certain heretics do who assert that he is the Word of God with a body, but without a human soul, the Word serving as soul for His body; or, as the Word of God with a soul and body but without a human mind, the Word of God serving as mind to His soul. You certainly do not understand Christ as man in this sense, but, as you expressed it above when you said that you accepted Christ as almighty God, with this formula of belief that you would not believe Him God if you had not believed him perfect man. Obviously, when you say perfect man, you mean that the whole human nature is there, for man is not perfect if either a soul is lacking to the body or a human mind to the soul (E 187.2.4).

Not only did Augustine find it necessary to defend the full human nature of Christ, he also had to engage in argument against those who denied the divinity: the Arians, the Photinians and the Eunomians.

As followers of Arius, a fourth-century presbyter of Alexandria who taught that the Logos-Son was God's primordial and perfect creature through whom all else was created, the Arians believed that the Logos-Son acted as a soul 'in Jesus' body'; as a creature it was able to undergo characteristically human experiences. By attributing to Christ no human soul, they denied his humanity; by insisting that the Logos was created rather than generated from the Father, they denied his divinity.

As followers of Photinus, a fourth-century Bishop of Sirmium who regarded Christ as only a morally perfect human being, the Photinians had been condemned at the Council of Constantinople in AD 381.

As followers of Aetius, a fourth-century deacon at Antioch, and of Eunomius, a fourth-century Bishop of Cyzicus, the Eunomians taught that the Father and Son are united in will but dissimilar (*anomoios*) in essence, and that just as the Son was created by the Father, so the Holy Spirit was created by the Son. Basil the Great (330–379) and Gregory of Nyssa (331/340–*c*. 395) firmly refuted this position, as did Marius Victorinus (b. AD 281/291). Augustine's Christology dissociated him from any and all of these positions concerning the human and divine states of Christ. As early as AD 391 Augustine preached the orthodox doctrine of the Church:

> A complete man, a rational soul and body was assumed by the Word in such a fashion as to be one Christ and one God, the Son of God, not the Word alone but the Word and the man, and this totality is the Son of God the Father according to the Word and the Son of Man according to the man . . . He is not only man but Son of God, but by the Word, by whom the man is assumed; and he is not only the Word but the Son of Man by the man assumed by the Word (S 214).

More precise language is used in a letter to Volusian around AD 412: 'He has appeared as Mediator between God and man, in such wise as to join both natures in the unity of one person . . .' (E 137.3.9). This letter has frequently been called a treatise *On the Incarnation*. Augustine continued tnis explicit terminology which was to become the classic vocabulary of council documents on the incarnation of Christ in his brief work *The Enchiridion* or *On Faith, Hope and Charity*:

> Wherefore, Christ Jesus, the Son of God, is both God and man. He is God before all ages; man in our own time. He is God because He is the Word of God, for 'the Word was God'. But he is man because in his own Person there were joined to the Word a rational soul and body. Therefore, so far as he is God, he and the Father are one; bɾ ɩ so far as he is man, the Father is greater than he. Since he was the only Son of God, not by grace but by nature, in order that he should also be full of grace he became likewise the son of man; and the one selfsame Christ results from the union of both. For, 'being in the form of God, he thought it not robbery' (Phil 2:6) 'to be' what he was by nature, that is 'equal with God'; but he 'emptied himself, taking the form of a servant', neither losing nor diminishing the form of God (En X.35).

In this union of the two natures, Augustine goes on to say, the human nature is graced beyond every other instance of it; taken up as it is into the unity of the only Son of God, this grace was obviously unmerited by human nature itself. So it is with all human beings; they are justified by grace which comes to them not through their own merits but through the free gift of God (En XI.36).

If it is established that there is only one Person in Christ, a divine Person, then whatever activity proceeds through any one of the two natures is the action of God and as such is a saving act. Thus the Son of God was crucified. And God having united himself to human nature died for the sins of all humankind. In his effort to understand what he believed, Augustine distinguished the one Person from the two natures. He understood a person to be an agent, the source of actions made possible by the nature possessed. Thus in his work *On the Trinity* he referred to the difference between 'nature' as something possessed in common with others of the same nature, and 'person' as something singular and individual (*aliquid singulare atque individuum*: DT VII.6.2).

In Letter 137 Augustine, without specifying Plotinus, reproduced his version of the union between soul and body to indicate how the human and divine natures are united without loss to either one. Plotinus had spoken of soul and body being united as light and air, and of the body being in the soul. When the air (i.e. body) travels outside the space where the light (i.e. soul) is, it leaves that space without retaining any light. While under the light, it is illuminated, so that it is correct to say that the air (i.e. body) is in the light, rather than the light (i.e. soul) in the air.[1] Following this tradition, Augustine stated in Letter 137:

> But there are some who request an explanation of how God is joined to man so as to become the single Person of Christ, as if they themselves could explain something that happens every day, namely, how the soul is joined to the body so as to form the single person of a man. For, as the soul makes use of the body in a single person to form a man, so God makes use of man in a single Person to form Christ. In the former person there is a mingling of soul and body; in the latter Person there is a mingling of God and man; but the hearer must abstract from the property of material substance by which two liquids are usually so mingled that neither retains its separate character, although among such substances, light mingled with air remains unchanged. Therefore the person of man is a mingling of soul and body, but the Person of Christ is a mingling of God and man, for, when the Word of God is joined to a soul which has a body, it takes on both the soul and the body at once. The one process happens daily in order to beget men; the other happened once to set men free (E 137.3.11).

Augustine believed in the value of such philosophical explanations as showing the non-impossibility of the realities made known by divine revelation. The pastoral import of the fact of the transcendent God manifested as a God-for-us by the sending of the Logos-Son to unite with human nature was too great to refrain from any possible intellectual clarification. It was through this incarnate Son that humankind was to learn of the intimate life of God as Father, Son and Holy Spirit. As early as AD 389, Augustine wrote to Nebridius that God became man through the activity of the whole Trinity (E 11). His mission was to be the mediator between human persons and the Trinity. It was appropriate for the Son-Wisdom of God to give to people consciousness of the Father so that in the gift of the Holy Spirit (*caritas*), people might participate in the life of the Trinity, a life of love.

To understand how Christ could be an authentic mediator is to appreciate the real union of divinity and humanity. The various heretical positions as previously described denied the former or the latter.

As mediator, Christ had to be that which possessed saving powers and that which was to be saved. His acts of redeeming from sin were accomplished through a human nature actuated by the divine Person of the Word of God. Christ as God suffered through his humanity for human persons in order that they could be divinized and so enter into friendship with God. Christ 'died because he is the Son of man, not because he is the Son of God. Nevertheless the Son of God died although he died according to the flesh and not according to the Word' (S 127.9). As a man-God he was able to expiate for human sins; as a God-man he gave the divine Spirit of love to draw men and women into divine life. God loved humankind before the Son became incarnate to manifest that love in his human life and suffering. That manifested love draws human persons to turn wholly to God.

Countless are the passages where Augustine speaks of divine love stooping to embrace humanity, and by that humility curing human pride. Christ substituted himself on the cross for all sinful human beings to reconcile them with God. This sacrifice is continually offered in Catholic liturgies in all parts of the world. By baptism Christians enter into the Body of Christ; by faith in Christ the fruits of his sacrifice are applied to human persons.

> The medicine for all the wounds of the soul, and the one propitiation for the offences of men is to believe in Christ ... They who believe in him become the children of God; because they are born of God by the grace of adoption, which is by faith in Jesus Christ our Lord (S 143.1).

Christ died for all people. This is the significance of the New Testament: the arrival of a way to God open to all.

> The blood of your Lord, if you will it, is given for you: if you do not will it, it is not given for you ... This is the important point, that he gave it once and for all. The blood of Christ is salvation to those who wish it, punishment to those who refuse (S 344.4).

The humiliations of Christ proved to be powerful forces in cleansing Augustine of the pride which permeated his youth and professional life. Although he emphasized humility as the basic moral lesson of the incarnation through constant references to St Paul's letter to the Philippians 2:6, he knew and taught that the example of Christ was efficacious only by his redemptive life and sacrifice which bridged the gap between God and humankind.

> For it profits us to believe, and to keep firmly and unshakenly in our hearts, that the humility whereby God was born of a woman and was led through such great insults to his death by mortal men, is the most excellent medicine by which the swelling of our pride may be cured, and the exalted mystery by which the chain of sin may be broken (DT VIII.7.5).

The texts of Augustine are the best evidence against thinking that he saw Christ solely as a man united by grace to the divinity, or considered that Christ's humility was more important as a moral example than his expiation of sins by dying on the cross. The following text adequately synthesizes the redemptive role of Christ:

> For certainly we would not be redeemed even by the 'One Mediator of God and men, the man Jesus Christ' (1 Tim 2:5) if he were not also God ... But once sin had created a wide rift between the human race and God, it was necessary that a mediator who alone was born and lived and put to death without sin, should reconcile us with God even to the extent of obtaining for us the resurrection of the body into life everlasting, in order that the pride of man might be rebuked and cured through the humility of God ... that the fountain of grace might be opened by the only-begotten taking the form of a servant ... (Phil 2:6; En 29.108).

Augustine read the New Testament as a record of the important deeds and sayings of Jesus of Nazareth as told and believed by those who wrote the record, inspired as they were by God. Like other patristic thinkers, Augustine tried to determine from the witness given in the New Testament what could truly be said about Christ's divinity, humanity and personhood, as well as his relationship to the Father and the Holy Spirit. The conclusions reached are scattered throughout his works and represent his Christology. The more essential ones have been retrieved for this presentation.

It is noteworthy that they were not arrived at for their own sake. It was necessary to know whether this Jesus of Nazareth had the divine power to save humankind and whether he could identify completely with humanity (body and soul). Gregory of Nazianzus taught that 'that which he has not assumed he has not healed; but that which is united to his Godhead is also saved'.[2] And Augustine taught that there was another way of denying the truth of the incarnation of God's Son, the way taken by those who assert the coming of Christ with their tongues and yet deny it with their deeds by a lack of charity which is the profound meaning of the incarnation. 'Greater charity has no man than this, that he lay down his life for his friends.' A true believer in Christ is 'he that maintains Christ's coming in the flesh, not in word but in deed, not by loud noises but by love' (JE IV.3).

That Mary of Nazareth was the mother of God, and that she was and remained a sinless virgin, was Augustine's constant teaching. He, like the teaching bishops before him, learned this by reflecting on the gospels of Matthew and Luke (DT XIII.23.18; S 5.6; DNG XIX.6.42). The doctrine that Mary was the mother of the Word made flesh and not merely the mother of the humanity (as Nestorius (c. 381–451) would later say) followed from the wholeness of the Person of Christ. As mother of Christ the head of the Church, his spiritual body, Mary is through love the mother of the members of the Church. No assertion of Mary's bodily assumption into heaven at the time of her death is in the texts of Augustine.

While the patristic tradition, both East and West, on the unity of the divine and human natures in the Person of Christ contributed to Augustine's Christology, his main source was, as usual, Holy Scripture. He saw the New Testament as proceeding from Christ to whom the Old Testament led. For him Christ was both the foundation of the Christian faith and the centre of all theology.

Of prime importance in the development of the theology of Christ were St Paul's letter to the Philippians 2:6–7 and St John's Gospel 1:1–14. Many before Augustine had reflected on the scriptural story of Christ: Justin, Tertullian, Clement, Origen, Alexander, Athanasius, Gregory of Nyssa, Ambrose. Of all these it may have been Athanasius and his influence upon Ambrose which brought Augustine to realize the centrality of Christ in all Christian doctrine as well as for salvation and spirituality. Like Athanasius, Augustine looked upon Christ as providing in openness to the Father and empowerment by the Spirit the exemplar for Christian self-understanding — a Christian concept of humanness. This concept he substituted for the one offered by the Platonic philosophers. And so he argued strongly for the Word taking flesh and rising after death as a pledge of the resurrection of all bodies against the powerful and popular Porphyry who advised all to 'take flight from all body' as from something injurious to the soul.

Because he died in AD 430 Augustine did not directly participate in the great christological Councils of Ephesus (431) and Chalcedon (451), but indirectly his insistence on the integrity of human nature and of divine nature united in the Person of the Logos-Son influenced the outcome of those Councils. The Council of Ephesus was called to deal with Nestorius who was accused of teaching that the two natures of Jesus were so sharply divided that there was a risk of concluding to two persons, of two centres of consciousness. This same belief was held some years earlier by a certain person in the West called Leporius, who in cherishing Christ's divinity feared for its corruption by any close union with human nature. He was advised to consult Augustine, who tutored him in the scriptural teaching on the incarnation. Leporius then confessed faith in the Word made flesh as a union of human nature with the Person of the Word. The Word was made flesh but this happened only personally and not by nature, not with the Father nor the Holy Spirit.[3]

This pupil voiced Augustine's final teaching that 'it is the pre-existent Person of the Word who is the focal point of this union and who "takes up" the human nature into the unity of his Person'; the unity was not merely the synthesis of two natures (*Persona una ex duobus substantiis constans; una in utraque natura persona*: JE XCIX.1).

THE TRINITY

Augustine's defence of the divinity of Christ promoted his research into the traditional teaching and liturgical practice of the Catholic

Church concerning the worship of a divine Trinity: Father, Son and Holy Spirit. The textual evidence shows that the Bible and various patristic interpretations of it acted as a continual source of his growing understanding of this doctrine. He learned whatever he could from his predecessors, especially from Tertullian (*c*. 160–*c*. 225), Jerome, Ambrose, Hilary of Poitiers (*c*. 315–367), Athanasius, Didymus the Blind (*c*. 313–398), Gregory of Nazianzus. Hilary is the only one he quotes explicitly in *On the Trinity*. Studying the many christologies available to him, he could not fail to be struck by the various functions they linked with Father, Son and Holy Spirit. Such an approach to the Trinity was normal for thinkers who had read what the Christ of the New Testament said about the Father and the Spirit. Beginning with faith in a three-personed God Augustine examined the things of nature for some reflection of the threeness of the God who created them. He saw that everything had being, a certain structure, and an activity or direction. In the book of Wisdom he read: 'You ordered all things by measure, number, weight' (11:21). This suggested to him the philosophical categories of existence, species, order (DD83 6; DNB 3 and 21–23; DGnL IV.3.7; DT VI.10.12), and he interpreted them as reflections (vestiges) of Father, Son and Spirit. We are awakened first to the third category — the ordering of our affections. Charity, breathed into us by the Spirit, leads to the Son who conforms us to himself and in whom we are united to the Father (DME I.13.23). Augustine linked this with Romans 11:36: 'All that exists comes from Him; all is by Him, and in Him.' The writings at Cassiciacum, Milan and Rome all show that by that time he held perfectly orthodox views concerning the distinctness and equality of Father, Son and Spirit. The linking of the distinct Persons of the Trinity with creation is present in *On the Morals of the Catholic Church*, *On Free Choice* I–II, *On Greatness of Soul* 34, and clearly asserted in *On Genesis Against the Manichees* I and *On the Literal Interpretation of Genesis: An Unfinished Book* I.2. The role of the creative Trinity is elaborated between 389 and 391 in *On True Religion* where the distinctiveness of the vestiges is not permitted to cancel out the unity of the creative activity.

> There is one God: Father, Son and Holy Spirit. When this Trinity is known as far as it can be in this life, it is perceived without the slightest doubt that every creature — intellectual, animal, and corporeal — derives such existence as it has from that same creative Trinity, has its own form, and is subject to the most perfect order. It is not as if the Father were understood to have made one part of creation, the Son another, and the Holy Spirit another, but the Father through the Son in the gift of the Holy Spirit together made all things and every particular thing. For everything — essence or nature or whatever better word there may be — possesses at once these three qualities: it is a particular thing; it is distinguished from other kinds of things by its own proper form; and it does not transgress the order of nature (VR VII.13).

The eighteenth of Augustine's *Eighty-three Different Questions* is said to have been written between 388 and 391. There he says that

... for every existing thing there is something responsible for its existing, something responsible for its distinctness, and something responsible for its coherence [order or value] ... But the author of every created thing we call God. Therefore it is fitting that he be a Trinity such that perfect reason cannot find anything more excellent, intelligent and blessed. For this reason also, in the search for Truth, there can be no more than three kinds of questions: 'Does a thing exist at all? Is it this particular thing or something else? Should it be approved or disapproved?' (DD83 18).

Not only did Augustine gain insight from Scripture into the Trinity as creative and reflected in all creatures; he also saw the distinctive saving roles of the three divine Persons. In a small piece written during the Thagastan period we read: 'One should investigate with great attentiveness the following sayings of the Lord Jesus: "No one comes to me unless the Father draw him" (Jn 6:44). "No one comes to the Father except through me" (Jn 14:6) and "He Himself [the Spirit] will lead you into all truth"' (Jn 16:13; DD83 38).

As early as the work *On the Morals of the Catholic Church* (388) and *On Greatness of Soul* (387–388) Augustine spoke of the Spirit in terms of *caritas* which unites one to God; love was later discussed as the proper name of Spirit in book 8 of *On the Trinity*. This naming of the Spirit as love is one of the most important and original aspects of his Trinitarian theology, since this was not done by previous writers. His fellow-African predecessor, Marius Victorinus, had explicitly identified the Holy Spirit with knowledge. Moreover, the Holy Spirit was not mentioned by the Neoplatonists (CD X.29).

Therefore in approaching the Trinity as he did through the economy or plan of creation and salvation, Augustine took seriously and spoke primarily of the distinctness of Persons in the Trinity. What was said of them in Scripture led him to detect the distinctive aspects of their unified creative activity. It was also a clue to whatever could be learned of the inner relationships of the three, now usually referred to as the 'immanent' Trinity. Augustine looked for an image of those relationships in human beings, aware as he was of the words of Genesis 1:26: 'Let *us* make man to *our* image and likeness.' Because God is Spirit, Augustine looked to the human soul's activities for the image. This linking of the image-doctrine with the doctrine of the Trinity which fills the pages of *On the Trinity* is often said to be original with him since it is not characteristic of Eastern Trinitarian theology. It might be more accurate to associate it with Western Trinitarian theology since it is certainly present in the Trinitarian treatises of Marius Victorinus. The latter, however, finds a more metaphysical than psychological image in the human person.

It was after 391 that Augustine turned to human consciousness for analogies of the Trinity. He did so with no claim that he was 'explaining' the Trinity, a doctrine of three Persons in one God which was proclaimed by Pope Damasus (d. 384) in the Council of Rome (AD 382) as the great Christian mystery. But because doctrines have practical significance, faith in them entails a probing for as much understanding as possible. That Augustine thought this is well known.

In the *Confessions* (397–401) he stated:

> Who can understand the almighty Trinity? Yet we all speak of it, if it really is the Trinity of which we speak. Rare is the soul which in what it says of the Trinity knows what it is saying. And men struggle and contend, and no one without peace sees that vision. I would like men to consider three aspects of their own selves. These three are something very different from the Trinity — The three things I mean are existence, knowledge, will. For I am and I know and I will. I am a being that knows and wills. I know that I am, and I know that I will. I will to be and I will to know. Now he who is capable of doing so will see how there is in these three an inseparable life — one life, one mind, one essence — and how, finally, how inseparable a distinction there is between them, yet there is a distinction (C XIII.2).

These three aspects were made more 'psychological' in *On the Trinity* as they became the mind — its knowing — its loving, followed by remembering, knowing, and loving oneself. Both are natural images of the Trinity, so that a human person is *capax Dei*, in Augustine's words. 'Remembering' refers to the intellectual rather than the sense-memory and is a kind of self-presencing. These triadic aspects are only illustrations or analogies of the Trinity. To be made to an image would entail an exemplar as origin, a likeness to the exemplar, and an immediate tendency toward the exemplar as a source of greater perfection. The human person as made in the image of the Trinity was therefore created in grace (that is, the Trinity dwelling within), and given new powers of faith, hope and charity. That is why Augustine finally described the image of the Trinity in the human soul as remembering, knowing and loving God. Once again 'remembering' here means one's awareness of the presence of God and conforming oneself to the Trinity of wisdom and love by knowing and loving them. Through love, gift of the Spirit (DT VII.10.14), one is united with the Trinity, and the more that love increases, the greater becomes the likeness to the Trinity. Said Augustine: 'I believe the Scripture when it says: "God is love, and he who abides in love abides in God"' (John 4:16; DT VIII.8.12).

This growth in love for God and neighbour is not the immediate result of conversion and baptism. It is a daily renewal of the image with the help of God's actual graces (2 Cor 4:16).

> If the last day of this life shall find anyone in such progress and growth holding fast to the faith of the Mediator, he will be received by the holy angels in order that he may be brought to the God whom he has worshipped, and by whom he is to be brought to perfection; and at the end of the world he shall receive an incorruptible body, not for punishment but for glory. For the likeness to God in this image will then be perfect when the vision of God will be perfect. The Apostle Paul says of this vision: 'we now see through a mirror in an obscure manner, but then face to face' (1 Cor 13:12). He likewise says: 'But we, beholding the glory of the Lord with face unveiled, are transformed into the same image from glory to glory, as through the Spirit of the Lord' (2 Cor 3:18). This is what takes place in those who are making progress steadily day by day (DT XIV.17.23).

With original sin grace was lost to the descendants of the first human parents, but the natural image or capacity for the relationship of friendship with God was not destroyed. For this reason Augustine insisted, against those who wished to reserve the term 'image' only to the Son of God and to speak of human persons as only 'to the image', that St Paul had called human creatures both 'images' (1 Cor 11:7) and made 'to the image' of God (DT VII.6.12). He compromised with this nomenclature by calling human persons 'imperfect images' while the Son was a 'perfect image' of the Father. As an imperfect image, a human person is oriented toward a daily renewal of the image toward the perfection of the exemplar. 'For one does not approach God across intervals of space but by likeness, and by unlikeness one draws away from Him' (DT VII.6.12).

In making Christ the exemplar of human imaging of God, Augustine Christianized the Neoplatonic doctrine of participation in the Divine Ideas of the Nous (divine intellect). He spoke of Christ as the Father's 'likeness' in whom all Christians were to participate, just as the world had participated in the wisdom of the Logos in being created in its manifold species, thereby being made intelligible. This transformation of a philosophical insight also involved a correction of the Neoplatonic notion that an image is always inferior, as it was in the emanation of the Nous from the One. Insight into spiritual reality and spiritual generation was undoubtedly gained from Plotinus's *Enneads* where the divine mind or Nous proceeded directly from the One and in turning (conversion) to contemplate its origin became an image so that it could emanate All-Soul. With All-Soul contemplating the divine mind it thereby emanated its own image — World-Soul. In writing his *Confessions* Augustine seemed unaware of the degradation implied in Plotinian emanation when he said that he had discovered the Trinity in the books of the Platonists. But as Victorinus demonstrated (*Against the Arians*), and Augustine's teaching maintained, if the Father's knowledge of himself is perfect, then there is nothing lacking in the Son as image, so that he is indeed equal to the Father.

The Plotinian notion of image had been changed not only by Victorinus but also by Ambrose (*Hexaemeron* 6.41). It was possibly between 394 and 395 when he was making a concerted study of the Pauline letters that Augustine wrote: 'not only is [the Son] his image, because he is from [God], and the likeness, because the image (John 14:27), but also the equality is so great that there is not even a temporal distinction standing between them' (DD83 74).

In addition to giving the Holy Spirit the proper name of 'Love' and using creation in the image of God to illuminate the inner life of the Trinity, Augustine is notable for having taught that 'relation' in the spiritual world transcends the categories of substance and accidents. It can therefore distinguish Father, Son and Spirit from one another without violating the simplicity of the Godhead, as it would do if it were an 'accident'; and without violating the unity of the Godhead, as it would do if it changed the substance in any way. Their relation is exactly what

Scripture says it is. The Son is born of the Father; the Spirit proceeds from the Father through the Son. If one must use an abstract term to speak of that whereby they are distinguished from one another, the term 'relation' is most appropriate. Years later Thomas Aquinas will emphasize the non-accidental qualities of these divine relations by calling them 'subsistent relations'. In doing so he was describing what Augustine said in many different ways, namely, that relationality in the Godhead is within the structure of one substance. In the various human activities cited by Augustine as imaging God, he pointed out that each activity is identical with the one mind (*mens*) or acting self and yet is relationally distinct from the other two activities.

This concept of 'relation' is analysed in Books V–VII of *On the Trinity*. It is thought to have been suggested by his reading around AD 413 of the Cappadocian Fathers of the Church, probably Gregory of Nazianzus (*Oratio* 29.16) and possibly the reading of *De Trinitate* I.16 of Didymus the Blind.[4]

In the discussion thus far the distinctness of the Persons has taken centre stage as it did in the early Christian faith-community. Yet Augustine is usually censured for featuring in his work *On the Trinity* the oneness of the divine nature. He certainly taught the unity of the Persons by insisting on their common actions in creation and salvation (technically called *ad extra*). This responds, however, to the surviving Arianism in fourth-century culture and to the more recent upsurge of Semi-Arianism and of Anomoeanism, akin to Arianism. Eunomius proclaimed the Son to be unlike the Father. He taught that since God was simple (without accidents),[5] all that was said of him must be said according to substance (DT V.4.5). Since the Father is unbegotten, he is unbegotten according to substance, and therefore the Son, who is begotten must be substantially different from the Father. Augustine responded by arguing that begottenness–unbegottenness characterize the relation between a human parent and child and do not describe the human nature of each one which in fact is held in common. The Semi-Arians did not call the Son a creature, as Arius did, but they refused him equality with the Father, preferring the word *homoiousios* (similar in substance) to the word *homoousios* (consubstantial) of the Nicene Creed. Augustine used the term 'relations' to express the fullness of divine life (its interpersonal reality); this term did not denote any addition to the divine Substance of Being.

For this reason Augustine often formulated the doctrine of the Trinity as one single divine nature subsisting in three Persons whereas the Greek Fathers spoke of the Christian God as three Persons having the same nature. Nevertheless, Augustine conceived of God concretely as Father, Son and Holy Spirit, as his Christology shows. There is no God other than the three divine Persons; that is why when God acts, they act in common.

The visible missions of the three Persons in creation, salvation and sanctification alerted Augustine to the divine processions — the Son from the Father, the Spirit from both. However, he looked to the inner divine life of knowing and willing to derive some understanding of the number and nature of the processions. The Son is born of an act of knowing: he is the Word. The Holy Spirit proceeds from the love of Father and Son: he is Love.

The fifteen books *On the Trinity* were written between AD 400 and 416. The first twelve books which were sent to Aurelius of Carthage (E 173) were circulated without any authorization and before being revised. Augustine had to be persuaded to complete the last three books. In Books I-VII he expounded the doctrine as found in Scripture and gave reasoned responses to various objections. In Books VIII-XV he pondered the inner life of the Trinity by using analogies from the knowing and loving human mind. This was a spiritual exercise of believing in order that he might understand.

Karl Rahner has criticized Augustine for not beginning his reflection on the Trinity as the divine Persons functioned within the economy of salvation. William Hill and Edmund Hill, both very competent contemporary theologians, do not consider Rahner's criticism valid. The former has stated: 'Edmund Hill . . . has rightly taken exception to the overly facile and somewhat arbitrary character of this dismissal, noting (i) that the early books of the *De Trinitate* are developed entirely from the New Testament; (ii) that there is a persistence throughout the whole work of the doctrine of the temporal missions; and (iii) that the doctrine of "appropriation" is far more subtle than Rahner allows.'[6]

There is evidence in *On the Trinity* that Augustine not only defended against Arianism the unity of Father, Son and Holy Spirit established by their common being but that he eagerly raised the consciousness of the faithful here and in homilies to the interpersonal unity established by the love of the Persons for one another. This unity all Christians are called to reflect. Not only did Augustine first suggest the loving-beloved-love triad in the human soul as an analogy of God. He highlighted the intimate connection between the final triad of remembering, understanding and loving God with the love of neighbour commanded in both Testaments. These two loves in all his writings he constantly kept together. Thus he wrote that through the Holy Spirit

. . . the begotten is loved by the unbegotten, and in turn loves him who begot him; in him they preserve the unity of Spirit through the bond of peace . . . And we are commanded by grace to imitate this *unity*, both in our relations with God *as well as among ourselves* (DT VI.5.7).

This call of Augustine is echoed in the Vatican II document on the Church and the Modern World *Gaudium et Spes*, which proclaims 'a certain likeness between the union of the divine Persons and the union of God's children in Truth and Charity' (n. 24).

The grace of baptism in the name of the Father, the Son and the Holy Spirit marks the Christian's visible mission. Sent by the Trinity into the world, the Christian is called to know and love God and the neighbour dear to God. In this way Christians reflect the Trinity in the world. Guided as he was by the ancient epistemological principle that 'like is known by like', Augustine's pastoral activity and his monastic rules were directed by his realization that human persons are called, with God's grace (*caritas*), to realize in themselves the divine image. A true remembering, understanding and loving of God opens that love to others as seen in the compassionate Jesus of Nazareth. Such is the dignity of human personhood: a vocation to share divine life, a life of love. The image that a human person is, a mirror for reflecting God, is distorted by disordered love. It is restorable by ordering one's love according to the scale of values: God first, then images of God (human persons), then traces or vestiges of God (non-human creatures). Since God's image in human persons was originally distorted by pride, only the humility of Christ and faith in the crucified and risen Christ can cleanse the mirror so that by the Holy Spirit's gift of himself as love, a human person may become a true image of the Trinity (Gal 5:6).

Notes

1 Plotinus, *The Enneads* (Cambridge, MA: Harvard University Press, Loeb edition, 1984), IV.3.21.

2 Gregory of Nazianzus, *Epistle 101 to Cledonius* as quoted in E. R. Hardy (Philadelphia: Westminster, 1954), p. 218.

3 A. Grillmeier, *Christ in Christian Tradition* I, tr. J. Bowden (Atlanta: John Knox Press/London and Oxford: Mowbray, 1975), pp. 464–7.

4 I. Chevalier, *Saint Augustin et la pensée grècque: Les relations Trinitaires* (Fribourg, 1940), pp. 141ff. as referred to in E. TeSelle, *Augustine the Theologian* (New York: Herder and Herder, 1970), p. 223.

5 An accident is that which cannot properly exist in itself; it needs another being or thing in which to exist as in a subject; it therefore forms with the subject a 'composition'; e.g., quality and quantity are accidents of material things. A substance is a thing which exists in itself and not in a subject.

6 E. Hill, 'Karl Rahner's "Remarks on the Dogmatic Treatise *De Trinitate*" and St Augustine', *Augustinian Studies* 2 (1971), pp. 67–80, as quoted in W. J. Hill, *The Three-Personed God* (Washington, DC, 1982), pp. 55–6.

7

Church and sacraments

Augustine had at his disposal the ecclesial doctrine of St Cyprian (d. 258), Bishop of Carthage, and of Optatus who was writing books about AD 367 when he was the Bishop of Milevis in North Africa. From them, and from his own reading of Scripture, Augustine learned that the Church was established by Christ the incarnate God and was given the authority to become the visible channel of the grace (divine life) of Christ through material signs called sacraments. Since it was a matter of Christ sharing his Trinitarian life of love with the recipients, Augustine understood that Christ was the invisible and main minister.

In all his teachings on the Church, therefore, Augustine spoke of two aspects: an external and an internal aspect of the one Church. The external aspect is visible through its ordered government, its observable congregations of women, men and children, its public worship and sacraments. The internal aspect is what the external aspect exists for and helps to achieve: the union of the baptized with Christ so as to constitute the whole Christ (*totus Christus*), the head and members (CEP IV.7). Augustine called this internal aspect of the Church the body of Christ (DGnM XXIV.57). This view of the Church was derived from the epistles of St Paul: 'A man never hates his own body, but he feeds it and looks after it; and that is the way Christ treats the Church, because it is his body — and we are its living members' (Eph 5:29-31).

To the members of the Church, his body, Christ communicates divine vitality and heals the wounds of sin. This begins at baptism when the Holy Spirit enters the soul of the Christian with his gifts of faith, hope and charity to bind the newly baptized with Christ and with all the other members of his body. Commenting on the descent of the Holy Spirit as a dove on Christ at his baptism (Mt 3:16), Augustine said: 'He then deigned to foreshadow his body, namely, the Church, in which those who are baptized receive the Holy Spirit in a special way' (DT XV.26.46; JE X.11). And when the Holy Spirit, after Christ's resurrection and ascension, was sent by the Father and the Son on Pentecost to animate the apostolic community as a universal Church, the Holy Spirit became the soul of this spiritual body of Christ (JE XXVI.13).

73

This doctrine of the Church as the body of Christ is present throughout the epistles of St Paul and became the traditional teaching of the Apostolic and Church Fathers. Later theologians were to call the Church the 'mystical body' of Christ to distinguish it from his physical body. Augustine welcomed this tradition as highlighting the dignity of the baptized person and Christ's desire for the intimacy of an exceedingly close presence to his creatures. To his congregation at Hippo Augustine said: 'Behold, therefore, by what admirable grace you are united with God — even through Him who, one with God the Father, wished to be also one with us' (EnP 142.3).

Just as there is an internal and an external aspect of the one Church, so is its foundation both invisible and visible. Augustine speaks of Christ as the invisible 'rock' or foundation of the Church and of Peter as the visible foundation. Christ had asked Peter: 'Who do you say that I am?' Simon Peter said: 'You are the Christ, the Son of the living God.' And Jesus responded: 'Simon, son of Jonah, you are a blessed man! Because it was not flesh and blood that revealed this to you, but my Father in heaven. So I now say to you: You are Peter and on this rock I will build my Church. And the gates of hell can never hold out against it. I will give you the keys of the kingdom of heaven: whatever you bind on earth will be bound also in heaven; whatever you loose on earth will be loosed in heaven' (Mt 16:16–20). And after his resurrection at his third appearance to the disciples, this time on the shore of the sea of Tiberias, Jesus said to Simon Peter: 'Simon, son of John, do you love me more than these others do?' He answered: 'Yes, Lord, you know I love you.' Jesus said to him: 'Feed my lambs' (John 15:15–16). A second and a third time this request was repeated by Jesus, and Peter is made the spiritual shepherd of the faithful (S 295.4.4). Augustine interpreted Peter's confession of faith in Christ as what takes place when one enters the Church. The Church is founded on Christ, the rock, whom Simon confesses to be Son of God and is called Peter, the rock. And so throughout his life at various times Augustine applied the word 'rock' to Christ and Peter. In his final review of his writings he reminded his readers that in an early treatise he said of the Apostle Peter: 'On him as on a rock the Church was built. This idea is also expressed in song by the voice of many in the verses of the most blessed Ambrose where he says about the crowing of the cock: "At its crowing he, this rock of the Church, washed away his guilt" ' (R XX.1).

Augustine recognized that Christ was intimately and invisibly united to his Church, which was founded on faith in him and in his saving power to be administered by Peter, the other apostles and their successors. Christ is spoken of as the bridegroom of the Church, his bride, to signify his intimate and permanent union with her. Augustine testified to the identity of this spiritual union with the visible Catholic Church when he said: 'Christ is the Bridegroom of this Church which is preached to all the nations and now blossoms and grows to the ends of the world, starting from Jerusalem. Of this Church Christ is the Bridegroom'

(S 183). As extended throughout the world this Church is the Catholic (universal) Church. In the same homily Augustine continued:

> After speaking the words with which he commended the faith of Peter and after revealing that Peter would be the rock on which to build the Church, He proceeded to tell his disciples that He would come to Jerusalem and suffer much and be rebuked by the elders and the scribes and the priests and that He would be put to death and rise again on the third day (Mt 16:21; S 183).

Augustine accepted the primacy of Peter among the Apostles as discerned in these scriptural directives. He realized that no visible society could remain unified and constant in its mission without a central authority. As early as AD 397 he referred in a letter to the Bishop of Carthage who 'could afford to disregard even a number of enemies conspiring against him, because he saw himself united by letters of communion both to the Roman Church, in which the primacy of the Apostolic chairs always flourished, and to all other lands from which Africa itself received the Gospel' (E 43.7). In another letter written in AD 400 Augustine names only the successors of Peter as representing the whole Church: 'For if the lineal succession of bishops is to be taken into account, with how much more certainty and benefit to the Church do we reckon back until we reach Peter himself, to whom, as bearing in a figure the whole Church, the Lord said: "Upon this rock will I build my Church, and the gates of hell shall not prevail against it" (Mt 16:18). The successor of Peter was Linus, and his successors in unbroken continuity were these' (E 53:2).[1]

Augustine concluded that since the keys of the Kingdom were given to Peter, representing the Church, the way to salvation is through the Church as the visible communicator of the grace of Christ. Although 'prevenient or actual grace' is given to those outside the Church, it is given to lead to the sacramental life whereby the Holy Spirit can enter souls and enrich them with faith, hope and charity. Indeed, the saving relation to God is a communal and not a purely individual matter. Just as both body and soul are essential to human persons, so also is there bodily and spiritual presence in the Church. To the baptized St Paul said: 'Know you not that you are the temple of God; that the Spirit of God dwells in you?' (1 Cor 3:1). And Augustine commented:

> Even if such as these are overtaken by the last day of this life before they attain to that spiritual age of mind when they will be fed solid food instead of milk, the One who dwells in them will perfect whatever they have lacked of understanding here, since they have not withdrawn from the unity of the body of Christ, who has become our Way (Jn 14:16) nor from their membership in the temple of God. In order not to withdraw from it they hold steadfastly to the rule of faith which is common to little and great in the Church' (E 186.29).

In the same letter he speaks of those who are 'born into the totality of the body of Christ as into a living structure of the temple of God which is his Church' (E 186.33).

Authority in the Church was recognized by Augustine when he appealed to the Bishop of Rome to ratify the African bishops' condemnation of the Donatists and the Arians. And in a letter he noted: 'Reports of the [Pelagian] controversy were sent to the Apostolic See from the two Councils of Carthage and Milevis ... In addition ... we also wrote a personal letter to Pope Innocent of blessed memory [d. AD 417] ... He answered all these communications in a manner which was right and fitting for the pontiff of the Apostolic See' (E 186.2). On another occasion he said:

> There are many things which rightly keep me in the bosom of the Catholic Church. The consent of peoples and nations keeps me, her authority keeps me, inaugurated by miracles, nourished in hope, enlarged by love, and established by age. The succession of priests keeps me, from the very seat of the Apostle Peter (to whom the Lord after his resurrection gave charge to feed his sheep) down to the present episcopate. And so, lastly, does the name of Catholic, which not without reason, amid so many heresies, the Church has alone retained; so that though all heretics wish to be called Catholics, yet when a stranger asks where the Church is, no heretic will venture to point to his own chapel or house. Such in number and in importance are the precious ties belonging to the Christian name which keeps a believer in the Catholic Church (CEM IV.5).

The visible communion with the Church was for Augustine a sign or sacrament of invisible communion with Christ. Augustine used the word 'sacrament' in many contexts. Christ is the sacrament of God (E 187.34); the Church is the sacrament of Christ. In the Church there are rites or sacraments instituted by Christ as sacred external signs to achieve an internal good effect (DCD X.5). In as much as only God can give grace, a participation in the Trinitarian life of God, Christ has to be the invisible minister of the sacraments. They are the source of holiness, of greater union with God, and of community among the faithful.

Augustine wished all to be aware of the internal change for the better in the recipient of a sacrament externally administered as a public action. He spoke of the Old Testament sacrifices as sacraments intended not to benefit God but to increase fidelity to him. 'A sacrifice, therefore, is the visible sacrament or sacred sign of an invisible sacrifice' (DCD X.5). It symbolizes 'a heart contrite and humble', a willingness to do what the Lord requires: 'to act justly, and to love mercy, and to walk humbly with thy God' (Micah 6:6–8). 'In the epistle to the Hebrews it is said, "to do good and to communicate, forget not: for with such sacrifices God is well pleased" (Heb 13:16). All the divine ordinances, therefore, which we read concerning the sacrifices in the service of the tabernacle or the temple, we are to refer to the love of God and our neighbour' (DCD X.5). And thus the daily Mass or Eucharistic liturgy is the perfect sacrifice or sacrament for the development of Christian love. 'For, as we have many members in one body, and all members have not the same function, so we, being many [persons] are one body in Christ, and all members of another, having gifts differing according to the grace that is given to us

(Rom 13:3-6). This is the sacrifice of Christians: we, being many, are one body in Christ. And this is the sacrifice the Church continually celebrates in the sacrament of the altar, known to the faithful, in which she teaches that she herself is offered in the offering [of bread and wine] she makes to God' (DCD X.6).

The so-called system of seven sacraments, so familiar today, was not made explicit until the mediaeval period. Augustine spoke of a sacrament as a sacred sign and a social bond. Signs are sacred and 'called sacraments when they refer to divine things' (E 138.7). Sacraments are social bonds when they bring together the Christian people. 'The Lord ... collected a society of new people by sacraments which are few in number, easy of observance, and excelling in significance' (E 54.1, 2). Augustine took a broad and narrow view of the term 'sacrament'. Broadly speaking, sacraments were many and included such signs as the blessed salt given to catechumens, exorcisms, the 'handing over' of the Creed and Lord's Prayer to catechumens, and, as previously noted, even events and persons in the Old Testament that foreshadowed Christ. Narrowly speaking, the sacraments were few; in this sense Augustine mentions baptism and the Eucharist as examples (E 54.1).

The sacrament of baptism which initiates the recipient into the body of Christ, brings an indwelling of the Holy Spirit, and the virtues of faith, hope and charity. These virtues are called 'theological' because they come directly from God and are directed to God. Since Christ is the source of baptismal grace, even an unworthy human minister cannot prevent this rebirth into the body of Christ if the adult recipient is disposed to have faith in him. Augustine maintained that baptism which brings forgiveness of original and personal sins is a necessity for salvation. Confirmation, that is, the strengthening of the soul by the gifts of the Holy Spirit, was in Augustine's time given at baptism. 'The sacrament of chrism ... is holy in the line of visible signs, like baptism itself' (CLP II.104.239).

In Augustine's day there were significant differences with respect to what we today call the sacrament of reconciliation. A reliable report of what was called 'second penance' has been given by F. Van der Meer: 'In 400 men believed more firmly than ever that after baptism the true Church could still forgive even the gravest of sins and that she did forgive them at least once.'[2] For this 'second penance' one could confess one's sins to the bishop privately. A public penance ceremony presided over by the bishop was required only when the sin had caused public scandal. Augustine preached that not only the three sins of idolatry, murder, and impurity, but that all grave sins against the ten commandments fell under the power of the keys — all sins, in fact, of which St Paul says that whoever commits them can have no part in the Kingdom of God.[3] 'The Church received ... the keys ... in the person of Peter, that is, the power of binding and loosing sins' (JE CXXIV.5). Whereas the sacrament of penance is necessary to forgive sins excluding one from the Kingdom of God and, therefore, called 'mortal', as signifying a second human death (the soul's death), less serious sins arising from human weakness are forgiven by repentance through prayer, assistance to the poor, fasting and good actions. Yet 'in the Holy Church the remission of even crimes themselves, no matter how great they may be, by God's mercy need not be despaired of by those who do penance according to the gravity of their sins' (En 65.17). The only sin that is unforgivable is the sin of denial that the Church has been given the power to forgive sins, a denial by one who 'scorns this great largess of divine bounty' — this is called the sin against the Holy Spirit (En 83.22). After the 'second penance' the Church merely advised penitents to impose penances upon themselves and to pray for forgiveness from God. Some people began to request a 'laying-on-of-hands' as a kind of general absolution as distinct from sacramental absolution, 'as though', Augustine said, 'the laying-on-of-hands could be of any benefit to anybody where there was no change in the manner of life' (S 232.7, 8; S 17.5; 131.7; 351.6). For ordinary people 'who led decent lives and gave offence to nobody, there was nothing in the nature of confession, except that which they made to God in their prayers'.[4] They heard their bishop preach that God always forgives the sins of weakness of those trying to do his will when there is prayer, fasting and almsgiving. Augustine when dying repeated the penitential psalms.

Of the real presence of Christ in the Eucharist Augustine preached: 'Not all bread but only that receiving the blessing of Christ becomes the body of Christ' (S 2343). Through the eating of this consecrated bread the physical body of Christ is received. To belong to the spiritual body of Christ is to participate in his life; by receiving with faith the Eucharist, an external offering of the Church, the divine life of love is nourished. And so of the Eucharist Augustine exclaimed: 'O sacrament of unity! O bond of charity!' (JE CXXIV).

He was keenly sensitive to the fact that Christ had made of the marriage union a symbol of his union with the Church. Like that union, it is indissoluble. This indissoluble bond gives a spiritual 'character' to Christian marriage. In promising permanent fidelity to each other in a bond of intimate love the spouses receive the grace of the sacrament. Interpersonal love and openness to the procreation of children are called for in marriage. Marriage is good, said Augustine, 'not merely on account of the begetting of children, but also on account of the natural society [community] itself in a difference of sex' (DBC 3.3). And so in speaking of the goodness of marriage he attributes it to the children born of it, to the chaste fidelity of the spouses, and to the sanctity of the sacrament received which makes of marriage in the Church a state of holiness. Such marriage brings obligations. For, 'a marriage once entered upon in the City of our God, where, even from the first union of the two, the man and the woman, it bears a certain sacramental character, can in no way be dissolved except by the death of one of them' (DBC 17).

The sacrament of Orders was conferred by a bishop. Since Christ chose the first bishops, it seemed to Augustine that only the successors of Christ who governed the Church could confer the sacrament of

Orders. This witnesses to the scriptural fact that Christ chose from his disciples the apostles whom he made pastors of the faithful. He therefore charged them with the mission of teaching what Christ had taught, of governing to protect the doctrine and the unity of the Church, and of administering the sacraments to increase the holiness of the faithful. The consecration to God in ordination is irrevocable, bringing a permanent sacramental 'character'. As no one can be re-baptized, so no one can be re-ordained. 'There remains in the ordained persons the sacrament of ordination; and if, for any fault, any be removed from his office, he will not be without the sacrament of the Lord once for all set upon him, albeit continuing unto condemnation' (DBC 24.32). If one's consecration to God has been neglected or repudiated, its renewal can occur through the grace of repentance and the sacrament of penance. In this spirit Augustine welcomed schismatic priests who wished to return to the Catholic Church. Whenever they give up their false views, then, 'we shall embrace our brethren, standing with them, as the apostle says, in the "unity of the Spirit, in the bond of peace" (Eph 4:3), and acknowledging in them the good things which are divine, like their holy baptism, the blessing conferred by ordination, their profession of self-denial, their vow of celibacy, their faith in the Trinity, and suchlike' (E 61.2).

Although this doctrine of Holy Orders is more complete than any other in early Church history, its elements came from traditional practice. Augustine names the three main 'Orders' as the episcopacy, the priesthood, the diaconate; but he also speaks of sub-deacons, acolytes, lectors or readers. Without ever using the term 'hierarchy', he alludes to a gradation among those holding offices. Frequently he spoke of Peter 'in whom the primacy of the Apostles shone forth with such excelling grace . . . For who does not know that that primacy over the apostolate is to be preferred to any other bishopric?' (DB II.1.2). To the bishops is confided the protection of doctrine and morals. This is ordinarily accomplished through general Councils 'called into plenary session from the whole Christian world' (DB II.3.4). The decisions of such Councils (today called Ecumenical) were final, guided infallibly by Christ governing his Church through the Holy Spirit who entered within her at Pentecost. In the matter of the condemnation of Pelagianism the Pope acted alone and his decision was accepted by the universal Church. In asking Pope Innocent I to ratify this condemnation which was originally made by an African Council, Augustine said; 'God deigns to direct you in your deliberation and to hear your prayers' (E 176.5).

So, as the Body of Christ, the Catholic Church is 'holy'; as the visible continuation of Christ confided to Peter, it is 'apostolic'; as fulfilling Christ's command to go and teach all nations, it is 'universal' or Catholic; as making available both the one true teaching of Christ and the sacraments he instituted as visible signs of grace to vitalize Christians and churches, the Catholic Church exhibits 'unity'. The members are responsible to God and to one another to retain the 'unity of charity in the bond of peace'.

The question of who are members of the Church founded by Christ became crucial in early fourth-century Africa long before Augustine's conversion. This question was linked to two doctrinal ones: (1) whether the ordination of a bishop or of a priest is valid when conferred by a sinful bishop; (2) whether baptism is invalid when conferred by a sinful minister. A group of African bishops declared that 'holiness', a basic mark of the true Church, depended upon the holiness of the members. If they were to lose the grace of Christ by sinful actions, they would cease to be members of the Church, and the sacraments they administered would be invalid. This group, later called Donatists, denied the validity of any ordination by Caecilianus, who was consecrated Bishop of Carthage in AD 312. They accused him of having complied with the demands of the authorities persecuting Christians under the Emperor Diocletian (245–313) that the Scriptures be handed over to them. Diocletian apparently thought that if he could destroy the Scriptures he could eliminate Christian belief. These Donatists rejected Caecilianus as a traitor. They left the Church directed from Rome and set up a rival government and priesthood throughout Africa. They declared that the Roman Catholic Church was no longer the true Church of Christ because it was not 'without spot or wrinkle', as Scripture described the Church. In separating themselves from the Catholic Church they became a schismatic one, but with members more numerous than those in the Catholic Church in Africa. The first notable leader of the party was Donatus, who acted as a schismatic Bishop of Carthage for forty years. According to W. H. C. Frend this was an African movement of independence from Roman ascendancy.[5]

When Augustine became Bishop of Hippo in AD 396 he had to deal with the increasing antagonistic actions of the Donatists. Bands of peasants called 'Circumcellions' took up arms against the Catholics. Augustine's first move was to reach out to them in an effort to bring them back to the Church. He composed a popular song to help the general public understand the history of the conflict and the errors of the Donatists. In trying to end the dispute by discussion he wrote many works: *On Baptism against the Donatists*; letters to a Donatist bishop; a letter to a Donatist layman; *On the Unity of the Church*; a long letter to the tribune Boniface, and many other letters and homilies re-enforcing the former ideas.

In these writings Augustine taught that the efficacy of the sacraments did not depend upon the holiness of the human ministers but upon the holiness of the divine minister, Christ himself. He pointed out that 'holiness' as a mark of the true Church was derived from its founder, Christ, the head of its spiritual body. To the Donatists the Bishop of Hippo insisted: 'Christ heals, Christ cleanses, Christ justifies' (S 292.6). He warned that by their accusations they were wounding charity, the mark of the Holy Spirit's presence in the hearts of the faithful, and by their schism they were destroying 'unity', an essential mark of the true Church.

Moreover, the Donatists were incorrect in their view that sinners are not members of the Church of Christ. It is true that those who sin gravely lose the grace of charity, the indwelling of the Spirit, and they lose living faith (since faith is alive through love). Yet, if they do not give up their belief in Catholic teaching, and if they continue to participate in Catholic worship, they remain members of the Church in its visible aspect and also in its internal aspect as the body of Christ. In this body, however, they are no longer 'living cells'. But they are closer to Christ than non-members because they can be re-vitalized if they choose to be. The Church prays and offers channels of grace for the holiness of the members but never excludes sinners from its membership. Sinners gravely offending God remain always materially united to the Church if they so wish; what they have lost is animation by the Holy Spirit, the soul of the Church. The baptized who act justly and desire to increase love for God and neighbour are animated by the Holy Spirit. Members who withdraw themselves from the Church by becoming schismatics, heretics, or persons excommunicated for their grave offences are excluded from the sacraments.

Augustine distinguishes 'the Church as it now is' from the Church as it will be, or the historical from the eschatological Church (En 9.12; CD XX.9.1; CEP III.3.17–18). He accuses Parmenianus of wanting to winnow the chaff from the wheat himself. The separation of the good from the wicked is reserved to God at the end-time.

In the historical Church Augustine distinguishes two planes, that of the sacraments, or external signs, and that of grace, interior reality. Grace or holiness is in the Church, but is also the transcendent Holy Spirit of Christ. People are bonded together by participating in the sacraments, referred to as *communio sacramentorum* (DC III.32.45). Augustine also speaks of the union of persons by grace as a *societas sanctorum* (JE XXVI.17). The communion of the sacraments is the order of the Church on earth, a participation in earthly realities derived from the work of Christ, the Word made flesh. The order of the society of saints is the order of participation in spiritual realities: peace, unity and charity. These spiritual realities derive from the gift and action of the Holy Spirit.

Clearly Augustine wished to use persuasion to lead these schismatics back to the Church. He wrote: 'It is indeed better that men should be led to worship God by teaching than that they should be driven to it by fear of punishment or pain' (E 185.6.21). Only when the Donatists increased their physical assaults upon the Catholics and their churches did Augustine ask the secular power to force the Donatists to give up their separate churches, relinquish their weapons, and to end the conflict. When they asked for re-admission to the Church they were not re-baptized or re-ordained (as were Catholics becoming Donatists). They were treated with respect and kindness. Augustine's own distress had not been so much with the damage to the churches as with the Donatist destruction of the 'unity' of the Church and of its 'universality' or catholicity. The Donatist church was for Africans only. Without unity where was charity, the very life of the Trinity and the very essence of the Church? To the returning Donatists he said: 'You do not indeed receive baptism which was able to exist in you outside the framework of the body of Christ, although it could not profit you; but you receive the unity of the Spirit in the bond of peace, without which no one can see God; and you receive Charity which, as it is written, "shall cover a multitude of sins" ' (E 185.10.43).

In a long letter to Boniface, tribune and count in Africa (417), Augustine explains his reasons for appealing to secular forces when the public disorder could no longer be contained. If the public peace had not been disrupted there would have been no appeal. Yet the intermingling of religious belief in this civic conflict created an unfortunate and dangerous precedent: that coercion was appropriate in religious disagreements. To look on this fourth-century African solution as a precedent for religious wars is, however, to abstract it from its unique historical circumstances.

Notes

1 Clement, Anacletus, Evaristus, Alexander, Sictus, Telesphorus, Igninus, Anicetus, Pius, Soter, Eleutherius, Victor, Zephirinus, Calixtus, Urbanus, Pontianus, Antherus, Fabianus, Cornelius, Lucius, Stephanus, Xystus, Dionysius, Felix, Eutychianus, Gaius, Marcellinus, Marcellus, Eusebius, Miltiades, Sylvester, Marcus Julius, Liberius, Damasus and Siricius, whose successor is the present Bishop, Anastasius: E 53.2. Augustine also speaks of the authority present in the People of God with their 'sense of the Faith'. He is quoted in chapter 12 of Vatican II's *Dogmatic Constitution on the Church*: 'The body of the faithful as a whole, anointed as they are by the Holy One (Jn 2:20, 27) cannot err in matters of belief. Thanks to a supernatural sense of the faith which characterizes the People as a whole, it manifests the unerring quality when "from the bishops down to the last member of the laity" (Augustine, *On Predestination of the Saints* 14.27) it shows universal agreement in matters of faith and morals.' It was in this sense that Augustine said: 'I would not believe in the Gospel unless the authority of the Catholic Church ordered it' (CEM V.6; CF XXII.79).

2 F. Van der Meer, *Augustine the Bishop* (New York: Sheed and Ward, 1961), pp. 382–7.

3 Ibid., p. 385.

4 Ibid., p. 387.

5 W. H. C. Frend, *The Donatist Church* (Oxford, 1952).

8

Monasticism

Many early Christians wished to imitate Christ as closely as possible. As individuals they freely dedicated their lives to loving God and neighbour. For some, this took the form of an ascetical way of life: the surrender of property, honours and marriage.

This group gradually became a distinct class in the Church, first in the East and later in the West. Solitude at first prevailed when Antony of Egypt (d. 356) entered the Libyan desert as a hermit. His holiness soon attracted many other hermits who received spiritual inspiration and instruction from him. By AD 320 Pachomius opened a large monastery in the Theban desert where some former hermits then gathered together as a community. Thus developed two kinds of monasticism, the eremetic (individuals) and cenobitic (groups). Hermitages and monasteries could be found in Palestine, Syria, Mesopotamia and Asia Minor. One leader of the cenobitic or community way of life was Basil of Caesarea. By the mid-fourth century there were monasteries in Gaul and in Italy where the way of life followed that present in Eastern monasteries.

Augustine became enamoured with the life dedicated to the pursuit of wisdom when in his nineteenth year he read the *Hortensius* of Cicero (C III.4). This essay was an invitation to philosophy. Philosophy, which literally means 'a love of wisdom', was in the ancient world a career or vocation, a way of life. To be a philosopher entailed the letting go of possessions, honours and sensual pleasures, not because they were considered evil, but because the pursuit of wisdom was incompatible with their pursuit. Pagan thinkers had early discovered that specifically human powers like intellect and will opened one to realities higher than those in the world of the senses. When Augustine began to realize this, his dissatisfaction with his enslavement to temporal goods increased. Feelings of frustration had already given him some inkling of it. He then became avid for discussion with others, and shared his thoughts with Alypius, Verecundus, Romanianus, Evodius and Nebridius. Later in Milan, when he had become Public Orator, there was a plan for ten friends to live a communal life in the search for and enjoyment of wisdom. They would combine all their riches and confide their material welfare to the stewardship of two members each year. The remaining eight could then concentrate on study. Because several of them were already married and others engaged to marry, the obstacles to the venture proved overwhelming (C VI.14; CA II.2.4).

The plan's failure, however, did not extinguish Augustine's desire for contemplation, which increased enormously after reading the 'books of the Platonists'. Plotinus possibly led him to regard celibacy as indispensable for an undivided search for truth (C VIII.3) and the happiness associated with it. He was deeply aware, however, that neither in Cicero's wisdom nor in Plotinus's quest for contemplative union with the One was the name of Christ present.

But the name of Christ became associated with the ascetical life on that memorable day when his fellow-African, Pontitianus, told him of the Egyptian hermit, Antony, and of all the hermits and cenobites in the desert region. He learned also that just outside Milan the Bishop, Ambrose, had established a monastery. From Pontitianus, Augustine likewise learned of the effect of Antony's way of life on two friends in the emperor's service: on reading Antony's life-story they immediately relinquished their careers and marriage plans to follow Christ more closely as hermits. Pontitianus told Augustine that Antony's vocation had originated as a response to what he read as he randomly opened the Scriptures. 'Go, sell all that you have and give it to the poor. Then you will have treasure in heaven. Then come, follow me' (Mt 19:21).

With all this in mind Augustine retreated hastily to the Milan garden and passionately entreated God's help (C VIII.12). Help came with the hearing of a refrain: *Tolle, lege*, take and read. He thereupon took up the book of Paul's epistles, opened it and read: 'Not in rioting and drunkenness, not in debauchery and licentiousness, not in quarrelling and jealousy, but put on the Lord Jesus Christ, and make no provision for the flesh, to satisfy its desires' (Rom 13:13–14).

In reading this text, contrary to what some say, Augustine was not converted from paganism to Christianity, since he had already been signed with the sign of the cross and seasoned with the salt of exorcism at birth (C I.1.17). To this he testified some time before the Milan garden experience: 'Yet the faith of your Christ, our Lord and Saviour, the faith that is in the Catholic Church, was firmly fixed within my heart. In many ways I was as yet unformed and I wavered from the rule of doctrine. But my mind did not depart from it, nay, rather, from day to day, it drank in more of it' (C VII.5.9). This Pauline text marked the occasion for the grace of conversion to Christ's way of life.

> For you had converted me to Yourself, so that I would seek neither wife nor ambition in this world, for I would stand on that rule of faith where, so many years ago, You had shown me to her [Monica]. You turned her mourning into joy far richer than she desired, far dearer and purer than that she had sought in grandchildren of my flesh (C VIII.12.20).

At that moment Augustine described the grace he received as 'being flooded with light' to embrace chastity and humility. Not only would he

make 'no provision for the flesh, to satisfy its desires', but the possessions and honours which often cause quarrelling and jealousy would be
renounced. From then on he prayed to desire the great gift of total
dedication to Christ as admonished by St Paul (C X.26.37), and he began
to experience the healing grace of Christ.

A year later when writing *The Morals of the Catholic Church and of
the Manichees*, Augustine revealed how the ascetical ideal which had
attracted him in the pagan philosophical and literary tradition (but had
not influenced his behaviour) had become realizable through its subordination to a positive value: the love of God in Christ Jesus. This
insight into love as the essence of virtue marked the beginning of that
transformation of the Eastern emphasis on the ascetical life as one of
renunciation into a primary emphasis in Western monastic life upon
charity. Christ became Augustine's treasure, 'sweeter than every pleasure
. . . higher than every honour' (C IX.1.1).

In the period between this wholehearted embracing of Christ and his
baptism by Bishop Ambrose at the Easter Vigil in AD 387, Augustine
enjoyed a prayerful and philosophical experience at Cassiciacum, not far
from Milan. His thinking at the time, permeated with Christian con-
victions and philosophical expressions, can be found in his writings *The
Happy Life*, *Against the Sceptics*, *On Order* and shortly after, the *Soliloquies* and the *Immortality of the Soul*.

After the death of Monica in the autumn of 387 and during the year
in Rome where he was forced to stay by reason of a blockade of the Ostia
port, Augustine became more acquainted with monasteries. This did not
happen accidentally in a manner similar to his first awareness of this
ideal way of life. Augustine made a point of visiting monastic communities around Rome because he and his friends had already decided
to live together in Africa in the service of God. So from the book written
during this Roman period, *The Catholic and Manichean Way of Life*,
we learn of his views on monasteries. While he praised the Eastern
ascetics, Augustine became attracted to the arrangements made by
Pachomius for a common life of shared ownership as well as a preference
for chastity and asceticism as providing an atmosphere conducive to
prayer and the study of Scripture. By this time he viewed monasticism
as an accepted Christian mode of life, and he highly esteemed the perfect
continence of many Christians 'particularly in the East and in Egypt'
(DME I.31.65). The monasticism of which he wrote was a lay-movement.

It was this kind of lay monastic life led by Augustine and his relatives and friends at Thagaste that was later described in the *Rule of
St Augustine*, a Rule which was to become a cornerstone in the evolution
of Western monasticism.

There in North Africa between 388 and 391, this small group settled
down to a life of prayer, Scripture reading, discussion and writing.
Augustine engaged in much letter writing, answering questions both
philosophical and theological. These letters increased throughout his life
to add up to a large collection. The answers to questions put to him from
388 onward to 395 or 396 were collected and published in a book entitled

Eighty-three Different Questions. The longest letters at that time were written to Nebridius, a great admirer of Augustine's wisdom, who frequently raised philosophical problems. Others were addressed to those whom he had misled into becoming Manichees. He tried now to bring them back to true faith in God.

Augustine's book *On True Religion* was written to influence his patron, Romanianus, to believe in the Christian doctrine of the incarnation of God and the doctrine of the Trinity, and to show the value of human reason in the effort to understand what is believed. *On Genesis against the Manichees* was written with the similar purpose of trying to remedy the effect of his own misplaced enthusiasm for a sect that claimed faith to be unnecessary. The love of learning which so well harmonizes with the desire for God is a striking feature of this early Western monastic experience in Africa. Its emphasis on studies was not present among the Italian ascetics visited by Augustine (CF VIII.6.13–15). Two other books written at this time were *The Teacher*, a dialogue between Augustine and his son, Adeodatus; *On Music*, a work previously begun and not finished even here at Thagaste.

The lay-monastery at Thagaste included Alypius, Evodius, Severus, Honoratus and Adeodatus (who died there at the age of seventeen), and others. There was community of possessions and no evidence of luxury. They lived according to Gospel values inspired by Acts 4:32–35.

In AD 391 upon Augustine's visit to a church in the coastal city of Hippo his name was called out by the congregation when Bishop Valerius announced that he needed a priest to assist him. Augustine agreed to ordination on condition that he could continue to live in a monastery. The bishop had a monastery constructed in the garden within the Church property. Some of the Thagaste community came with Augustine to this garden-monastery at Hippo where laymen joined them.

On becoming a priest Augustine's first desire was to become qualified to preach the Gospel as well as possible, and so he asked for a period of time to study Scripture. This would prepare him for sharing God's word with others, a high priority for him. 'We should not so surrender ourselves to the leisure of contemplation that we forget to help our neighbours; nor should we become so immersed in activity that we lose our longing to contemplate God in recollection' (CD XIX.19). This period of Scripture study resulted in a first attempt at exegesis: a commentary on *The Lord's Sermon on the Mount*, two commentaries on the *Epistle to the Romans*, one on the *Epistle to the Galatians*. During this first period of priesthood (391–395) Augustine completed the work begun in Milan, *On Music*, one begun in Rome, *On Free Choice*, and he wrote a small treatise *On Lying*. Intellectual questions continued to arouse discussion among the brothers; some of these are included in the work, *Eighty-three Different Questions*.

Ordained coadjutor bishop in 395, he succeeded Valerius as bishop in 396, and began to live in the bishop's house now converted into a monastery of clerics: priests, deacons and sub-deacons. About this time he composed his *Rule* based upon the spirit and actions of the apostolic community at Jerusalem as described in the Acts of the Apostles (4:31-35). All undertook the obligation to live according to the Rule. In the opinion of F. Van der Meer,[1] we cannot be certain whether Augustine knew of the uniting of monastic discipline and clerical ministry by Bishop Eusebius of Vercelli, around AD 340, and in his own day by Bishop Paulinus of Nola. Augustine was the first, however, to introduce into Africa the idea of clergy living in community. Until then each priest lived in individual quarters. Augustine's clerical monastery, however, gave rise to others and provided places where candidates for the priesthood could receive intellectual training. The clergy in Africa were both numerous and respected. The African Church gradually gained ten bishops from Augustine's monastery at Hippo and they in turn established their own monasteries for clerics. Also at Hippo Augustine established the first monastery in North Africa for women.

In successive stages, therefore, Augustine lived in a monastery as a layman, a priest and a bishop. In Acts he found a call to the 'interior life' of love for God expanding into a community life of love and respect for one another. He viewed this love for one another as a positive indicator that those entering the monastery were 'intent upon God'. Dedication to God and neighbour excluded the self-assertion which manifests itself in possessiveness and the pursuit of honours and power. 'Let love, which will not pass away, preside over everything' (*Rule* 5). The centrality of love in his monastic ideal prompted Augustine to say very little in the *Rule* about prohibitions and ascetical practices. Marriage was renounced not as an expression of disdain for its value but for the sake of giving undivided attention to God and neighbours. One can detect echoes of St Paul: 'He who is unmarried thinks of the Lord's business and the ways in which he can please Him ... The unmarried woman is concerned with the Lord's claim, that she be holy in body and soul' (1 Cor 7:32, 34). Religious life aims to bring Christian love to maturity. 'Before all else, dearest brothers, God should be loved, and then your neighbour, for these are the chief commandments that were given to us' (*Order of the Monastery* I).

In an ardent homily on the Psalms, one can overhear Augustine articulating the monastic ideal to the Hippo congregation:

'See how good, how pleasant it is for brothers to live together in unity' (Ps 132:1) ... These words of the Psalm, this alluring song, this melody pleasant both to the ear and to the mind, this has also brought forth the monasteries. By this sound the brethren who desired to dwell together were stirred up. For them this verse was like a trumpet blast resounding over the whole earth and gathering together those who were separated. It was a cry from God, a cry from the Holy Spirit, a prophetic cry ... heard all over the world ... All the disciples were from the [Jewish race], and they were the first to dwell together in unity. They sold all they had, and laid the price of their goods at the Apostles' feet ... And what is 'together in unity'? They had, he says, one mind and one heart Godwards. So they were the first to hear, 'Behold how good and pleasant it is that brethren dwell together'. They were the first to hear but not the only ones to hear (EP 132.2).

Such oneness in mind and heart generates community, according to Augustine. From its literal meaning the word *monachus* signifies a spiritual unity of many persons and not 'one' who lives for God alone in isolation from other persons. 'Those who live in community in such a way that they form but one person, *monachus*, one single person bring to life what is written, "of one mind and one heart", that is, many bodies, but not many minds, many bodies, but not many hearts' (EnP 132.5). That is what Augustine meant by a monk.

This oneness generates a religious community when it originates from many single intentions of living for God with an undivided heart. It entails a striving day by day for greater intimacy with God, thus sharing ever more deeply his love for all creatures in the divine image and likeness. A religious community is not a spatial concept but a reality of interpersonal relationships among those focused on God and his interests. Such persons share a fundamental belief in God's love for them and they share one another's hopes and disappointments. Their community of goods and their common life constitute the outward signs of their spiritual unity. As contemplatives living in harmony and praising God, such servants of God reflect an image of the Church as it exists in heaven. In their prayer and ministry they respond to a special call to work for the perfection of the Church here on earth, the Body of Christ.

The contemplative environment of a monastery was valued by Augustine for promoting the search for God. Wisdom as the terminus of the human search for truth, gleaned from Cicero and Plotinus, was radically transformed by Augustine with his realization that the Word of God is Wisdom. To participate in this Wisdom the human person was created in the image of the Trinity, that is, with memory, understanding and will so as to be *capax Dei*, receptive of God. And the human person was originally created in the likeness of the Trinity, that is, participating in the Trinitarian life of love; 'not by its own light, but by a participation in that highest light, will it [the human person] be wise, and where the eternal light is, there it will reign in blessedness. This wisdom is called the wisdom of man, as to be also that of God. For it is then true wisdom, since if it is only human wisdom, it is vain' (DT XIV.123.15). And with Job Augustine says: 'Behold the worship of God is wisdom' (Job 28:28). But there can be no true worship of God without faith, hope, and love which bring intimacy with the three divine Persons. By these virtues one is mindful of the inward presence of God whom one knows through faith expressed in love. To foster the pursuit of this wisdom Christian monasteries were formed. As the brothers grew closer in likeness to God, they progressed in the love that enabled them to contemplate him (EnP 99.5). Augustine referred to this as the renewal of the image of God.

Whoever then is being renewed in the knowledge of God ... by making progress day by day, transfers his love from temporal to eternal things, from visible to intelligible things, from carnal to spiritual things, and constantly endeavours to restrain and to lessen the desire for the former, and to bind himself by love to the latter. But he does so in proportion to the divine help that he receives, for the saying of God is: 'without Me you can do nothing' (John 15:5; DT XIV.17.23).

Augustine likened this renewal to being transformed from a 'fleshly' to a 'spiritual' man. No Neoplatonic overtones of a flight from the body or repudiation of it are rightly heard here. It is the Holy Spirit who makes 'spiritual' men through the love he pours into the hearts of the faithful and by his sevenfold gifts (Rom 5:5).[2] Here knowledge depends upon love. Faith, for Augustine, was never purely speculative. He distinguished between 'believing God' in his teaching and 'believing in God'. The loving Christ not only makes God's revealed Word credible but inspires trust in himself, God's incarnate Word (John 6:29; Gal 5:6; JE 29.6). All Christian life and, therefore, monastic life is the taking up of the cross to follow the Lord (E 243.11).

In the *Rule of St Augustine* there was only one vow mentioned, the vow to live a common life. Religious 'profession', however, included the obligation to live an unmarried life dedicated to God. According to A. Zumkeller, 'we do not know if a vow to this effect was taken, but this is not improbable since those in the outside world who were living lives dedicated to asceticism and virginity were familiar with such a vow'.[3] If possessiveness, sensuality and self-assertiveness are forms of distorted love, their elimination by practising the virtues of poverty, chastity and obedience is for the sake of a life of true love, a life for others. Since pride stifles love, humility was greatly encouraged as essential for conformity to Christ. Religious life is not a good in and for itself but has its worth from its concentrated espousal of the essential Christian value: love of God and neighbour. If one becomes proud of living such a life, its purpose is vitiated, its value lost: 'A humble married woman is better than a proud woman consecrated to virginity' (EnP 99.13).

Yearning for an intimate friendship with God was considered the origin of each brother's request to enter the monastery. Few people are unfamiliar with Augustine's famous words concerning this restlessness of heart (C I.1). Such yearning he equated with the prayer of the heart which should accompany all vocal prayers and never ceases. The continuation of this yearning furnishes evidence of the gift of perseverance in prayer. Such perseverance was promoted in the *Rule* by the arrangement of fixed times for community prayer and by opportunity for private prayer in an Oratory not to be used for other activities. In a homily Augustine remarked: 'Longing is always at prayer even though the tongue is silent. If your yearning is constant, then you are praying always. When does our prayer sleep? Only when our desire cools' (S 80.7).

> In faith, hope, and love we are praying always with uninterrupted longing. But at particular hours and times we entreat God also with words so that through these verbal signs of the reality, we may impel ourselves to greater effort, help ourselves become aware of how much progress we have made in this yearning, and rouse ourselves to grow in it with greater vitality ...

Therefore at certain times we call our spirit back to prayer from the other cares and activities which in some way diminish our yearning (E 130.9.18).

In Augustine's *Rule* for the servants of God the word 'Superior' was not used. Christ was the Superior, the teacher of all, and the group listened to the gospel and to the prompting of the Spirit dwelling within each one. The 'man-in-charge' (*praepositus*) or 'woman-in-charge' (*praeposita* in the feminine version) was responsible for the welfare of the community. This one-in-charge was intended to live out the community ideal so well as to be a leader or model for the others. He also made decisions concerning the appropriate punishment when the religious ideal was forsaken by an individual. Each person, however, was responsible for the others in the sense of speaking to them of any serious failures to follow the *Rule*. Within the monastery there were no social classes, as indeed there were at that time in the Roman Empire. The *Rule* enjoined that God was to be loved within each member of the community. And because God dwelt within the leader, the leader was to be obeyed with love. To him was given the greater opportunity to render service to God by placing himself at the feet of all.

Love for God and neighbour: such is the essence of Christianity. In religious life Christians dedicated themselves totally to this end according to the counsels of the Lord. Life in a monastery was intended to facilitate this total dedication. All the rules for living this life were for the sake of concretizing such love.

There has always been controversy surrounding the authorship of the various elements which make up the dossier of the *Rule*. There is also a question as to which version of the *Rule* was the original and fundamental one. Widely held was the opinion, passed on by Erasmus (c. 1469–1536) and St Robert Bellarmine (1542–1621), among others, that the only *Rule* written by Augustine was the one for nuns, as this is presented in Letter 211. Recently, however, the late Luc Verheijen OSA, an expert on the *Rule of St Augustine*,[4] argued persuasively that the original text was a rule for men. Verheijen published a careful study of it in its manuscript tradition. In the English language George Lawless OSA has presented a scholarly discussion of these matters in a recent book.[5]

The *Rule* in its feminine version is found, as noted, in Letter 211. Verheijen calls this *Rule Regularis informatio*. It may have been adapted by Augustine or by someone else, but the text is basically the same as that of the *Rule* for men, called *Praeceptum* by Verheijen. There is another *Rule* called *Regulations for a Monastery* which Verheijen ascribes to Alypius, Augustine's student, friend and fellow bishop. This has two small additions made by Augustine. Scholars are far from a consensus regarding both the provenance and authorship of this last document.

A first monastery for women was founded by Augustine in the 390s. Soon there were more communities of women ascetics in North Africa than of men. 'The sisters copied books; they spun and wove, and . . . elsewhere directed a home for foundlings.'[6] The Augustinian life for the sisters was likewise inspired by the 'common life' of the early Christians.

The name given to the woman-in-charge of the convent was, as we have seen, *praeposita*; the spiritual direction of the sisters was confided to a cleric. Augustine spoke of the sisters as *virgines Christi*. Widows as well as virgins were admitted to the convents. As in the brothers' monasteries, all joined in the canonical 'hours' of prayer. There was daily Mass at Hippo, but it was celebrated in the Basilica Pacis. Augustine preferred the chanting of the psalms and hymns as able to 'move one's spirit of devotion and to enkindle the heart with divine love' (E 55.18.34). At the time of her death, Augustine's elder sister, a widow, was in charge of the convent where some of his nieces and relatives also lived. When the new *praeposita*, Felicitas, gave a rebuke which disturbed the sisters (about AD 420), Augustine intervened and adapted the *Rule* for them to follow.

Some of the regulations might seem too minuscule to those outside a monastery. But the monastics obeyed them in an effort to purify their hearts for the 'seeing' of God. Such regulations had to do with common life. They were directed ultimately toward that inner community of thoughts and affections from which God's love is expressed for each one. As God dwells in the temple of each one's heart, so he dwells within the community as in a temple, to witness to the oneness of Christ and his members. The aim of 'living in freedom under grace' remains always the ideal toward which the various regulations in the *Rule* are directed.

The *Rule of St Augustine* was the first monastic regulation in the West. The lay monastery at Thagaste was the first of its kind in Africa. Augustine set up a similar monastery at Hippo on going there as a priest. And on becoming a bishop, he established for the first time in Africa an episcopal community of priests who renounced personal wealth and marriage to live ascetically and contemplatively while working for the salvation of others in humility, charity and peace. About AD 400 he wrote a brief treatise (at the request of Bishop Aurelius of Carthage) on the necessity for the brothers to live by their own work rather than from gifts of the public. They were also to give time to works of mercy. This treatise emphasizes not only the duty of labour but the dignity of manual labour. Entitled *The Work of Monks*, it was directed to the lay monks who were not engaged in Church ministries. Augustine did not hold that work itself was a punishment for the sin of Adam; prior to the Fall, however, it was done with greater pleasure. The cultural achievements of Western monasticism owed much to Augustine's insistence on using one's talents within the monastery. The principal function of a priest, however, was to be 'a dispenser of the Word and the Sacrament' (E 21.3). There was a great need for educating people to read and write and to understand the Christian faith. He pointed to the special responsibility of the 'servants of God' for the moral and religious instruction of Christians. This was a ministry of assisting the laity to become ever more perfect members of the Body of Christ, the Church. But the primary responsibility of monastic Religious is to form a community where the ideals of Christian life and love are given concrete expression.

Writers in Gaul, Spain and Italy made use of the *Rule* in the two centuries following Augustine's death. Between the ninth and the eleventh centuries groups of Religious adopted it as their mode of spiritual life. It was used among the Canons Regular of the eleventh and twelfth centuries and in the Mendicant Movement of the twelfth and thirteenth centuries. This *Rule* guides the religious life of the Order of St Augustine (OSA), organized in its present form in 1256 by Pope Alexander IV, and known originally as the Order of the Hermits of St Augustine (OESA), a title that prevailed until 1968. Among others who adopted the *Rule* were the Premonstratensians (1120), the Dominicans (1235), and the Servites (1256). In the fourteenth century it was adopted by confraternities of hermits: the Pauline Fathers, the Ambrosians and the Apostle-Brothers; by confraternities of lay people: the Alexian Brothers, the Jesuates and the Voluntary Poor. In the sixteenth century it was adopted by teaching orders: the Fathers of Christian Doctrine, the Piarists and, more recently, by the Augustinians of the Assumption of Mary, called the Assumptionists (nineteenth century). The Discalced Augustinians and the Augustinian Recollects form two branches of the original Order. The *Rule* is followed by Augustinian contemplative nuns and by countless religious orders of women who are engaged in an active ministry. The attraction of the *Rule* consists in its scriptural origin. There are 'not less than thirty-one [references to Scripture], of which twenty-seven are from the New Testament'.[7]

To follow the *Rule of St Augustine* enables its adherents to make a spiritual ascent to Beauty or God, the splendour of truth. Spontaneous generosity responds to this Beauty as it is reflected in a community of one heart and one mind in the one Christ, after the model of the first Christians at Jerusalem. Thus a fervent monastery is conceived of as a microcosm of the City of God, the heavenly Jerusalem. In the first Christians Augustine saw a model and a call to authentic Christianity: an 'interior life' of love for God which externalized itself in a community life of respect and love for one another. As fundamentally Christian, the *Rule* is spiritually liberating. Toward its end Augustine prays: 'May the Lord grant that, filled with "longing for spiritual beauty" (Sirach 44:6), you will lovingly observe all that has been written here. Live in such a way that you spread abroad "the life-giving aroma of Christ" (2 Cor 2:15). Do not be weighed down like slaves straining under the law, but live as free persons under grace' (Rom 6:14–22). Thus the *Rule* both anticipates and recapitulates Augustinian spirituality.[8]

Notes

1 F. Van der Meer, *Augustine the Bishop*, tr. B. Battershaw and G. R. Lamb (London: Sheed and Ward, 1961), p. 199.

2 That Augustine is referring to 'spiritual' men as those 'mature in grace' can be inferred from the statement in Sermon 71.18.30: 'I, brethren, was unable to speak to you as people of the Spirit. I treated you as sensual men, still infants in Christ. What I fed you with was milk, not solid food, for you were not yet ready for it.'

3 A. Zumkeller OSA, *Augustine's Ideal of the Religious Life* (New York: Fordham University Press, 1986), p. 240.

4 L. Verheijen, *La Règle de Saint Augustin*, I: *Tradition manuscrite* (Paris, 1967), II:

Recherches historiques (Paris, 1967). Cf. T. J. Van Bavel, *The Rule of St Augustine*, tr. R. Canning. (London, 1984).

5. G. Lawless, *Augustine of Hippo and His Monastic Rule* (Oxford: Clarendon Press, 1987; paperback 1990).

6 Zumkeller, op. cit., p. 217.

7 T. Van Bavel, 'The evangelical inspiration of the Rule of St Augustine', *Downside Review* 93 (1975), p. 83.

8 Writings of Augustine relating to monasticism: *The Rule of St Augustine*; *Holy Virginity* (CSEL 41); *The Work of Monks* (CSEL 41); *Sermons* 75, 355 and 356; *Letters* 48, 60, 78, 83, 111, 157, 210, 211 and 243; *Expositions on Psalms* 83, 99, 103, 131, 132, 343, 355 and 356.

The relevant passages have been assembled by Zumkeller, op. cit., pp. 283–422. Cf. M. T. Clark, 'Augustinian spirituality' in M. Downey (ed.), *The New Dictionary of Catholic Spirituality* (Collegeville, MN: Liturgical Press, 1993), pp. 66–73.

9

City of God

Historical narrative was used by Augustine in two major works. They are his *Confessions* and the *City of God*. In the *Confessions* we have seen him trace the story of his own life from his African birth until, as a newly baptized Catholic in Milan, he returned to Africa in order to live with other laymen in semi-monastic style. In this personal history he is selective rather than comprehensive, highlighting the events in which with Christian insight he recognized divine providence at work to bring him safely into port.

In the *City of God* he traces the story of the human race from the creation of Adam and Eve in the region of the Tigris–Euphrates river, through the election and political development of the Jewish people, the ascendancy of the Greek city-states and of the Assyrian and Macedonian Empires, the rise of Rome, the birth of Christ, the establishment of the Catholic Church until the shaking of the Christian Roman Empire in AD 410 when Alaric the Goth sacked the city of Rome. Here too he sees God in his providence working in secular history, and at first through the Christian Empire, to bring about the salvation and fulfilment of human individuals. The salvation-history of humankind as told in the Bible was accepted by Augustine for what it was: a sacred history of God's love for human beings and of the way to happiness. He did not view the Bible as the work of trained historians prescinding from all literary forms of expression. With all the means at their disposal — factual knowledge, poetry, symbols, metaphors, stories — the human authors transmitted the message of God's providential plan for the human race, culminating in his heavenly Kingdom.

Because the origin of the human race preceded all recorded history and its future was non-observable, Augustine considered it reasonable to accept on faith whatever God revealed of the creation and culmination of the world through the writers of Scripture. In this way he divided history into six periods: (1) from Adam to Noah; (2) from Noah to Abraham; (3) from Abraham to David; (4) from David to the Babylonian Captivity; (5) from the Babylonian Captivity to the birth of Christ; (6) from the birth of Christ to the Last Judgement.

In the periods described in the Old Testament God added to the good angels who constituted the City of God those human citizens who lived in fidelity to God the Father and prophetic faith in the coming of the Messiah. Through the book of Genesis Augustine understood that by being made to the image of God human persons are distinguished from animals and plants which are only traces of their Creator. The spiritual souls of human beings give access to a saving truth and goodness when they freely adhere to their Creator in friendship available through grace, a loving relationship to God in which the first Adam was created and which was restored by the second Adam, Christ.

In reading the New Testament Augustine realized that the Trinity of Father, Son and Holy Spirit, the origin and end of all reality, is calling humankind to peaceful co-existence where knowledge and love for God and neighbour are appreciated as the highest values, and, as the mark of Christian personhood, can cast out fear and greed. This community of the lovers of God on earth was embodied physically, historically, in a visible Church with the descent of the Holy Spirit, the Spirit of Love, ten days after the ascension of Christ into heaven. It was to expand with the Holy Spirit's entering the hearts of the faithful at every baptism to bring the gifts of faith and hope in God, love of God and neighbour. If they reject these gifts the baptized may *appear* to be Church members but are not citizens of the City or Kingdom of God.

The call to God's City witnessed to transcendent capacities in human nature, but it was not seen by Augustine as a summons to abandon temporal existence. The faithful are not intended to disparage the temporal world (God's creation) but to direct all natural and human things to the building of God's City by dealing with them according to their natures, that is, for their natural purposes. Time, space, matter, spirit — each makes its own contribution to the achievement of history's purpose as movement toward God by pilgrims on their way.

In his reflections on history in later life Augustine placed himself at the greatest possible distance from the Platonists. They divorced soul from body; he kept them united, with body belonging to human nature. While they saw matter in motion as irrational, he saw it as purposeful. For them, motion was merely process; for him it was ambiguous, but it could be progress through right human choices. He departed from an ancient view of history as cyclic and affirmed the view of his Christian predecessors — the biblical view of history as linear. Consequently, he underscored the import of history's goal as transcendent; history began from 'above' the earth and would culminate 'above' the earth. This was a philosophical decision to attend to the final cause (*telos*) as well as the efficient causes of events to discover the meaning of history. Recognizing that the end (*telos*) or purpose of history was made known through God's revelation in the Scriptures, he saw faith in God's word as key to the understanding of history's meaning. The Scriptures, he discovered, were future-oriented, a future made possible, however, by God's action in the present: the risen Christ as head of the Church, his body, and the Holy Spirit active in baptized souls who respond in faith to God's will.

It is in that light, the light of faith in God's Word — the written word and the incarnate Word — that Augustine wrote the *City of God*. As John O'Meara has forcefully shown, this book emitted rays of optimism in the darkness of Rome's greatest crisis. It was a 'Charter for a Christian future, not only for Rome but for all the world'.[1] We shall see below Augustine's mature interpretation of the 'Christian future'.

Contrary to a widely accepted opinion that this book is directly and chiefly about the sack of Rome and the exoneration of Christians from any blame for it, and that it contains Augustine's political theory, it is really about the City of God as being shaped and guided by the indwelling Spirit of God even in the midst of natural disorders and human follies. Rome in its success and Rome in its failure — both in their own way were part of history's forward movement. Augustine saw the so-called barbarians seeking their place in the sun as an appropriate movement of history calling for the sharing of education and the gift of faith and bringing new energy into God's City.

In discussing the suitable attitude toward temporal goods and toward the government for a Christian in the world, a theme never outdated, Augustine produced his most fact-filled and best structured work. To embrace the historical experience of humankind in the past, the present and the future (as prophesied), he wrote 22 chapters. It was not a case of pitting Christian against pagan values but of reconciling human values, so much appreciated by pagans, with God's transcendent purposes in creating the world. Augustine saw this world as one where intellect should be as keenly developed as it was with the Greeks, order as deeply sought for as it was with the Romans, and trust in God's Revelation as necessary as it was for the Hebrews. He would never cease promoting a Christian–classical culture although he would lose enthusiasm for a Christian government as able to establish God's Kingdom. A Christian culture, however, gives priority to the values of faith, hope and all-inclusive love without rejecting the philosophical, literary, artistic achievements of classical culture. Christianity added true religion to classical culture, enabling human persons to know and worship God as Father, Son and Holy Spirit, source of creation, salvation, sanctification and giving a truer self-image to persons than was found in classical culture.

In chapters 1–10 Augustine responds to the pagan charge that Constantine's declaration of a so-called Christian Empire had angered the Roman gods and led to Rome's fall in AD 410. In chapters 11–22 he traces with the aid of Scripture the origin, development and destiny of the City of God and the ungodly city, symbolized by Jerusalem and Babylon, one led by God, the other by Satan.

In the first five chapters, with the help of Varro, Caesar's librarian and the author of 490 books, Augustine gives evidence of many misfortunes befalling the Roman Empire while the pagan gods were being worshipped. These chapters deal in detail with the polytheism of Rome. From all that was said by the pagans when Rome fell in blaming the forsaking of the gods for this disaster, it became obvious that earthly happiness was the motivation for such worship. The following five chapters concern the Roman worship of certain gods in order to obtain eternal life. Augustine argues that if the gods were unable to bring earthly fortune, they can scarcely have power over eternal life. In fact they are men or parts of nature who have been deified. A truer conception of God has been given by the Platonists who are also good moral philosophers, but some of these philosophers worship demons to obtain good fortune (Porphyry). Three of these five chapters are devoted to Greek philosophy. It is praised for its intellectual achievements but shown to be unable to fulfil its aspirations to truth. Pride keeps it from submitting to the authority of Christ as the way to the transcendent world it had discovered to exist.

In the following four chapters the origin of the two cities is traced. The City of God originated with the good angels who loved God with a love of preference. The ungodly city began with the rebellion of Satan and the fallen angels against God. Within these chapters Augustine once again discusses the creation of the world bringing the opportunity for human members of the City of God with the possibility of their becoming citizens of the ungodly city.

The next four chapters pertain to the historical course of the two cities from the time of Cain and Abel to the Deluge, from Noah to Abraham to the Kings of Israel and the Prophets, from Samuel to David to Christ. This is followed by an analysis of all the prophecies of the coming of Christ.

In the final four chapters the ends of the two cities are discussed. Augustine recalls the failure of the philosophers to give happiness to themselves. He then portrays the peace and happiness of the heavenly city in the fellowship of the saints where all enjoy the vision of God. This supreme good is contrasted with the supreme evil of separation from God in the ungodly city. The two cities are not to be identified with temporal societies or institutions. Symbolically and rhetorically, Augustine sometimes speaks of Rome as the new Babylon and of the Church as the new Jerusalem. But, strictly speaking, only the eschatological Church is at one with the City of God. Nevertheless, the historical City of God, the Church, as the chosen channel of God's grace, is to be fostered, strengthened, increased and protected. To the City of God all the world is on pilgrimage; the way was barred to it until the King of that city made himself the Way to it. 'I am the Way, and the Truth, and the Life.'

Cain is cited as the first human member of the ungodly city (DCD XV.7.17), an association of the rebellious angels and those human persons whose selfishness leads them to reject God and his plan for their true fulfilment (DCD XIV.13). The two cities are formed by free wills being used well or abused by angelic and human persons. When the angels became demons, they henceforth used their no small power to influence human beings to turn to false gods. 'Accordingly, two cities have been formed by two loves: the earthly [or ungodly] city by the love of self, even to the contempt of God; the heavenly [or godly] city by the love of God even to the contempt of self. The former glories in itself, the latter in the Lord' (DCD XIV.28).

Since the direction taken by human wills is a dynamic force in whatever happens, it is a part of history, albeit an invisible part. Augustine does not propose the City of God, therefore, as a figment of the imagination or as a projection of philosophical speculation. It is not an ideal archetype; it is composed of living persons. In God's city human and angelic persons are related and mutually influential. The love of humankind shown by Christ in his earthly life and death inspired the first generation of Christians to become citizens by returning love for love. This intimate relationship to Christ, forged by the Holy Spirit who pours love into the hearts of the faithful, establishes interpersonal relations and constitutes as an organic totality the Body of Christ. By accepting the authority of the Catholic Church which exhorts faith in the canonical Scriptures (DCD II.8), one admits the reality and importance of the City of God which is invisible to the senses and unaided human reason.

Because persons are created to exist to the image of the Trinity by their capacity to know and love God, in an outpouring of grace God built a divine City where citizens participate in truth and adhere by love to God and one another.

The questions most frequently raised concerning the City of God are the following: does the existence and praise of this city entail a repudiation of the achievements of Rome and of classical culture as well as a disdain for governments that are not Christian? Is the City of God as a community of the lovers of God co-extensive with the Catholic Church? Is membership in the City of God an escape from temporal responsibility and a devaluation of the material and natural world?

There is no doubt that Rome was featured in the history provided in the *City of God* text. Rome was taken throughout the text as the outstanding historical embodiment of purely secular values, fortified, as they were, by the Greek philosophical tradition. As symbolizing the high point of civilization in the eyes of an African nurtured in the Latin culture, Rome could not but be somewhat admired by Augustine. His attitude toward it is nonetheless ambivalent, as when he terms it the new Babylon. He attributed the successes of the Republic (500–27 BC) and of the Empire (27 BC–AD 476) not to the favour of false gods but to the moral standards to which the earlier Roman rulers held their citizens. He was aware of the discipline inculcated in families and of Roman courage, willingness to work, loyalty to law, and generosity to the poor. At first he spoke of Roman achievements as the work of divine providence preparing for a Christian civilization.[2] There were virtuous Romans: Marcus Cato and Caius Caesar. Rulers claimed descent from Aeneas who came to Italy after the fall of Troy.

Rome fell not solely by outside forces but mainly by losing the moral stamina which urged patriotic Romans to sacrifice personal satisfactions for the common welfare. Augustine recalled the words of Roman writers — Sallust and Cicero — to testify to the gradual decline of Roman society (DCD II.21). Yet rulers often lacked moral leadership.

Remus was murdered by his twin brother Romulus, the first king of Rome, to which he gave his name. D. Junius Brutus (d. 43 BC) was murdered by Antony; civil wars in the first century BC were marked by unusual cruelties. With the triumph over Carthage in the Punic wars (264–146 BC) a period of material prosperity promoted every kind of indulgence and stirred up the lust to dominate other peoples. In the first three centuries after Christ's birth, Christians were thrown to the animals to entertain those in the amphitheatres throughout Roman lands. By the third century Rome, the embodiment of secular culture, was tottering from self-inflicted wounds and on the brink of death. Augustine attributed its survival to the triumph of Constantine in AD 313 and the Edict of Toleration at Milan.

Lacking true religion the Romans deified Aeneas, Romulus and the emperors and worshipped many gods in the mistaken belief that they could ward off all threats to economic and political prosperity. The worship of pagan gods was not offered to attain power to live good moral lives (DCD II.22).

Augustine's view of religion was utterly different. He thought that religion is an indispensable part of the virtue of justice: a rendering to all of that which is their due. To him it was clear that to the creator of the world, the one true God, worship is due. Thus the Romans were guilty of a travesty of justice: they gave God's due to demons or to human beings. 'Rome never was a republic, because true justice had never a place in it' (DCD II.21). True justice is the obvious virtue of the City of God: 'the City of which Holy Scripture says, "Glorious things are said of thee, O City of God"' (DCD II.21).

This analysis of justice as entailing the virtue of religion is Augustine's reason for saying that Rome was never a state according to the definition of Scipio (b. 125 BC) who defined a true state as reported in Cicero's *De Republica* as an association of persons in acknowledgement of a 'right' and in their common interest (DCD XIX.20). And Augustine asked: 'Where, then, is the true justice of man, when he deserts the true God . . . Is this to give everyone his due? Or is he who keeps back a piece of ground from the purchaser and gives it to a man who has no right to it, unjust, while he who keeps back himself from the God who made him, and serves wicked spirits, is just?' (DCD XIX.21).

In order to speak of unjust states realistically it was necessary to redefine a state as 'an assembly of reasonable beings bound together by a common agreement as to the objects of their love; then, in order to discover the character of any people, we have only to observe what they love' (DCD XIX.24). In this way Rome could be called a state, as could the Greek city-states, the Egyptian states and early Assyria, Babylonia and all other public governments, to be graded as superior or inferior people according to the higher or lower status of the interests and values each promotes. Where power alone is loved by rulers, Augustine thought it logical to conclude: 'Without justice, what is sovereignty but organized brigandage?' (DCD IV.4).

Theodosius the Great (b. c. AD 346), who reigned from 378 to 395, is praised for opening up the possibility of justice in a government that no longer worshipped false gods nor required that others do so. Theodosius made laws promoting moral life, and this Augustine admired; pagan and heretical worship were also suppressed (DCD V.26). Augustine taught that there were definite duties incumbent upon Christian rulers: to uphold truth and goodness in public life and to support those who directly promote them.

Did Augustine's view of Rome as an imperfect state lead to a disdain for government in general? Quite the contrary. Augustine welcomed the classical world's cultivation of order and viewed the state as working in history for the attainment of earthly peace needed by all citizens (DCD XIX.17). He considered it a duty to participate in political life and presided as bishop in judgement of civil cases. All the while he recognized that government can better prevent disorder than inculcate virtue. Virtue is fostered through the 'order of love' whereby greed and anti-social behaviour are uprooted at their source in the human heart. The need for order in a healthy social life entails an obligation to obey even evil rulers. Had not St Paul upheld the role of governments in the prevention of evils (Rom 13)? Moreover, governments which enact just laws are vestiges of the eternal law. They do not legalize torture and capital punishment. Nor is war the right way to settle differences between states. War should be waged only when unjust aggression threatens human values intrinsic to true community. It is only fully justified under certain conditions: that the war is defensive; that the injuries inflicted are as few as possible and actually necessary for ending the war; that the enemy is not so overcome that revenge will initiate a new war. Because of the possibility of aggression, military service is needed for self-defence.

As to whether the City of God is co-extensive with the Catholic Church, Augustine indicates that, strictly speaking, it is not a synonym for the visible, historical Church. Certain facts demonstrate this. The good angels and pre-Christian people are also citizens of the City of God. And since the interior dispositions of human persons are paramount in becoming citizens, the mere fact of being a 'sociological' member of the Church does not suffice. Until the Last Judgement the cockle will not be separated physically from the wheat (DCD XVIII.48). It is also possible for non-members of the visible Church to be citizens of the City of God if their absence from sacramental communion is not a personal rejection of it. Moreover, baptism which unites one to Christ, the head of the City of God, can be received outside the visible Church.

Nevertheless, since *caritas*, the love of God, as the supreme value, is a gift through the indwelling of the Holy Spirit in the hearts of the faithful, a grace coming chiefly through the sacraments, Augustine saw the Church as God's chosen means to bring citizens into his Kingdom. There is, moreover, another way of looking at the Church, one which does not take into account the interior dispositions of all its members. In this way the Church stands for God's revelation in Christ concerning the worship of the Trinitarian God and the obeying of the divine commands. In this respect — its faith and morals — the visible Church is equivalent to the City of God (DCD XIII.16). One passage where Augustine speaks directly of God's Church as the City of God is DCD XIII.16: 'But the philosophers against whom we are defending the City of God, that is, His Church . . .'

Augustine revered the Church as the authoritative representative of Christ; he therefore looked to the universal Church as a guide for the acceptance of the various scriptural books prescribed as God's word (DDoC II.8.12). The unity of the episcopate and of the Church was derived from St Peter whom he called the first of the apostles and the representative of all Christians. Just as the dissent of one man, Adam, alienated his descendants from God, so the assent of one man, Peter, reunited those descendants to God in the Church. Thus Augustine refers to St Peter as the 'Rock' and at times to Christ as the 'Rock' on which the Church was founded: St Peter's successor is visible, Christ is invisible (S 76.1). That he attributed true authority to the Bishop of Rome is evident from his request to the Pope to condemn Pelagianism and by his appeal to Rome against the Donatists (E 177, 181, 182, 183).

The relation of the Church to the state was an issue on which Augustine apparently changed his mind while he was writing the *City of God*. We have seen that he had attributed Rome's survival to Constantine's inauguration of a Christian Empire. This optimistic attitude went even further at first. Absorbing the earliest Christian appraisal of the Constantinian empire as God's intervention in history to accomplish the coming of his Kingdom, Augustine tended to regard the empire as an ally of the Church in the development of the City of God. The question of the relation of 'state' to the City of God (symbolized by the historical Church) was eventually answered by Augustine in a way quite unlike his early opinion which had coincided somewhat with the opinions of churchmen who regarded Constantine and Theodosius as originators of a 'Christian era'. This shows that all his changes of mind are not made explicit in the *Retractations*.

It was indeed tempting to think that the Christian Empire which evolved between Constantine and Theodosius was a giant step toward the coming of the Kingdom of God promised by Christ. That Christ through the empire was renewing the face of the earth was firmly held by Eusebius, Bishop of Caesarea, in the East and by Ambrose, Bishop of Milan, in the West. Robert Markus has provided references from Augustine which show his early adherence to this 'imperial theology'.[3] In commenting on Psalm 6:13 (AD 392), Augustine showed his pride in Christianity's triumph by speaking of the *power* of Christ 'who turned the idolatrous persecutors of the Church to the faith of the Gospel within so brief a period of time'. In the work *Consensus of the Evangelists* (AD 400), he wrote of the Roman Empire as 'converted to the defence and service of the Christian faith' (I.14.21). Markus sees Augustine as admitting the action of the Christian empire into sacred history, making the empire's actions part of salvation history. In writing to Boniface in 417, Augustine tried to justify the government's use of coercive methods against the Donatists by referring to 'the changing order of times', a Christian order.

But from AD 420 onwards, according to Markus, Augustine took the position that there can be no legal enforcement of Christianity; what is needed is spiritual rebirth. The most decisive repudiation of 'political theology' is present in Letter 198.6 and *City of God* XX.5. Institutional Christianization is illusory. Markus states: 'The King's service of Christ, far from securing the Church's glory, is dismissed [by Augustine] as constituting a "greater and more dangerous temptation" ' (*The Perfection of Human Justice* 15.35).[4]

To understand why Augustine loosened the tie between the Christian Empire and the Church is to realize the continuing influence of his own conversion experience as resulting from God's providence working in daily events to prepare him to accept Christ through the words of St Paul (Rom 13:13). Reflection on the evil ways of many in the service of the Christian Empire and the fall of Rome in AD 410 stimulated a deeper consideration of the role of institutions in the coming of God's Kingdom. Augustine found nothing in Scripture which indicated that governments were instruments of salvation history. He squarely faced the fact that neither the City of God nor the ungodly city could be identified with any earthly institution. Members of the City of God can function in the government, as can members of the ungodly city. Likewise there can be members of the ungodly city who are members of the visible, historical Church. Therefore, the state and the Church have in them people who love opposite values. Some regard temporal things as of ultimate value; others know that eternal realities participated in on earth by faith, hope and charity will alone satisfy the longing of the human heart. This harmonizes with the primacy that we saw Augustine giving to love in his moral theory. But both groups share a common objective in securing an earthly peace for which the state is primarily responsible. They work together in the political order to secure such peace. Within a restricted sphere the government is autonomous, but all citizens, including Christians, have a stake in how the government uses its power. Although theologically neutral, the state should protect the lives and property of all persons; Christians as well as non-Christians are obliged to make sure that it does so. So membership in the City of God is not an escape from temporal responsibility nor a devaluation of the temporal world. In so far as justice is related to temporal peace, Christians have a responsibility for justice in all the social institutions in which they participate. They must be concerned with political order in so far as it relates to heavenly peace (the Kingdom of God). 'Both cities use the same temporal goods, both suffer the same calamities, but they do so not with the same faith, nor with the same hope, nor the same love' (DCD XVIII.54.2; XIX.17; I.8.2).[5] These cities will not be perfectly visible as societies until the Last Judgement; hearts are known only to God.

The City of God is multi-cultural and multi-national (DCD XIX). The Church is not linked to any one state, nor is it confined within any one culture. Augustine very early had argued against the Donatists who wished to make the Church African. Later he insisted that it should not be identified with the Roman state. The Greeks, as Markus emphasizes, looked to the *polis* to achieve their perfection; Christians become perfect through the grace of Christ, grace available to barbarians and slaves.

The originality of Augustine's mature attitude to the Roman Empire once he began working out his theology of history has been well documented by Robert Markus. All who are interested in the origin of political theology should read his entire book. From him we learn that Christians of the fourth and early fifth centuries 'could follow in the footsteps of Eusebius [and Ambrose and Jerome] and give the Empire a sacral significance in terms of the history of salvation. Alternatively they could follow the ancient apocalyptic tradition of hostility to the Empire, assimilating it to the *Saeculum* of apocalyptic literature.'[6] Augustine did neither. He avoided any proleptic 'spatialization' of the divine promise by individualizing and spiritualizing the object of Christian hope.

Wolfhart Pannenberg recalls the early Old Testament election of the people of God (Deut 7:68) as well as the emphasis on individual righteousness after the capture of Jerusalem by the Babylonians, and also Jesus' choosing of the group of apostles (12), a 'fresh start for the historical conception of election' by God.[7] He thinks that Augustine in the *City of God* managed to combine the two traditions: historical community and the individual. The City of God is a spiritual community, an invisible one of the 'chosen' dispersed among all nations. It also existed at one time, according to Pannenberg, as the people of Israel and exists at present in the form of the Christian Church. Pannenberg holds that the historical continuity disappeared in the post-Augustinian doctrine of election. However, he believes that the historical and social aspects of the people of God as representing 'chosenness' did not completely disappear. It went underground and exerted a formative influence on the political history of the West.[8]

The concept of the people of God, indicating all of Christianity, as found in the Vatican II documents, is an important event of our times, according to Pannenberg. He asks, however, for a theology that includes the political life of Christians. Indeed that should be a development from Augustine's teaching that Christians should contribute to the stability of the earthly peace which is government's direct concern. The fact that Augustine insisted that salvation comes from the grace of Christ (not from historical material achievements) does not entail a lack of interest by Christians in good government and the preservation of natural resources. Pannenberg is right that Christians share a common responsibility with all people for peace and justice for all humankind. As soon as the first Covenant was made, there was a social order, that is, certain conditions for belonging to God; love of neighbour was fundamental. Augustine's constant emphasis on love of neighbour implies his belief that the future Kingdom of God, characterized by concord and love, should begin and develop on earth.

Benedict Viviano explains Augustine's notion of the City of God as an eschatological rather than a visible entity, and related to the Johannine theology of eternal life and resurrection.[9] Augustine did not see the Kingdom of God as coming into existence as a temporal phenomenon. Even to the end he retained his early Christianized and socialized notion of happiness as the beatifying shared vision of God in heaven. Viviano thinks that Augustine's theology made the Church freer but more privatized.[10]

Langdon Gilkey asserts that in 'in large part on the basis of the Christian interpretation of history, as formed largely by Augustine . . . the modern consciousness of history arose'.[11] Of course the new view of time and history came with Scripture, but Augustine made it an object of theological reflection. He affirmed time and history as creative and good under the Lordship of God for the purpose of transforming individuals into the divine image. God not only created the world but works in human history. He does not work as an external cause but functions within various dynamic realities, including and most of all, freedom. This divine providence is concerned with God's eschatological goal for humankind. Each moment of time is therefore of ultimate significance. The more a human being participates in God through grace the better does it become. Thus Gilkey recognizes that for Augustine history becomes meaningful through the work of divine providence and grace (DCD XX.6 and 9). The Church is the sacrament of history making visible the presence of grace in history. Gilkey highlights the fact that Augustine became very conscious that the conquest of sin is an achievement far beyond the power of political action. After all, Augustine's central teaching, as we saw in the chapter on morality, is that only a new relation of the human being to God, to self, to neighbour can conquer sin. The lack of freedom in its many forms is not the basic problem of historical existence. It is, Gilkey sees, the corruption of freedom by sin as affirmed by Augustine. Unjust social structures are the consequences not the causes of human greed and pride. Political and social action can indeed reduce the suffering that sin causes. Surely, then, Augustine was working for the true peace of the temporal world also when he was zealously teaching the true source of the power to attain a right relationship to God, self and neighbour. True peace depends fundamentally on the right use of freedom.

No secular success, no wealth, no political power can make good Christians — this was Augustine's view. During the early centuries of persecution by the government, the blood of Christian martyrs became the seed of Christians. The development of the City of God as a community of the faithful took place by a reorientation of human affections from earthly realities as ends-in-themselves to Father, Son and Holy Spirit, in whom Christians are empowered to see the world as the created reflection of divine love. Adhering to God in this way changed the lives of men and women from within and influenced all their outward actions for the better. The fourth century blossomed with saints from all cultures and from every social class. Many lived in the world letting their lamps of faith shine to illuminate the path for others. Some became hermits or monks. In a number of lands there arose the communities discussed in the chapter on monasticism, anticipating the heavenly Jerusalem where all love Christ as with 'one mind and one heart'.

It is one thing to say that human values are not the ultimate ones for members of the City of God and quite another to say that they are depreciated by them. Augustine was quite sure that values like knowledge, freedom and friendship are desired by members of both cities. The classical philosophers had blamed the human body for defects in such values and taught that matter was a force opposed to the rational aspirations of the human soul. The most influential philosopher of the fourth century, Porphyry, insisted that human life be organized as a flight from the body and declared that Plotinus was ashamed of being in a body. Not so Augustine. He wrote of the beauty of body, of the exquisite intricacy of its working.

> Moreover, even in the body . . . what goodness of God, what providence of the great Creator is apparent! The organs of sense and the rest of the members are they not so placed, the appearances and form, and stature of the body as a whole, is it not so fashioned, as to indicate that it was made for the service of a reasonable soul . . . And even apart from its adaptation to the work required of it, there is such a symmetry in its various parts, and so beautiful a proportion maintained that one is at a loss to decide whether in creating the body, greater regard was paid to utility or to beauty (DCD XXII.24).

Holding, as he did, that the divine creative energy is operative in all natural things, Augustine sincerely appreciated the material world in all its aspects. And so he wrote:

> How can I speak of the rest of creation, with all its beauty and utility, which the divine goodness has given to man to please his eyes and serve his purpose . . .? Shall I speak of the manifold and various loveliness of sky and earth and sea; of the plentiful supply and wonderful qualities of light; of sun, moon and stars; of the shade of trees, of the colours and perfume of flowers; of the many birds, all unlike in plumage and song; of the variety of animals . . .? Shall I speak of the sea . . . what shall I say of food . . . the breezes . . . the clothing? Who can name all the blessings we enjoy? (DCD XXII.24)

It is doubtful that such realities would appear in a list of cherished values drawn up by a Neoplatonist! As a mature thinker Augustine was influenced more by Scripture than by the Manichees and Neoplatonists. It was logical for him to accept on faith the redemption of the whole human being — body and soul — and their future resurrection. The apostles and the women disciples of Christ had experienced him as risen and recognizable in his wounded body. St Paul taught that in the power of this resurrection all human persons would rise from the dead. The earth with all the values he cherished and praised was to be transfigured — their ephemeral character disappearing with the gift of renewal and permanence (Rom 8:21).

Yet Augustine firmly believed that the temporal blessings so highly praised were to be succeeded by greater ones lasting forever. That is why he devoted the last three chapters of the *City of God* to eschatology, that is, a theological reflection on the future realities at the end of the world, as made known in the Christian revelation: the resurrection of the body, the Last Judgement, hell, and heaven.

After the Last Judgement the cockle at last will be separated from the wheat: citizens of God's City, now his heavenly Kingdom. While appreciative of the temporal blessings and good things given by God, they preferred the giver to the gifts and embraced his providential plan for his creatures. The cockle will stand apart as citizens of the ungodly city, who, under the stimulus of Satan, took themselves and all temporal goods as ultimate values. All will receive celestial bodies, so changed as 'to be as the angels of God in heaven' (Mt 22:23–25). Such bodies are incorruptible (1 Cor 15:52–53); there will be no more illness nor death; even in hell-fire, incorruptible bodies endure forever.

Everyone will rise in a body renewed and recognizable as one's own (Luke 24:29). All temporal values will be redeemed and transfigured according to St Paul's words: 'Creation itself will also be delivered from its slavery to corruption' (Rom 8:21). There will be a 'new heaven and new earth'. Certain human activities − contemplation of the creator, love of others for their own sake, prayer or giving thanks and praise to God − not valued by ungodly citizens but valued by those on pilgrimage to heaven, anticipate heavenly life. They continue in risen life in an even more perfect way. The greatest human values − knowledge of God, self-knowledge, love, freedom, friendship − are found enhanced there, making actual a dynamic society − the communion of saints. This is the eternal peace longed for as greater than domestic peace, civic peace, international peace, because it is the ultimate 'tranquillity of order', the order of love. It is therefore a life of the highest and most intense personal activity: a participation in the knowing and loving of Father, Son and Spirit.

The City of God as a community will, in the end, enjoy the fullness of truth and goodness. And since that which is most personal about Father, Son and Spirit is their relationship to one another, persons created in their image are relational. Thus the survival of human persons includes the survival of their relationships. Of this Augustine assured a friend who had just lost a loved one: 'We do not lose those who have gone before us out of this life; we send them on ahead, as it were, into that other life where we shall rejoin them and where they will be all the dearer to us for our knowing them more intimately'.[12] Augustine also taught that the dead are aware of the living whom they loved, either through the new arrivals from earth or through divine revelation.

In this treatment of eschatology it is clear that Augustine does not blame the body for sin but the soul or, more truly, human persons who reject God's will as made known by God to Adam or to humankind through his word in Scripture or in his incarnate Son. Nor is sin due to any defect in nature. Sin originates in history. History is an ambiguous reality. Only through history do persons develop their full potential as true images of God. And yet history is a record of decisions that impede personal fulfilment. There are decisions for non-being, made by persons created *ex nihilo* with openness to Absolute Being. Augustine confessed to making such decisions himself until through God's providence he found in Christ, the Word made flesh, the exemplar of all humanness and the Logos through whom all things are made and made valuable. As noted by an eminent early Church historian at the Sorbonne, Augustine has 'an urgency to mount . . . as directly as possible towards Him who is First Cause and Highest Good — Cause of all that is, and Final End which fills to overflowing all need, all aspirations, all expectations'. But, as noted, this does not entail the repudiation of human values; it points rather to how they can be truly realized and rendered permanent. 'This Augustinian spirituality can well be defined by the verse of St Matthew's Gospel, "Seek first the kingdom of God and His justice, and all these things", that is, all these human values "will be given you besides".'[13]

For Augustine, as for St Paul, these human values were redeemed and enhanced to flourish forever in the City of God, the Heavenly Jerusalem, whose citizens enter into the happiness of the perpetual enjoyment of God and of one another. In the words of the liturgy, the joy of the resurrection has renewed the whole world.

Notes

1 J. O'Meara, *Charter of Christendom* (New York: Macmillan, 1961), p. xi.
2 C. N. Cochrane, *Christianity and Classical Culture* (New York: Oxford University Press, 1957), pp. 359–455.
3 R. A. Markus, *Saeculum: History and Society in the Theology of St Augustine* (Cambridge: Cambridge University Press, 1970), pp. 29–30.
4 Ibid., p. 40.
5 Ibid., p. 63.
6 Ibid., p. 55.
7 W. Pannenberg, *Human Nature, Election, and History* (Philadelphia: The Westminster Press, 1977), Part Two.
8 Ibid., p. 60.
9 B. Viviano, *The Kingdom of God in History* (Wilmington, DE: Michael Glazier, 1988).
10 Ibid., p. 56.
11 L. Gilkey, *Reaping the Whirlwind* (New York: Seabury Press, 1976), pp. 159–75; 216–38.
12 T. E. Clarke, 'Saint Augustine and cosmic redemption', *Theological Studies* 19 (1958), pp. 133–64.
13 H. I. Marrou, *The Resurrection and Saint Augustine's Theology of Human Values* (Villanova, PA: Villanova University Press, 1965), p. 2 and p. 39, n. 3.

10

Augustine and Neoplatonism

While Visiting Professor at Manhattanville College in 1966, speaking for Christian philosophers, Hilary Armstrong said: 'The common inheritance which binds us in a special kinship with Jews and Moslems does not only include all that comes to us from the Old Testament, but also the marks and memories of our several encounters with pagan Hellenic philosophy.'[1]

Augustine awakened to Neoplatonism with his reading in his thirty-second year of some 'books of the Platonists' – interpreted by Paul Henry to be principally *Ennead* I.6 'On Beauty', and asserted by John O'Meara to include also extracts from Porphyry's works, perhaps his *Sententiae* ('Propositions') but almost certainly a work that has been known as the *De regressu animae* ('On the Return of the Soul'). Whatever they were, they had been translated from Greek into Latin by the pagan Marius Victorinus the African, a famous orator-teacher in Rome, later a Christian theologian, whose career strangely paralleled in many respects that of Augustine himself. We shall consider briefly the Neoplatonic movement and its influence upon Augustine's view of reality.

Neoplatonism is the result of a mingling of Platonism, metaphysically interpreted, with elements from Stoicism, Aristotelianism and Neo-Pythagoreanism. It was launched in the *Enneads* of Plotinus, whose thought was developed and modified by others from the third to the sixth century. Previously the 'divine' Plato had been revived as supreme religious and theological authority by the Middle Platonists (Plutarch, Albinus, Atticus, Numenius) in the first and second centuries AD. They posited a divine mind as the transcendent First Principle, and they placed within this mind the Platonic forms, or Ideas. This was to become the basis for kataphatic (or positive) theology and for a doctrine of divine providence.

Neoplatonism's most distinctive doctrine is opposed to the primacy of the divine mind. Unlike Middle Platonism it holds that the First Principle and source of reality, the One or Good, transcends being and thought. This position became the basis for apophatic (or negative) theology, and it was taken even more firmly by later Neoplatonists such as Iamblichus and Proclus.

In his *Enneads* Plotinus presents an ordered structure of living reality proceeding from the transcendent and infinite One and descending in continuous stages from the Nous or divine Intellect, with its living forms, through Soul, with its various levels of experience and activity, to the last and lowest realities, the forms of bodies.

From the *Enneads* we learn that Plotinus posited this triad by hypostases — the One, the Nous, the All-Soul as a result of experiencing these levels of reality within himself. As with all serious philosophers, experience was the basis for his assertions, an experience interpreted by reason in the light of the philosophical tradition, mainly Plato.

In Paul Henry's opinion the Plotinian One corresponds to the Good of *Republic* 509b and the First One of *Parmenides* 142. The Intellect corresponds to the God of Aristotle (*Metaphysics* XII.9.1074b33). The Soul corresponds to the immanent Universal Reason of the Stoics. But Plotinus himself said (V.1.8) that they correspond to the diverse intensities of unity explained in the three hypotheses of *Parmenides*: the One which is not (*Parm.* 141E), the Multiple One (*Parm.* 155E), the One and the Many (*Parm.* 155E).

The ambivalent individual human soul (IV.8.4) is a wanderer on three levels: (1) that of sensitive–rational knowledge; (2) that of the intellectual grasp of being and beings; (3) that of unity with self and union with the One, which is more *presence* than thought, more *contact* than consciousness (III.4.3). Such are the experiences which promoted Plotinus's interpretation of the intelligible world.

Plotinus thought long and hard about the difference between his sense perception, his discursive reason, and his intuition, that is, a direct and instantaneous vision of truth which he found described by Plato in his *Seventh Letter* (341c–d). With Plato he concluded that this world is an image of the intelligible world, and he added that the origin of all things is the One or Good containing all things but in a transcendent mode. This Good is the object of all aspiration, that is to say, an *élan* or *erōs* toward the One, a desire given with existence. As to the 'why' of existence, Plotinus tells us that perfect beings give off an image of their internal activity. The Nous, the All-Soul, the human soul, nature are the offspring of the One's spontaneous emanation. Plato's rather off-the-cuff remark in the *Sophist* is given centrality by Plotinus, namely, true being is endowed with life and intelligence (II.5.3).

The Nous comes forth from the One and turns towards the One in contemplation, thereby being perfected with the multiple forms or Ideas, thus generating All-Soul which in its contemplation of Nous generates World-Soul. On every level emanation results from energy produced by the contemplation of those above (III.8.3–4). The origin of the human soul is not described consistently by Plotinus. Was it sent down to order individual bodies? Or is it embodied by some wilful departure from the intelligible world? Whatever the answer, its highest level has not descended; the soul is called to self-identity so that it may contemplate the One and once again participate in the Soul's mission of ordering the cosmos.

Plotinus offers two ways of regarding the human soul — a static way and a dynamic way. Having said that only the lower soul animates the body and that the higher soul has two operations, that of intuition and that of rational thought or reasoning, Plotinus states that, statically speaking, we are the rational soul, but dynamically, we are the kind of soul which corresponds to our attention. There is continuity here, not separation: intellect, reason and sense are continuous, dynamic through the three.

The intuitive soul or the Nous in us has never descended. If we attend to the life of contemplation which is our life at its best, we become that higher self, the Nous, and can be raised to the contemplation of the One. In speaking of the dynamic soul, Plotinus is referring to the human ego. This 'I' is located at the conscious level immediately below that which rules it unconsciously (its *daimōn*). The ego can will to identify with the higher soul, the rational soul or the lower soul. E. R. Dodds has said that Plotinus was the first to distinguish the concepts of soul (*psychē*) and ego (*hēmeis*). The soul is a continuum but

> . . . the ego-consciousness never covers the whole of this continuum; it fluctuates like a spotlight, embracing now a higher, now a lower sector . . . In ordinary life there fall below it the functions of the physiological life-principle which directly controls the body: not only breathing and digestion . . . but Plotinus recognizes (anticipating Leibniz) that there are sensations which do not reach consciousness unless we specifically direct attention to them (IV.4.8; V.1.12), and also (anticipating Freud) that there are desires which 'remain in the appetitive part and are unknown to us' (IV.8.8.9). The same is true of the permanent dispositions which result from past experiences of mental acts. Such dispositions, he says, can exert the strongest pull when we are least conscious of them . . . when we have them without knowing it, we are apt, he observes, 'to be what we have' (IV.4.4). This recognition that consciousness and mental life are not co-extensive is surely one of his most important psychological insights.[2]

And so for Plotinus the return to the One is accomplished by realizing that one's higher self belongs to the intelligible world and by awakening to that self. This involves discipline, virtuous actions, contemplation. Only then does the human soul experience freedom. Plotinian freedom is the tending spontaneously and with full knowledge toward the realization of one's true good, and this contrasts with actions performed under compulsion or under constraint from one's irrational forces (III.1.9; VI.8.4). If one has to think and choose between alternatives, then in that case the irrational soul has blocked the judgement and interfered with one's doing the right thing spontaneously. In this philosophy evil is located in the privation (absence) of the Good. In a sense one can find in Plotinus an early distinction between metaphysical and moral evil. For although in some respects he speaks of matter as evil, it is not in the gnostic mode of not-coming-from-the-divine, but rather of being, through disunity, the last and least vestige of any likeness to the One. On the other hand he places responsibility for evil on the individual human being not because of mere embodiment but with reference to undue attention to and absorption in the body.

And so we see that in explaining human reality, Plotinus went beyond the individual alone to offer a metaphysics of the universe with repercussions in human reality. He was to be the only Neoplatonist who claimed that there are forms of individual human beings in the Nous, archetypes to be identified with as the way to happiness, which is achieved by becoming open to mystical union with the One. Essential to this metaphysical understanding of human reality was the insight that our surface consciousness is only one of several levels of awareness, so that many elements in our mental life normally escape our notice. Much occurs on the sub-conscious level, to be sure, but we are also active, Plotinus maintains, on the super-conscious level.

Faced with the natural human desire to transcend form and limit, and faced with the classical Greek view of these as the essence of perfection, the Neoplatonic challenge was to retain Greek classical thought while adapting the categories of Greek thought to the world of inner experience.

The Neoplatonists' recognition of a realm transcending conceptual thought did not entail any loss of critical rigour in their thinking. If they held out the possibility of attaining the divine through identification with the higher soul, the Nous that never descended, they insisted that those who would unite with the One must first be thoroughly human, and that meant being rigorously intellectual. Thus Neoplatonism offered the purest form of philosophical theology in the ancient world and one constructed on the basis of an experience which could be called religious.

The *Enneads* of Plotinus (54 treatises edited by his student Porphyry), in the midst of the declining material resources of the Roman Empire, emphasized the power and the glory of the human individual's inner resources. These teachings (in the nineteenth century given the name 'Neoplatonic') became the basis of a humanism that is validated not by the denial of the transcendent but by the experience of it. Plotinus showed that religion, the cultivation of one's relationship to God, far from being in conflict with humanism is in fact an essential aspect of true humanism.

In Book VII.9 of the *Confessions*, Augustine says that in the books of the Platonists he found truths about God and human beings, truths also present in the Prologue of St John's Gospel, as we saw above in the chapter on knowledge. 'I found there', said Augustine, 'that your only begotten Son was before all times and beyond all times and remains unchangeable, co-eternal with you, and that of his fullness souls receive.' It is a problem for all Augustinian scholars who read this testimony to know how Augustine could have identified the Word or Son of God, equal to the Father, with the Plotinian Nous who is subordinate to the One. He is obviously interpreting Neoplatonic texts by means of the Christian doctrine he knows, and not vice versa. He does not think that he is correcting Plotinus; evidently he did not see the sharp distinction Plotinus makes between the One and the divine

Intellect which is real being. In *Ennead* VI.4–5 this distinction is not emphasized.

What was the immediate effect upon Augustine of this encounter with Neoplatonism? He says:

> I was admonished by all this to return to my own self, and with You as my guide, I entered in the innermost part of myself . . . I entered and I saw with my soul's eye . . . an unchangeable light shining above the eye of my soul and above my mind not as oil floats on water or as the heaven is above the earth. It was higher than I because it made me, and I was lower because I was made by it. He who knows the truth knows that light, and he who knows that light knows eternity (C VII.10.16).

This connection between a transcendent light and the experience of truth was never broken in Augustine's epistemology, as we have seen. But this connection will remain according to his personal assimilation of what he read in the books of the Platonists, always in relation to Scripture. Plotinus's explanation for the experience of truth is related to the presence of the intuitive soul in the intelligible world, thus remaining open to intelligible reality. Augustine did not consider the human soul an inhabitant of the intelligible world but in holding that the divine ideas influence human thinking he formulated the doctrine of divine illumination.

This first contact, as Augustine noted, led him to go from the exterior world to the interior world to experience his own interiority or subjectivity. It was from 'within' that he developed a metaphysics of divine reality as imaged in the substance and activities of the human soul. This could never have happened if he had retained his pre-Neoplatonic view that to be real is to be corporeal, a view taken from both Manichees and Stoics. The first intellectual effect of Augustine's initial contact with Neoplatonism was a liberation from materialism as a world outlook. He records this great reversal in the *Confessions* when he says:

> Is truth therefore nothing because it is not extended through any kind of space, whether finite or infinite? And from far away you cried out to me . . . 'I am Who I am.' And I heard as one hears things in the heart, and there was no longer any reason at all for me to doubt. I would sooner doubt my own existence than the existence of that truth which is clearly seen by those things which are made . . . (C VII.10).

There followed his admission of a new notion of reality:

> But then after reading these books of the Platonists which taught me to seek for a truth that was incorporeal, I came to see your invisible things, understood by those things which are made. I fell back again from this point, but still I had an apprehension of what, through the darkness of my mind, I was not able to contemplate; I was certain that You are and that You are infinite, yet not in the sense of being diffused through space whether infinite or finite \ . . that You truly are, and are always the same . . . also, that all other things are from You, as is provided most certainly by the mere fact that they exist (C VII.20).

What a contrast these statements are to those in Book III.7:

I did not know that God is a spirit and not one with parts extended in length and breadth, nor one of whose being can be used such words as size ... weight ... bulk ... Then, too, I was ignorant of what in us is the principle of our existence (soul) ... and what is meant by the words of Scripture ... (our being made) after the image of God ... As to that I was entirely ignorant.

In these fundamental ways Neoplatonism provided Augustine with a metaphysical view of the world and its spiritual principle. All these views, however, were assimilated to knowledge gained from Scripture and from Bishop Ambrose's interpretation of Scripture and indirectly from the writings of Hilary of Poitiers and of the Greek Fathers, Basil and the two Gregorys. The writings of Porphyry were also influential in a variety of ways.

We have spoken of Augustine's philosophical conversion through Neoplatonism. This had mainly the effect of removing certain intellectual obstacles or road blocks to his acceptance of Christian teaching. Later, a moral conversion took place, as described in previous chapters. This was to bring about the conversion of Neoplatonic thought to Christian thought.

Whereas Plotinian metaphysics is a view of the real as unity, with absolute unity identified with the One, less perfect unity in the hypostasis called Nous, and still less unity in All-Soul, Augustinian metaphysics is Trinitarian, with intellect and will on the same level as being, which is now the First Principle. The primary influence on Augustinian metaphysics is, as noted in the chapter on creation, Yahweh's answer to Moses' question 'What is your name?', as recorded in the Book of Exodus: 'I am who am'. A second influence which was fully discussed in that same chapter was the fact of creation derived from the Book of Genesis. Plotinus had deprived his First Principle of Ideas, placing them only in Nous, the Second Principle or Hypostasis. Augustine speaks of *esse*, of being, in the sense of unlimited perfection, a metaphysical infinite, a meaning applicable only to God. Such a being would not be moved by another nor would it engage in perfection-seeking action. In that sense we noted that Augustine speaks of God as immutable. Such immutability (that he is always himself, the fullness of existence) does not connote inactivity. Infinite spiritual being is being that is knowing and loving. From Scripture Augustine learned that such love manifested itself in creation and salvation. The Neoplatonic texts brought out the necessity of finite beings tracing their origin to an Infinite Principle. The doctrine of conscious creation made Augustine see the necessity for the archetypes or exemplars of all things being in God's mind insofar as is reconcilable with a Simple Being. Exemplarism became basic to Augustine's thought about God. He is closer to the Middle Platonists here. And by identifying the divine knowledge with the divine essence as he does very firmly in the *De Trinitate*, declaring that whatever God has, he is, the multiplicity of the divine ideas introduces no complexity into the divine being.

Augustine treats of this exemplarism in q. 46 of *Eighty-three Different*

Questions, written between AD 389 and 396. Plato was the first to give the Ideas their name, but as all know, with him they were not within the divine mind. Augustine realized that since God does not act unknowingly, he created according to ideas. If these ideas did not belong to the creator, God would have to look outside himself for a model or exemplar of what he was creating. Each thing therefore participates in existence as limited by a certain divine form or idea.

In the creation doctrine, unlike the emanation theory, all things are given existence by the Supreme Principle, God as Father, Son and Holy Spirit. Things do not come to be in a descent through three Intelligible Hypostases. Nevertheless, Augustine has retained from Plotinus the teaching on the absolute simplicity of God and on his nature as best known only negatively. This is made clear in the *De civitate Dei* and in the *De Trinitate* (DCD XI.10; DT XV.17; XV.13).

While God in his wisdom knows all things, his act of knowing is not like a human knowing. He does not move from thought to thought, or from knowing one thing to knowing another. He understands all at once (DT XV.14; XXV.17). God embraces all things, Augustine says, in one eternal and ineffable vision. But God's act of understanding is the same as his being. Augustine's theory is not without influence from Plotinus's Nous, described as a unity containing multiplicity and equated with each of its ideas. In identifying the ideas with the divine essence, Augustine taught that all things are created in the light of the divine essence as imitable. This foundation for the ontological truth of things is deeply related to his doctrine of illumination, as fully discussed in the chapter on knowledge.

Later in life Augustine took steps to differentiate this view from the Platonic two-world theory, stating that the wise would know the need for divine ideas if creation is not to be considered irrational (DD83 46). Lest anyone take Christ's words as reported in John 18:36: 'My kingdom is not of this world' to imply the existence of another intelligible world, Augustine took care to identify Christ's kingdom with 'the new heaven and the new earth', namely, this world as it will be when glorified at the end of time (R I.3.2).

Although never relinquishing the over-all metaphysical pattern present in Plotinus − of all things coming forth from the Supreme Principle and returning thereto − Augustine originated a new metaphysics through his reading of Yahweh's self-description as 'I am who am' interpreted as 'I am he who never changes'. He recognized that since nothing can be equal to God, things had to be created rather than emanating as from an overflowing fountain. The giving of less being to some, more to others, resulted in a chain of being: the divine, the psychic, the corporeal, as we noted in the chapter on creation.

The various ascents of the soul to God, described in Augustine's early writings, are journeys up this scale of being from the wholly mutable to the somewhat immutable to the wholly immutable.

In addition to the 'being' of things as just discussed, and their form in relation to Ideas, Augustine is very appreciative of a third dimension, an ordering toward the Supreme Principle or final cause, an orientation arising from an *erōs* toward the Good, awakened by an experience of beauty. Here again one can detect a distinctive Augustinian mode of assimilating Neoplatonic insights to scriptural teachings, resulting in a total transformation of doctrines. Being, form, and order are linked up with the biblical text 'Thou hast ordered all things in measure, number, and weight' (Wis 11:21). In his literal commentary on Genesis Augustine transposes these into *modus, species* and *ordo*, and speaks of God limiting, forming, ordering all things. The teleological dimension of 'ordering' entails a progress in goodness. In the human world the ordering is to be freely assumed as expressed in the famous Augustinian quotation 'My love is my weight'. The law of gravity, yes, but counterpointed by the love-relationship between the divine and the human which makes the way of return to the Good quite other than the Neoplatonic way. In the contemplation described by Plotinus in *Ennead* III.8 we find that the causality or dynamism of contemplation of the higher by the lower initiates a return to the One. This contemplative activity is grounded in the soul's desire for the One. In the Augustinian return as highlighted on almost every page of the *Confessions*, it is God's desire for all human beings to know and love him as constituting their true happiness which initiates their return. The love that brings about the human person's return to God is a free and graced response to God's love as that love is manifested in creation and the incarnation of the divine Son. To return to the communion of Father, Son and Holy Spirit, human love has to be graced by a participation in divine love − *caritas*, given when the Holy Spirit enters the soul at baptism, uniting it with the Son-mediator and thereby giving it a filial relationship to the Father. Paradoxically, at the moment of the Plotinian union with the One, contemplation is transcended in a movement of love, while for Augustine, when love, responding to divine love, leads to the enjoyment of God, there is given an intellectual intuition of the Trinity, the beatific or happy-making vision.

We recall that after finding in the Neoplationists much that seemed harmonious with Scripture, Augustine mentioned what he found missing there: 'Where was that *caritas* which builds upon the foundation of humility, the foundation which is Christ Jesus?' (C VII.11.21). He did not find in Neoplatonic books that the Word was made flesh, that he took the form of a servant, suffered and was delivered to death out of love for all. This was the mediator which he discovered to be the universal way to God. He criticized Neoplatonism for having found the goal of human existence − union with the Infinite origin of all reality − but failing to recognize the only universal way to it: the Father's incarnate Word or Wisdom, source of the soul's formation and re-formation.

This brief excursion into the 'way of return' serves to show how greatly Augustine was inspired by Neoplatonic themes to search the Scriptures for similar teachings which enabled him ultimately to transform doctrines central to Neoplatonism.

Augustine was generous in his praise of the Platonists as the most noble philosophers of all. This praise was based upon the effect they had on him and upon those teachings of theirs which helped him to understand the Christian faith. In the *De beata vita*, he said: 'When I had read a very few books of the Platonists ... I was so kindled that I wished to break away from all those anchors which held me, but for the influence of certain persons.' *Ennead* I.6 permeates the whole introduction to this first completed dialogue. And in the next one, the *Contra Academicos*, Augustine described the revival of Platonism, saying: 'Plato's countenance — which is the clearest and brightest in philosophy — suddenly appeared, especially in Plotinus' (III.18.41). In that same work he later says: 'I am so minded that I impatiently desire to grasp the truth not only by believing but also by understanding, and I have confidence that I shall find in the Platonic philosophers that which is not contrary to our mysteries' (III.20.43). Soon after in the *De immortalitate animae*, in a discussion of being and non-being, the influence of Porphyry can be inferred.

In his dialogues and in the De vera religione Augustine's doctrine of creation represented a distinct change from the emanation Plotinus had taught. This drastic difference is reflected also in his literal commentary on Genesis (393) where he quite definitely rejected the pre-existence of souls (VI.9.5), a position commonly known in Christian Neoplatonic circles, so that it would have been strange for Augustine not to refer to it now and then. Plotinus referred to the 'fall of the soul' in speaking of the origin of the human soul in the body. Yet even in AD 397 when he began writing the *Confessions* Augustine could still say that 'the Platonists in many ways led to the belief in God and his Word'.

By then he knew that their awareness of the transcendent destiny of the human being was accompanied by ignorance of the way for its achievement, a way involving charity and humility. Some Platonic insights, however, were never to be repudiated: the origin of all things from a transcendent principle to which all are called to return; the spirituality of God and the soul; the return to the self and the steps toward self-transcendence; the moral imperative of becoming 'like unto God'; a kind of knowledge of the Trinity (CD VII.7.11 – 8.12); a conception of evil as absolute non-being; a metaphysics of the degrees of being; an appreciation of the Beatific Vision (DCD VIII.11; X.1) (*Ennead* VI.7); their teaching on divine illumination (*Ennead* V.1 and V.6) (DCD IX.10; X.2); the immanence of God in the world (innerworldly, not otherworldly); the relation of freedom to the Good.

All this was taken over by Augustine while other teachings of the Platonists were rejected, just as the gold of Egypt was taken out by the Hebrews and not the idols of Egypt.

The charges against the Platonists to be found in the *City of God*, in *On the Trinity* and in the *Retractations* represent Augustine's awareness that he could not find in the Platonists what he once thought he could: an adequate understanding of Christian faith. Porphyry rejected Christ's divinity, incarnation, death on a cross, resurrection, and the resurrection of any human body. Christ who was the universal way to salvation, for which Porphyry was seeking, was rejected. For the Platonists, only through the rising to the intelligible world can one return to God and only by one's own efforts. Instead, Augustine found in Paul that the mystical experience was a gratuitous act of God and that all progress toward the Beatific Vision was by the grace of charity. No longer did the ray of truth suffice. The human soul is not a natural subordinate divinity. The soul's disorder was not to be explained by its being in the body as Porphyry taught, but by Adam's sin of pride and by one's personal sins. Augustine said:

> Platonism manages to avoid the cosmic dualism of the Manichees by attributing all the elements of the visible and palpable world to God as architect. Nevertheless, the Platonists suppose that souls are so affected by their earthly joints and moribund members that they attribute to these the diseases of desire, fear, joy and pain, the four passions in which are contained all the vitiation of human conduct (DCD XIV.5; V.9; XII.9).

In defending the human body, the incarnation of the divine Word, and the resurrection of the body, Augustine consciously rejected the Porphyrian norm of incorporeality for perfect humanness. The acceptance of the Neoplatonic framework of separation from God by unlikeness to him, and return by conversion through likeness, underwent a crucial transformation when Augustine learned that God is Love. He then realized that divine love (*caritas*) was given with the Holy Spirit in baptism to reform the image of God to which human beings were created. In receiving and exercising this love of benevolence, which God shares with human creatures, this likeness to God becomes the way of return to him. This was an instance of pouring new wine into old bottles. It was linked to Augustine's growing understanding of the role of the Holy Spirit as the one who pours *caritas* into the hearts of the faithful as contrasted with the Son as the World-illuminator. The most radical departure from the Neoplatonic way of access to God was taken when Augustine finally declared in the *De Trinitate* that man finds God in fraternal love. 'He cannot love God whom he does not see, who does not love his brother whom he sees' (1 John 4:7–8, 20). 'That he does not love his brother is indeed the reason why he does not see God . . . If, however, he loved him whom he sees by human sight with a spiritual love, he would see God who is love itself, with that inner sight by which He can be seen' (DT VIII.8.12).

It can be said that insofar as Plotinian monism delivered Augustine from the affliction of Manichee dualism and seemed at first to resonate with the Christian teaching heard from Ambrose, he welcomed it with whole-hearted praise. Insofar, however, as he recognized the Arian heresy against the divinity of Christ in Porphyry's teaching, and as he gradually recognized in Neoplatonism the Pelagian heresy of no need for grace to reach the kingdom of God, he separated himself radically from Neoplatonism. This is the thrust of these remarks in the *De Trinitate*:

> There are certain ones, however, who think themselves capable by their own

strength of being purified, so as to see God and inhere in God, whose very pride defiles them above all others . . . For they promise a purification of themselves by their own power, because some of them have been able to penetrate with their mind's eye beyond all created things and to touch, though it be ever so small a part, the light of the unchangeable truth, while many Christians, as they mockingly assert, who live in the meantime by faith alone, have not yet been able to do so. But what does it profit one who is proud and is, therefore, ashamed to ascend the wood (of the Cross), to perceive from afar his native land across the sea? Or what harm is it for a humble man if he cannot see it from so great a distance, but yet is coming to it on the wood (of the Cross), by which the other does not deign to be carried? These men also rebuke us for believing in the resurrection of the flesh, and would rather have us believe in them even in questions of this nature, just as though they should, therefore, be consulted about the transformation of changeable things, or the orderly succession of the ages, because they have been able to grasp the sublime and unchangeable substance through those things which have been made . . . Nor have these philosophers, who are better than others in their understanding of those sublime and eternal exemplars, gazed upon them . . . (DT IV.15.20 and 16.21).

Aquinas was right on target, therefore, when he said: 'If Augustine, who was imbued with the teaching of the Platonists, found any of their pronouncements fitting in with the Faith, he took them, but what he found against our Faith, he changed for the better' (*Summa Theologiae* I.84.5).

John O'Meara has summarized the controversy over Augustine's being classified by some as a Neoplatonist in this way:

In 1888 A. Harnack and G. Boissier had put forward a view (taken up later by Alfaric in 1918) that it was not until long after his conversion that Augustine accepted the Christian faith in opposition to Neoplatonism. From the time of C. Boyer's counter-attack in 1920 this view became gradually untenable. When the Augustinian Congress was held at Paris in 1954 most of the attending scholars would have agreed that at the time of his conversion, Augustine's acceptance of Christianity was sincere and that he was deeply impressed by Neoplatonism. He, along with others, thought that there could be a synthesis of Christian faith and Neoplatonic reason since the one God is the source of authority and reason . . . To us he now seems to have been a Christian of his time who held certain views that were abhorrent to Neoplatonism but nevertheless had been much influenced by Neoplatonism in not unimportant ways.[3]

We have specified some of those unacceptable positions which prompted Augustine to think out a Christian philosophy in his own very personal way, related to his experience and to Scripture. Etienne Gilson is therefore correct when he says that Augustine inhibited rather than transmitted Neoplatonic influence in the West.[4] But may we not say that the philosophical realization of spiritual reality, of divine transcendence, of human self-transcendence as capable of promoting a possible mystical experience of God is, in the Christian thought of Augustine, a valuable contribution from Neoplatonism?

Notes

1 A. H. Armstrong, 'Reason and faith in the first millenium A.D.', *Proceedings of the American Catholic Philosophical Association* (1966), p. 104.
2 E. R. Dodds, 'Tradition and personal achievement in the philosophy of Plotinus', *Journal of Roman Studies* 50 (1960), pp. 5–6.
3 J. J. O'Meara, 'The Neoplatonism of Saint Augustine' in Dominic O'Meara (ed.), *Neoplatonism and Christian Thought* (Albany, NY: State University of New York Press, 1982), p. 35.
4 E. Gilson, *History of Christian Philosophy in the Middle Ages* (New York: Random House, 1955), p. 67.

11

Retrospect

Any reader of this book is probably one who desires to know what Augustine thought about the major issues of human life, death and destiny. This interest is sparked, however, by a more fundamental craving, one shared with Augustine, the desire for truth.

In his writings (95 works, over a thousand sermons, more than 276 letters, some only recently discovered), Augustine bequeathed whatever truths he himself had embraced through faith and/or reason along with the arguments or evidence substantiating them.

In the last few years of his life he reviewed 93 works in order to reject or modify any statement which later information or reflection had shown to be erroneous or exaggerated or misleading. For each work he stated the circumstances promoting its writing, the purpose and plan of the work, and his own criticisms. This review was completed in AD 427 and called *Retractations* (as mentioned on p. 12 above, Henry Chadwick thinks *Reconsiderations* a more apt title). Two major works were later completed: *The Predestination of the Saints* and *The Gift of Perseverance*, AD 428/429. Augustine's death in AD 430 halted his final work against Pelagianism, called *Unfinished Work against Julian*.

An author's self-criticism is important for indicating intellectual development and also for keeping the record straight as to his final positions on themes put forward early in life. Augustine's criticisms may be unified under such specific topics as (1) opinions of the philosophers regarding happiness, sensible reality, pre-existence of souls, the need for high intellectual achievement; (2) his own statements defending free will in so far as they were open to Pelagian misinterpretation; (3) his inaccurate statements in need of modification or rejection; (4) his ever greater realization of God's great mercy and of everyone's need of his help until the end of time.

Augustine readily admitted that his criticism of what he once said or implied derived from his greater knowledge of Scripture at the end of his life. Such knowledge made him more sensitive to the human condition resulting from original sin, and to the human vocation to the communion of saints made possible by Christ, the incarnate Word of God. This led him to reject some expressions absorbed from Roman literature and Greek philosophy and not in harmony with the full picture available through divine revelation. Thus he expressed regret for so often using the word 'fortune' in describing good events which he knew to have occurred through divine providence (R I.3.2). Likewise he wished to withdraw references to the Muses 'as some sort of goddesses' (R I.3.2).

On a more serious note, he apologized for having overpraised the philosophers: 'Plato or the Platonists or the Academic philosophers beyond what was proper for such irreligious men, especially those against whose great errors Christian teaching must be defended' (R I. 1.4). Another philosopher mentioned was Pythagoras whom Augustine first thought to have no errors but in whom he later discovered 'many and fundamental ones' (R I.3.3). He wished he had not spoken of these philosophers as having 'shone with the light of virtue' (R I.3.2).

The philosophers here in question wrote of the best human life as one lived according to the highest human activity and therefore placed happiness in the highest functioning of intellect. In early writings Augustine was swayed by such opinions and wrote: 'What do you think to live happily is . . . if not to live in conformity to the best in man?' (CA I.2.5). He once wrote: the 'highest good is in the mind' (CA III.12.27), when he truthfully should have said that the mind's highest good is God (R I.4.3). And so he retracted the earlier statements with the remark that to attain happiness, one 'should live as God lives' (1 Pet 4:6). To do this the mind cannot be self-sufficient but subject to God (Ps 36:7; Jas 4:7; R I.1.2). After all, do not Christians read in Scripture: 'Be perfect as your heavenly Father is perfect'? Augustine felt obliged also to retract an early opinion that there could be complete happiness on earth through the soul's knowledge of God even while suffering many bodily miseries. From St Paul (1 Cor 13:12–13) he learned that perfect happiness is in the life to come when the body also will share in that happiness (1 Cor 15:42–44; R I.2).

Certain Platonic attitudes toward the sensible world cannot be wholly identified with Christian teaching. The recognition of this was lacking in Augustine's earliest works. Having learned from Plato of two worlds, sensible and intelligible, he had identified this doctrine with the Lord's teaching that his 'Kingdom was not of this world' (John 18:36). This would make God's Kingdom a solely intelligible world and leave the earthly world out of God's concern. Scripture does not warrant any such depreciation of the created world. So Augustine retracted his too-facile reconciliation of Christian and Platonic teaching by saying: 'If another world was intended by the Lord Jesus Christ, it can more appropriately be understood as that in which there will be "a new heaven and a new earth" (Isa 65:17; 2 Pet 3:13; Apoc 21:1) when what we pray for when we say, "Thy Kingdom come" will be fulfilled' (R I.4.2). And again in the *Soliloquies* he had written: 'These sensible things must be totally forsaken'. This statement, he later thought, might identify him with 'the opinion of the false philosopher, Porphyry, who said: "*omne corpus fugiendum"* (every body must be fled from)' (R I.4.24; DCD X.29; XXII.26). He feared also that certain expressions of his regarding knowledge as a 'digging out' of what was 'buried in oblivion' might link him to Plato's theory of knowledge as recollection whereas he believed that knowledge is better explained as an openness of human reason to the illumination of eternal reason.

It may have been his increased awareness of the heresy of the Manichees, who taught that corporeal things were to be avoided as contaminating forces, that galvanized Augustine to be wary of Platonic positions which could be interpreted (as they have been in oversimplified secondary sources) as denying any value to sensible things. At any rate, he took pains to dissociate himself from any expression of his which seemed to entail such a repudiation. In reconsidering his fifteen books on *The Trinity* the only statement he regretted making was one which claimed that to love the visible body is to be estranged from God (DT XI.5.9); 'it is not estrangement', said Augustine, 'to love corporeal beauty unto the praise of the Creator' (R II.41.2). He even felt it necessary to explain why he so often spoke of turning *away* from sensible things in order to grasp intelligible realities. He considered such advice needed because the soul is weak and not as capable as it will be in the next life to attend simultaneously to the sensible and the intelligible. He also knew through personal experience that corporeal things are ambiguous; they can remind one of their Creator, but they can also lure one to shameful pleasures. Such ambiguity will disappear in the next world where bodies will be more beautiful and more enjoyable than they are here on earth.

Another teaching originating with Platonic philosophers and absorbed into the late ancient culture was that of the pre-existence of human souls. In the *Retractations* Augustine repeated his rejection of this position and reiterated his ignorance from his earliest days of just how the human soul, admittedly created, had originated. He pointed out that in the dialogue *Against the Sceptics* he should not have referred to the 'return' of the soul into heaven but should have said 'will go'. He found this correction necessary 'because of those who think that human souls, having fallen from or having been driven out of heaven in punishment for their sins, are thrust into bodies here below' (R I.1.3). As to the soul's origin, 'how it came to be in the body, whether it came from that one man who was created first when "man became a living soul" (1 Cor 15:45) or whether, similarly, individual souls are made for individual men — I did not know at that time nor do I know now' (cf. DLA III.21.59 and 62; E 166). Although in AD 415 Augustine wrote *Origin of the Soul* he admitted that he did not solve the problem he raised (R II.71). He both asserted that the soul was created and leaned toward spiritual traducianism as a way to account for the transmission of original sin. No Church decree about this existed; Augustine therefore frequently asked others for their opinions. Whatever solution proved acceptable, he knew one thing as certain, namely, that baptism is necessary, for this had been the traditional practice in the Church since the earliest days of Christianity.

In quite another line, yet still with regard to the influence upon him of the philosophers and of Cicero, Augustine took a second look at his earlier identification of intellectual prowess with the attainment of human destiny. He confessed that early in life he had attributed too much to the liberal arts when many saintly men do not know them, whereas 'some know them and are not saintly' (R I.3.2). This emphasis on intellectual power appeared heavily in the dialogue *On Order* where he aimed to analyse the mysterious direction of divine providence. Unable to penetrate its very mysterious workings, he turned instead to an 'order' of studies which could promote the ascent from the corporeal to the incorporeal. To achieve this he projected a series of treatises on the liberal arts. After having written six books *On Music* he gave up the project. As early as AD 388 he began to be less enamoured of forsaking the corporeal than of embracing the embodied Word of God, Christ the only way to the Father. In this mind he regretted having written that 'there is more than one way of attaining union with Wisdom' (SO I.13.23) 'as if there were another way besides Christ who said "I am the Way" ' (John 14:6; R I.4.3). In fact, he flatly contradicted the opinion he had expressed in *On Music* that the knowledge of God is restricted to those who use their intellectual power to ascend from created things to God's invisible attributes. 'For those who do not possess the power, and yet live by "faith in Christ" (Rom 1:7; Gal 3:11; Heb 10:38), gain a perception of these realities more certainly and more happily after their life; but if faith in Christ who is the "one Mediator of God and men" (1 Tim 2:5) is lacking in those who possess the power, they perish with all their wisdom' (R I.10.1).

It is not surprising to find the topic of Pelagianism very much present in the *Retractations*. Augustine addressed this topic in two ways, first, by a defence of the need for grace along with a reminder that his earliest defence of free will was directed to the Manichees who saw evil as coming from opposing material forces external to the human will. Secondly, he listed reliable authorities all of whom taught the existence of original sin and from whom he learned of it.

Augustine's position regarding free will was midway between that of the Manichees and that of the Pelagians. He was therefore subjected to abuse from both sides. His work *On Free Choice* was written against the Manichees who thereupon argued that if evil derived from the human will, it had to be attributed to God. As previously noted, Augustine argued that a human agent, in turning away from God, the Last End, was responsible for his own immoral act. The Pelagians, on the other hand, regarded Adam's sin as one that affected only himself. They therefore rejected any need for grace to do good actions meritorious of heaven. Because in *On Free Choice* he was upholding free will's responsibility for evil against Manichee determinism, there was no long discussion of grace. In his review of this work Augustine emphasized that in no way should the Pelagians boast as though he had 'pleaded their cause' (R I.8.3). Among the 17 Italian bishops who refused to accept the condemnation of Pelagius was one Julian of Eclanum. He called

Augustine a Manichee because the Manichees condemned marriage, and he charged Augustine with condemning marriage because he believed that the guilt of original sin was inherited. Augustine responded that far from condemning marriage, he had described it as a great good (R II.88). He refused to accept authorship of the doctrine of original sin and defended it by arguments based on the testimonies of the Greek and Latin Fathers.[1] In his second book *Against Julian* Augustine supported his position 'by making use of the opinions of ten illustrious writers, among whom were Irenaeus, Hilary, Gregory of Nazianzus, and Jerome'.[2]

The final topic which troubled Augustine pertained to his own inaccurate statements. In speaking of the Trinity he should not have said that the Father and Son *is* one (SO I.1) but *are* one, as Christ said: 'I and the Father are one' (John 10:30; R I.4.3). From Origen's opinion that all people will eventually return to God (R I.6.6), Augustine explicitly separated himself, and he wanted it known also that although sins harm human nature, they do not corrupt it (R I.9.2). And he wished to correct his early opinion that human beings would not have generated children if Adam had not sinned (DGnM I.19.30) and to state without qualification that the command 'Increase and multiply' was given as a blessing (R I.9.2; I.11.8). In opposition to former statements, he affirmed that food was needed in paradise (R I.18.9), that miracles have taken place since the time of Christ (R I.11.7; I.13.5), and that God will be seen with bodily eyes in the risen life (R II.67). In formerly arguing against a Manichee that there was no contradiction between the Old and the New Testaments, Augustine admits having exaggerated in saying that no precepts and divine promises are found in the New Testament which are not also found in the Old Testament. In this he was wrong because the Kingdom of Heaven was not promised in the Old Testament. Moreover, one reads in the New Testament: 'You have heard what was said to the Ancients, but I say to you' (Mt 5:21–22; R I.21.2). Augustine greatly regretted that in his *Literal Commentary on Genesis* he gave the impression that by sin Adam lost the image of God to which he was made (DGnL VI.27.28). He did not mean that no image remained, but that it was deformed and had to be reformed (R II.50).

A major correction of his early misunderstanding of grace as a reward for faith was spelled out when Augustine reviewed his comments made in AD 394 on Romans 9:10–29. There he had said: 'It is ours to believe and to will; it is God's to give to those who believe and are willing the power to do good works through the Holy Spirit by whom love is spread abroad in our hearts' (R I.22.1). In AD 396 when re-studying these Pauline passages Augustine realized that not only the power to do good actions, but faith itself, is God's gift. He referred to this development in his understanding of grace in his last two works (DPS IV.8; DDoP XV.52), but from 395 on he had incorporated it into his teaching and explicitly retracted the early misunderstanding in AD 427. He would not have said that faith came from the will alone 'if, then, I knew that this faith is also among the gifts of God' (R I.22.1). His retraction of the early view, however, does not mean that free choice is not involved in the acceptance of the grace of faith. For 'both [faith and works] are ours, then, because of free choice of the will and both, moreover, have been given because of a "spirit of faith" (2 Cor 4:13) and charity' (R I.22.3).

> And what I [earlier] said, For it is we who believe and will, but it is He who gives to those who believe and will the power of doing good 'through the Holy Spirit' through whom 'charity is poured forth in our hearts' is indeed true; but because of this rule, He does both because He himself prepares the will (Prov. 8:35), and we do both because we do only what we will (R I.22.3).

Two striking motifs throughout the *Retractations* provide a seldom advertised view of this reflective bishop. They are his conviction of the mercy of God as unlimited and his realization that no one in this life, not even a saint, is in perfect peace but is always in need of God's help to resist temptation. Augustine denies that access to truth is limited only to moral knowers. 'I certainly disapprove of what I said in the prayer: "O God who has willed that only the pure know the truth" (SO I.2), for it can be said that many, even those not pure, know many truths' (R I.4.2). In the *Soliloquies* Augustine did not explain, as he did in later works, the kind of truth (saving) open to the pure alone, nor did he explain what knowing is. And in another section: 'we must not despair of anyone, no matter how wicked, while he lives but pray with confidence for him' (R I.18.7). Thus Augustine expressed sorrow for any limitation he might have placed upon the mercy of God. He deeply regretted having written that God is attentive to those who live well (DOR II.20.50) 'because this was stated as if God does not hear sinners' (John 9:31; R I.33). In fact, God helps all to find him (R I.12.4).

In addition to the vivid description in the *Confessions* (X) of his own daily temptations even as a bishop, he retracted the statement 'that in this life all vices are burned out by the flame of divine love' (DME I.30.64; R I.6.5). There will always be a struggle to resist the attempted movements against reason (R II.27). Otherwise, our prayer could not be as it must be: forgive us our trespasses — 'a prayer the entire Church will say until the end of the world' (R I.18.2). This reflection is climaxed with the frank statement: 'therefore, all the commandments are declared fulfilled when whatever is not fulfilled is forgiven'. 'And so in saying that God has chosen for himself "a glorious church, not having spot or wrinkle", I did not mean that in all respects the church is now in such a state, but after Christ shall re-appear, it will be' (R I.18.19). Augustine, therefore, wished to modify his expression formulated in AD 407: 'To the mass of weeds (Mt 13:36) among which *all* heresies are to be understood' to read: 'among which *also* all heresies are to be understood. For, in fact, there are weeds [scandals] in the Church as well. Even though we see such scandals, they should not weaken our faith or our charity so as to make us withdraw from the Church' (R II.54).

And finally with regard to his remarks on the difficult question as to how the seeing of God will take place in the risen life, he said: 'Only whatever is presented in the course of my argument which is supported by the authority of divine Scripture is to be believed without reservation' (R II.67). And he intended this to apply to all his statements in all his works.

From all the above it is obvious that Augustine considered himself to be open to correction. He commented on his self-criticism in this way:

> I do not wish that anyone should accept all my opinions in such a way that he or she follows me blindly, except in those points where the reader has become convinced that I was not mistaken. This is the reason why I am now writing books [*Retractations*] in which I revise my own works in order to show that not even I myself have followed myself in all points. I think that — with the help of God's mercy — I have written books constantly making progress. But I did not start off perfectly, and to claim that now, in my old age, I write perfectly and without any error would be more a sign of conceit than of truthfulness (DDoP XXI.55).

A special assumption absorbed from Augustine's fourth-century culture is that of the subordination of women to men. In the interest of truth, he would welcome being corrected for that today. Anyone familiar with ancient history and literature knows that women were universally considered the weaker sex, socially inferior to men and owing them obedience. Because the biblical narratives were also culturally conditioned they could not liberate Augustine from popular opinion on this matter. Yet he took pains to associate this prevailing opinion with bodily sex rather than with female gender. In a recent article, 'Augustine's view on women', T. J. Van Bavel has noted the positive elements in Augustine's view which made him more progressive than his contemporaries.[3] There is, first and foremost, his affirmation of their intellectual equality with men. 'Because of her reasonable and intelligent mind she would have equality of nature' (C XIII.32.47). It is in virtue of their rational minds that all human beings are images of God (EnP 96.12; 48.2; CF XXIV.2). In declaring women to be images of God Augustine differed from some of his predecessors (DGnL III.2; VI.7) as well as from those who cited St Paul as teaching otherwise in respect to an obligation for a woman to cover her head. The latter, according to Augustine, is to be interpreted figuratively. Both reason and the authority of Paul recognize that it is not in 'its bodily form or in any one part of the soul but according to the rational mind where the knowledge of God resides' that the human being is 'made after the image of God'. And as to the renewal of the image (Eph 4:23-24; Col 3:9-10), 'we become the children of God through the baptism of Christ . . . Who, then, would exclude women from this fellowship, since they with us are co-heirs of grace?' (DT XII.7.11-12).

In affirming the creation of women to the image of God, Augustine was well aware that this had been denied. 'It does not escape me', he wrote, 'that some eminent defenders of the Catholic faith before me . . .

asserted that the man was the mind, but that woman was the bodily sense' (DT XII.8.13). Van Bavel points out that not only did Augustine never deny women the dignity of imaging God on the level of creation or grace, but that he frequently attributed female gender characteristics to God. 'The Psalmist made God father; he made God also mother. God is father because he created, because he calls, because he commands, because he governs. God is mother because God cherishes, because God nourishes, because God suckles, because God embraces' (EnP 26.18). Unlike Aristotle who regarded the female as an imperfectly developed male, and unlike those ecclesiastics who thought that, in the resurrection of the body, women will be changed into men, Augustine taught that woman was fully planned by God to be a female human being (DCD XXII.17–18; XIII.19–20).

The moral superiority of women to men was openly championed by Augustine. He was struck by the strength of faith in the great women martyrs of the first centuries and also by the virtue of ordinary Christian women who could serve as models and teachers for men. 'Many husbands are surpassed by their wives; wives remain chaste, and men do not even want to be chaste' (S 9; 280). Augustine dismissed the 'double standard' and urged 'Christian women not to show patience with their adulterous husbands and not to remain indifferent to such a situation' (S 292). One of the first to take up the cause of discrimination against women, Augustine spoke out against the Roman law which punished women for adultery while the men went free (S 153; 392). He also opposed the Roman law which allowed remarriage while both spouses lived (DNu II.8.7; S 9).

Finally, Van Bavel maintains that the most important contribution to changing the subordinate relationship of the wife to a husband was made by Augustine when he emphasized interpersonal love in married life and interpreted the conjugal relationship as friendship. Before him, this was seldom or never done. He took his cue from Scripture, where God admonishes husbands to love their wives (Eph 5:25). Marriage becomes personal, not merely the result of social nature and biological attraction. Although he did not entirely eliminate the social subordination of women which continued in marriage as obedience, Augustine 'made more of a breakthrough in the Christian understanding of sexuality and marriage than any other theologian of the patristic era. Christian theology . . . acknowledges the bishop's triple enumeration of marriage blessings in the form of mutual fidelity, offspring, and sacrament.'[4]

There is always hope that a discovery of new manuscripts of Augustine's works will increase our understanding of the development of his thought. Yet the two most recent findings of sermons and letters do not seem to have helped in this regard. The sermons found at Mainz in Germany are mainly from the first fifteen years of his episcopal life. This means that some were being preached while he was engaged in writing the *Confessions*.[5]

Around 1980 Johannes Divjak, in the course of cataloguing the Augustinian manuscripts in France, discovered at Marseilles 27 of

Augustine's previously unknown letters. Most of the letters date from 415 to 430. Their value comes from the light they shed on the social conditions of the late Roman world. We learn in them of the plight of the poor and defenceless who sought sanctuary in the Church, the violence and the injustices inflicted by slave-dealers, the custom of parents leasing for up to 25 years the labour of their children, who as serfs gradually became enslaved. Letter 24* concerns this practice. Augustine wrote it to a layman, a lawyer, and asked legal counsel pertaining to a case on which Augustine in his episcopal role as arbitrator in civil cases had to pass judgement. Ever since Constantine's decree of AD 318, all bishops in the Christian Empire were authorized to be judges in civil disputes. This responsibility absorbed much of Augustine's time.

The letters bring to the fore the concerns of an African bishop trying to be a worthy shepherd of his flock and also of those whom he hoped to become members of the Church. In letter 2* to Firmus, a non-Christian, ever seeking more 'knowledge' before believing in Christ, Augustine observes that knowledge, even of the highest good, will not release one from evil. Sins, not ignorance, are the obstacle to salvation. Liberation from sin comes only by rebirth in Christ, 'the Mediator who, although so remote . . . by the divine majesty, deigned to become close to us through human weakness' (E 2*.5).[6] Notice Augustine's apt use of words and his direct approach as he concludes: 'Therefore, you must commit yourself, without further delay, not to yourself, O infirm Firmus, but to him who can do all things, to change your life for the better and receive the grace of rebirth' (E 2*.7).[7]

One of Augustine's major concerns as highlighted in these letters is to have more priests in Africa, especially in the rural areas. He is emphatic, however, in not wishing quality to be sacrificed to quantity. He laments the scandals arising from time to time among the clergy and wants to find ways to assist them in maintaining their first fervour. But

> . . . it is up to God to grant the increase (1 Cor 3:6), even if not all make progress and persevere to the end; still, as the Apostle says, the Lord 'knows who are his own', he who foretold all these scandals to come which sadden us. He warned us not to be discouraged, and promised the reward to us who persevere with his help in order that we may live with him for eternity, there where there will be no temptation and scandals, but only joy, and the certain assurance of eternal joys; and blessed immortality, and happiness without end (E 18*).

* * *

As one looks back at the whole span of Augustine's life, how can it be best expressed? Possibly as a journey from multiplicity to unity. It was a journey directed by the single-hearted desire to know the soul and God. Augustine's intense interest in philosophy was one with his consuming interest in religion. Obviously, he thought it important to seek a *true* philosophy, for only true philosophy is true religion, and vice versa. In uniting these two, a human person's concrete existence manifests a harmonious union of faith and reason. We know that in the ancient world philosophy was not viewed as a system of abstract principles, nor as a methodology. It was a way of life. How else could the dialogues of Plato, the *Ethics* of Aristotle, the *Enneads* of Plotinus have been written? Precisely because in Christ's life the fullness of truth shone forth, he was recognizable as the universal way to truth to which the pagan philosophers aspired. That is why Augustine viewed Christianity not as a rival to ancient thought but as its fulfilment. With him Christian philosophy was launched. It met both the requirements of reason and of Scripture.

Materialism, scepticism, rationalism were present in the age of Augustine as indeed they are today, with rationalism more accentuated in this post-Enlightenment, post-modern era. The experience of truth in its immutable character was the witness Augustine called to prove that there is more to reality than the changing, living beings we are, more than animals, plants and the material world. Truth-experiences signified an interior relation to God through the mind; faith-experiences established a relation to God by love through the will. To see the beauty of the world is to see it not only in its nature but in its right order. Anything in right order is fully itself as intended by God. On the human level this means a loyalty to the desire for God, to which the conscious desire for happiness is an unconscious aspiration. Knowing the soul means knowing this. Knowing God through Scripture means knowing him as Father, Son, Holy Spirit, one in nature, one in love. These divine Persons are the source not only of the truth which guides human judgements but also of the love intended to prevail in social relationships. In origin and in order, the primacy is with love, for love is creative and unitive. It is a personal spiritual disposition flowing from life in God. Through his humanity Christ imparts to his Church the Trinitarian life of love he shares with Father and Spirit. With this life comes a new consciousness with the added powers of believing, hoping in and loving God. A new body for Christ is the Church enabled to continue his ministry to all wishing to be saved.

As Augustine's understanding of Scripture increased, he realized love to be God's own being and the point of everyday life and eternal life. Just as persons need immutable divine truth as the source of correct human judgements, so also do they need infallible divine love as the source of their love for God and for each other. In the perennial human search for knowledge of God, Augustine began with the philosophers. The Augustine of the *Soliloquies*, who dialogued with Reason to arrive at a knowledge of God, soon became the Augustine of *True Religion*, who realized through faith that God becomes knowable in the personal relationship made possible in the Spirit's gift of *caritas*.

The incarnation of God's Son can be understood as making possible this gift of love. In sending the Holy Spirit of truth and love into the world, Christ did not intend to eliminate the good of nature as divinely created. Nor does the new consciousness operating through faith, hope and love eliminate the human need to know and will in the natural order.

In praying, thinking and writing to keep faith and reason united, Augustine never sought to avoid the resulting tensions by easy solutions. What he bequeaths to us, however, are not dichotomies, but simply polarities with distinctive characteristics not truly deniable. One such polarity is that of Grace–Freedom. Others may view these two as incompatible; Augustine viewed them as inseparable. He retracted his early position that faith is our own doing (R I.23). But he also taught that there is no faith without our willingness to believe. Grace is not merited by our good acts; yet it is never received without our wanting it. This leaves grace available to more than the righteous. Sinners, as Augustine himself experienced, continue to be loved by God. Thus one final polarity vividly described in the *City of God* can be called the Mercy–Misery polarity. The unhappiness of the human condition is more than counterbalanced by the mercy of God. Augustine's final works on *Predestination of the Saints* and *Gift of Perseverance* may seem to many to restrict the divine love. If so, they need to be counterbalanced by Augustine's most fundamental conviction, namely, that the mercy of God is above all his works. For surely Augustine was right in saying 'Love may despair of no man' (DCG XLVI).

We have seen that Augustine's influence was theological, philosophical and pastoral. He upheld both the distinction and the necessary union of faith and reason for the fulfilment of human life in its temporal responsibilities and in its highest aspiration for that divine friendship which enhances every human relationship. All true love, he maintained, is a participation in divine love. If God's love is rejected and he is not loved, neither is anyone so loved as to ensure that love's survival unto eternal life.

Augustine's influence through the ages has been traced by Henri Marrou from the end of the late Roman Empire into the early Middle Ages, through high Scholasticism and the Renaissance to the recovery of Augustinian themes in the Reformation (along with exaggerations of his anti-Pelagian writings) to the Counter-Reformation's return to the 'teaching of the "Doctor of Grace" as the Church's tradition had understood it'.[8] Then came the revival of his emphasis on spiritual life and mysticism filling the whole seventeenth century and nourishing the Christian renaissance of the nineteenth century with its many new religious orders.

Despite the misunderstandings arising from Augustinianism, the Catholic Church has never ceased venerating him as one of its greatest Doctors. He was solemnly praised in panegyric and encyclicals in 431 by Pope Celestine, in 1930 by Pius XI, in 1954 by Pius XII, and in 1986 by John Paul II.

Etienne Gilson (1930), Maurice Nédoncelle and André Mandouze (1954) advised all students of Augustine to appeal constantly from 'Augustinianism' in all its manifestations to St Augustine himself. In putting forward the overall thought of Augustine in this small volume, I have tried to be guided as closely as possible by the writings of Augustine himself. So I hope that readers will also turn to those writings.

Augustine's legacy was a doctrine that is a consistent totality and a life that witnessed to Christian personhood — consciousness of self, and freedom exercised in a love that transcended self-centredness through the Spirit's indwelling power. He remained forever grateful to the Greek-Roman tradition which bequeathed to him many truths attained by human reason. His embracing of scriptural revelation did not entail relinquishing the fruits of human reason created by God. In Augustine we of the twentieth century discover our intellectual and spiritual ancestry. A high point of that heritage is the appreciation of the human person as created to the image of the Trinity, and the realization that God is the source of truth and of the freedom not only to choose between alternatives but to do the truth in love.

Notes

1 Augustine, *Retractations*, tr. Sr M. I. Bogan (Washington, DC: Catholic University of America Press, 1968), p. 261.

2 Ibid.

3 T. J. Van Bavel, 'Augustine's view on women', *Augustiniana* 39 (1989), pp. 5–53.

4 G. Lawless, 'Augustine of Hippo: an annotated reading list', *Listening: A Journal of Religion and Culture* 26/3 (1991), pp. 173–88.

5 *Revue Bénédictine*, 101 (1991), pp. 240–56; 102 (1992), pp. 44–74. *Revue des études Augustiniennes*, 36 (1990), pp. 355–9; 37 (1991), pp. 37–78; 261–306; 38 (1992), pp. 50–79.

6 *Saint Augustine: Letters 1–29**, tr. R. B. Eno (Fathers of the Church 81; Washington, DC: Catholic University of America Press, 1989), p. 21.

7 Ibid., p. 23.

8 H. Marrou, *St Augustine and His Influence Through the Ages* (New York: Harper/ London: Longmans, 1957), pp. 147–80.

Index

Abel 97
Abraham 94, 97
Academics 4, 121
Adam 23, 28, 37, 44, 48, 50, 52, 53, 55, 56, 91, 94, 95, 101, 106, 123, 124
Adeodatus 2, 8, 10, 18, 27, 86
aesthetics 39
Africa, Africans 1-3, 5, 6, 9, 15, 73, 75, 79, 80-2, 85, 87, 90, 91, 94, 98, 103, 108, 128
Alaric the Goth 94
Albinus 108
Alexander 65, 82, 92
Alexandria, Alexandrians 6, 17, 58
Alexian Brothers 92
Alfaric 118
Alypius 3, 7, 8, 11, 83, 86, 90
Ambrose 4-8, 11, 14, 47, 53, 58-60, 65, 66, 69, 74, 84, 85, 101, 103, 117
Ambrosians 92
Ambrosiaster 48
Amelius of Carthage 71
Anderson, J. 40, 41
angels 25, 95, 97, 100
Annaba 10
Anomoeanism 70
Antony 7, 8, 83, 84, 99
apocalyptic tradition 103
Apollinarists 60
apophatic theology 108
Apostle Brothers 92
apostles 75, 79, 87
Apostolic 79
  Fathers 74
  See 76
Apuleius 3
Arians, Arianism, Arius 12, 58-60, 70, 71, 76, 117
Aristotle, Aristotelians 2, 3, 14, 20, 21, 26, 36, 39, 44, 108, 109, 127, 129
Armstrong, A. H. 108, 119
ascetic, asceticism 6, 83-5, 87, 89, 90
Assumptionists 92
astrology 4, 14
Athanasius 58, 65, 66
Athens 4
Atticus 108
Augustinian tradition 21
Augustinianism 130
Augustine
  early life 1-6

conversion 7, 8, 84
  at Thagastan monastery 10
  priest and bishop 10-11
  self-criticism 120-6
Aurelius of Carthage 9
authority 8, 10, 24, 56, 73, 75, 76, 97, 126

Babcock, W. S. 57
Babylon, Babylonia 2, 94, 96, 99, 103
baptism 4, 8, 29, 42, 44, 46, 48, 53, 63, 71, 73, 77, 79, 80, 82, 85, 95, 100, 115, 117, 122
Basil, St 61, 83, 124
Basilica Pacis 91
beatific vision 28, 29, 115-17
beauty 3, 24, 26, 37, 40, 92, 105, 115, 122, 129
being
  Absolute 107
  finite 37
Berber 1
Bible 51, 94
  see also Scriptures
body 13, 58, 117
  see also Jesus Christ
Boethius 12
Boniface 80, 82, 101
Bourke, V. 33, 40, 57
Boyer, C. 20, 118
Burns, J. P. 57

Caecilianus 80
Caesar 96, 98
Cain 97
Calvin 52
Canons Regular 93
capital punishment 100
Cappadocian Fathers 70
caritas 46, 47, 54, 62, 67, 100, 115, 117, 129
  see also charity; love
Carthage 1-3, 10, 12, 13, 73, 75, 80, 99
  Council of 52, 76
  Synod of 52
Cassago 8
Cassiciacum 8, 15, 66, 85
catechumen 1, 2, 6, 14, 59, 77
Catholic Church 6, 8, 14, 75, 76, 79, 80, 84, 94, 98, 100, 130
  see also Church
Catholic faith 5, 13, 14

132